BEST WAYS TO CATCH MORE FISH IN FRESH AND SALT WATER

BEST WAYS TO CATCH MORE FISH IN FRESH AND SALT WATER

VLAD EVANOFF

DOUBLEDAY & COMPANY, INC.
GARDEN CITY, NEW YORK
1975

Library of Congress Cataloging in Publication Data

Evanoff, Vlad.
    Best ways to catch more fish in fresh and salt water.

    Includes index.
    1. Fishing.   I. Title.
SH441.E845   799.1
ISBN 0-385-01975-0
Library of Congress Catalog Card Number 73–9155

To my wife *Betty*,
who understands fishing and fishermen

Foreword

More has been written about the sport of fishing in magazines, fishing guides, books, and other publications than any other sport, and n‸   ‸′ in the United States, but also in other countries; f   ′ truly an international pastime and is one of th‸   ′ced in almost every country in the world.

So wh‸   ‚ book like this one comes out, the natural reac‸   ‚, "Oh, no! Not another fishing book!" What else can t‸   ‚ to write about that hasn't been written before? Many anglers feel that if they already own a fishing book or two they don't need any more.

Well, having written quite a few fishing books, I also feel that there isn't much sense or logic in just writing another fishing book that is already on the market. Unless I can write a new or different book, why duplicate a book that already exists? So when I got the idea for this book, I decided to impart to anglers some new and helpful information they can't find in other fishing books.

So I feel that this book is different in one very important way. Instead of dwelling for pages on end about fishing tackle —rods, reels, lines, lures, and other things needed in fishing— the emphasis throughout the book has been on the actual *use* of this tackle. Fishing tackle is mentioned or outlined briefly, but most of the book has been devoted to the methods, techniques, and skills needed in actual fishing. After all, most anglers have little trouble buying a fishing outfit, but they do have difficulties in learning how to use this tackle and the lures and baits in the most effective way.

This book differs from other fishing books in another way too. Instead of just covering only fresh-water fishing or only salt-water fishing or only a single fish or method of angling, it covers all the best ways of catching fish almost anywhere. No matter where you live or what kind of fish you hope to catch, you'll find the information you need in this book. As the title indicates, the purpose of this book is to show you how to catch *more* and bigger fish.

VLAD EVANOFF

Contents

BEST WAYS TO CATCH MORE FISH IN FRESH AND SALT WATER

1

Still Fishing

Still fishing usually means that the angler fishes from an anchored boat or from shore in one spot and lowers or casts his bait—usually a natural worm, minnow, or insect—into a likely spot, and then sits and waits for a fish to come along and take it. Most of the time there's a float or bobber attached anywhere from a couple of feet to several feet above the hook. But you can also still fish without this float and let the bait sink deeper or even use a bottom rig with a sinker to cast out farther and get the bait down to the bottom. And you don't have to fish from a stationary boat anchored to one spot. You can drift along with the wind or current or even paddle or row your boat every so often to change spots.

You usually think of a still fisherman as a boy, man, or woman with a long bamboo or cane pole held out over the water. And while cane poles or even glass poles or metal poles are used by the majority of still fishermen, you can also use a wide variety of other fresh- and even salt-water tackle for still fishing. Spinning, spin-casting, bait-casting, fly-fishing tackle, light salt-water rods, and even hand lines or drop lines or trot lines can be put to good use in still fishing depending on what kind of fishing you are doing and what kind of fish you are after.

Most still fishermen seek panfish such as sunfish or bream, shellcrackers, yellow perch, white perch, white bass, and crappies. For them a cane pole or glass pole or fly rod or spinning rod is good. Most cane or glass poles run about 10 to 20 feet in length. The longer ones are best when fishing from shore or a pier or dock where you have to flip the bait out a good distance.

The shorter ones are better from a boat where you are usually right over the fish.

There are many types of floats or bobbers available for still fishing. They are made of cork, plastic, or styrofoam and they vary in shape and size. Use as light and small a float as possible, since a fish will not feel the pull or resistance as much as with a larger float. Even when casting a bait with a float using a spinning, spin-casting, or bait-casting outfit, you don't need too big a float because the weight of the bait itself is often enough to get it out quite a distance.

You'll also need an assortment of hooks for fresh-water still fishing. Such patterns as the Sproat, Eagle Claw, Aberdeen, Carlisle, and Model Perfect or round bend are the most widely used and can be stocked in various sizes.

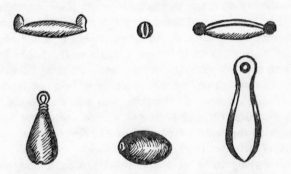

Sinkers used for still fishing include Top row: Clincher, split shot, rubber core Bottom row: Dipsey, egg or oval, bank.

Various kinds of sinkers, such as the clincher or clamp-on sinker, rubber-core sinker, split-shot sinker, dipsey sinker, round and egg or oval sinker, and bank sinker, are used for fresh-water still fishing. Most of these range from a fraction of an ounce up to 2 or 3 ounces in weight. Occasionally when fishing in big rivers and strong currents you may need heavier ones.

Many still fishermen seek sunfish, of which the bluegill or bream (pronounced "brim" down South) is the most popular. They are found in most lakes, ponds, and sluggish rivers and canals, and reach a good size and make fine eating. Bluegill fishermen usually use a cane or glass pole, tie a monofilament line about the same length as the pole, and add a bobber or float about 3 to 6 feet above the hook. The hook can be sizes Nos. 10, 8, or 6. The usual bait is a garden worm or a piece of a nightcrawler.

Although bluegills are found in many different spots in a lake, most of them are close to shore, among lily pads, weed beds, sunken trees, and logs, and under piers, docks, and bridges. In the spring and early summer they come close to shore to spawn, and their beds or nests can be seen.

While bluegills are fairly easy to catch, there are little tricks and tips and know-how that will enable you to catch more and bigger fish. First in importance is to always use fresh or lively bait—a worm that wriggles is much better than one that is still or dead. It is also a good idea to move your line or float a foot or so every so often to give the bait some movement to attract fish.

If worms don't work too well, try "bonnet worms," which are found in the upper stalks of "bonnets" or lily pads. Another highly effective bait for bluegills is a catalpa worm. This big caterpillar is found in catalpa trees and is cut in half and turned inside out, and one of the halves is placed on a hook.

Still another top bait for bluegills is a fresh-water shrimp. These tiny shrimp live in many fresh-water lakes, especially in the South, where there are hyacinths. They can be netted under these plants with a fine mesh net.

And live crickets make a great bait for bluegills. Either the wild variety found in the fields and pastures can be used, or you can buy the so-called "gray" crickets, which are raised commercially and are sold by bait dealers and tackle shops. If you can't get crickets, try grasshoppers.

Most of these baits work best when used on small, light wire hooks such as the Aberdeen. You can use crickets and grasshoppers without any float or weight and let them kick around on top of the water and then slowly sink. But if you want to catch a lot of big bluegills, add a split shot or two about a foot above the bait and let it sink to the bottom.

Another popular fish caught by still fishermen is the crappie (called "speckled perch" in Florida). In most lakes there is a period of hot crappie fishing lasting a few weeks, usually in the spring, when they move close to shore and into coves and in the mouths of creeks to spawn. This may occur as early as February in Florida and as late as June in the North. Crappie like to hang around weeds, lily pads, hyacinths, sunken trees, or brush and rocky areas. During the summer months look for them in shady spots such as under docks, piers, rafts, and overhanging trees.

The top bait for crappies is a small live minnow about 2 inches long. They also take various insects such as grasshoppers, crickets, mealworms, and nymphs. At times they will also take worms. These baits can be fished several feet below the surface using a float or bobber to keep it suspended at that depth.

In northern waters the yellow perch is often caught still fishing in lakes and sluggish rivers. The best fishing for them is also in the spring soon after the ice melts. They swarm inshore and up creeks and streams to spawn. Like crappies, they prefer tiny minnows for bait but will also take worms and insects. They are also school fish, and if you locate a good-sized school you can have some fast fishing. Look for yellow perch in water anywhere from 4 to 5 feet deep to 50 feet or more in depth. Look for them over weed beds, over bars, in coves and channels, under bridges, and along dropoffs. In rivers they hang out in the quieter sections and side coves, where the current isn't too strong.

White perch are caught by many still fishermen both in fresh-water lakes and rivers and brackish waters in bays and rivermouths. Sometimes they can be spotted moving along the surface of a lake. They tend to move closer to shore at dusk and feed at night. Worms, minnows, and insects make good baits in fresh water. In brackish waters they bite well on tiny grass shrimp, seaworms, pieces of crab, or clam. You can also try cutting a small strip from the first white perch you catch and use this for bait.

The fish that are made to order for still fishing are the bullheads and catfish. Being mostly bottom feeders, they move slowly along the bottom, dragging their whiskers in the mud.

When they taste or "feel" food, they grab it. Most boys and many a man have spent many happy and productive hours fishing for the small bullheads or the larger catfish.

Bullheads and catfish like muddy bottoms and quiet sections of rivers and streams. But they will also hang out over gravel and sand bottoms. The bigger catfish prefer the deeper holes and pools and channels, and that is where your bait should be. They also congregate below dams and high falls. Although cane poles serve well for the smaller bullheads, heavier-spinning bait-casting, spin-casting, and even light salt-water outfits are better for the bigger catfish.

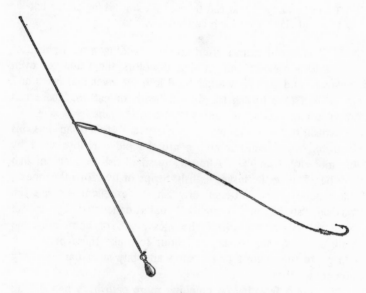

Basic rig used for still fishing on the bottom.

With casting outfits a bottom rig with a sinker and a hook tied a few inches above the weight are best for reaching the hot spots and for holding a bait in a strong current. Another good rig is the "sliding sinker" rig, making use of an egg sinker, which slides on the line. Tie a barrel swivel about 14 to 16 inches above the hook so that the sinker on the fishing line doesn't slide down to the hook.

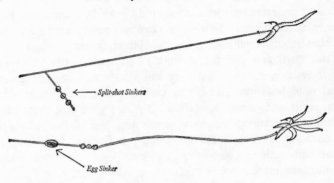

Two types of rigs that can be used for still fishing on the bottom, especially good for rocky bottoms.

Bullheads and catfish often go on a feeding spree right after a heavy shower or rain, which discolors the water or even makes it muddy. This washes food into the river and lakes and is the best time to fish for the bullheads or catfish. These fish are also more active on cloudy days and at night.

Catfish baits are many, and every still fisherman has his favorite. Worms and minnows are the old standbys used by the majority of anglers. Almost any small fish or piece of fish can be used for the larger catfish. Strips of liver or other meats make good baits. Soft-shell crayfish are excellent. So are the various "stink" and doughball baits concocted by catfish regulars. To save yourself the messy job of combining the stale meat or fish, cheese, and flour to make these baits, you can go to the nearest tackle shop and buy such baits already prepared.

Here are a few tips on catching more catfish: When fishing in lakes, fish the side toward which the wind is blowing. The waves often carry insects and other foods toward this shore. When going after big catfish, first catch a bullhead and put this on a big hook after clipping off its sharp spines. They are tough and stay alive longer than most fish and often attract their bigger relatives. When fishing rivers, wait until the river is low and fish the deeper holes and pools. Catfish will gather in such spots during a drought. Finally, when you catch your first catfish, cut it open and examine its stomach. Catfish often show a preference for a certain kind of food and feed on that for extended periods. So it's a good idea to use this for bait.

One fish that will test a still fisherman's know-how and skill is the carp. These fish are very wary, smart, and clever at stealing a bait off a hook. You have to be very quiet and patient and often wait hours for a bite. A spinning outfit is ideal for carp fishing because you can often cast doughball baits without any added weight. However, in rivers with currents, bottom rigs with sinkers such as those mentioned in the section on catfish above are needed.

Most expert carpfishermen prepare their own doughball baits using cornmeal and flour and add honey, sugar, molasses, or a similar sweetener or flavoring. One highly effective recipe calls for adding strawberry-flavored gelatin to the cornmeal and flour. These ingredients are usually mixed wiith water and kneaded or cooked in boiling water for a short time. Then the mixture is rolled into a big ball and kept in aluminum foil in a refrigerator until used. The bait is formed into doughballs shaped like small pears around a single or treble hook.

Carp will also take corn kernels strung on a hook; parboiled vegetables such as potatoes, parsnips, and green peas; mulberries; soft-shell crayfish; fresh-water clams and mussels; and even worms at times. But doughball baits are usually best.

Carp like muddy bottoms and a lot of weeds or vegetation so fish such shores along lakes and rivers. In rivers the carp will be found in the quieter stretches. They also come close to shore to spawn in the spring. They can often be seen lying near the surface or actually spawning. Best fishing is usually early in the morning and toward evening.

Carp will bite very delicately at first, and many fish are lost when an impatient angler tries to set the hook too soon. Wait until the light nibbles stop and the carp starts to move away with the bait, usully indicated by the line rising out of the water and becoming taut.

Many so-called gamefish can also be caught by still fishing. Even trout will pick up a lively worm from the bottom of a lake or stream. And if you want to catch small-mouth bass consistently the year 'round, you should still-fish using such baits as worms, hellgrammites, crayfish, minnows, and frogs.

They are especially effective and deadly during the summer months when the fish are down deep.

You can fish for small-mouth bass with a live minnow on a small hook and a light spinning outfit and 4- or 6-pound-test line. Cast the minnow into likely spots from shore or a boat. Then don't close the bail, but hold the line on the spool with your forefinger. When a bass picks up the minnow, let it swim away for a few feet before trying to set the hook.

Still another deadly bait for small mouths is a lively frog fished deep in a lake among rocks or ledges or other bass hangouts. Add a couple of split shot or a small clincher sinker a foot or two above the hook to get the bait down near the bottom.

Small-mouth bass in rivers are partial to hellgrammites and crayfish. Here the best way to fish them deep in holes or pockets or below rapids is to add a small dipsey sinker on the end of your line, then tie a hook on an 18-inch leader a few inches above the weight. You can use several small worms or a big nightcrawler the same way. Here again, wait until the bass starts moving out with the line before setting the hook.

Large-mouth bass are also caught by still fishing in lakes and sluggish rivers. Minnows make a great bait for largemouths and can be hooked through the back or lips and cast into likely spots with or without a float. This can be done from a drifting or anchored boat. Some of the biggest bass in Florida waters are caught still fishing with live shiners. You can bait the shiner through the nose or back with a single hook. But because of the size of the shiner (usually 6 to 10 inches long), a treble hook will miss fewer fish. Run this through the tail of the shiner. Then add a cork or plastic float about 6 feet above the hook. Cast this out toward the edges of lily pads and hyacinths, or near shore or into deep holes, and let the shiner swim around. If a bass grabs the shiner, let him run with it and wait until he stops. Then when he moves off again, set the hook.

Large-mouth bass can also be caught on frogs. These can be fished on or near the surface by hooking them through both lips or a leg and casting it out among the lily pads or weeds, letting it swim around on top. Or you can add a clincher sinker a couple of feet above the frog and let it sink toward the bottom.

One of the best ways to catch a steelhead along the West Coast during the winter months and when the waters tend to be muddy or roily is by still fishing. Called "plunking," it is simply another form of bottom fishing, with a sinker and hook rig to keep the bait down deep. Up to 5 to 6 ounces of lead may be needed to hold bottom in swift or strong currents. The best bait for plunking are salmon eggs or eggs taken from a fresh-caught steelhead itself. These are put on a treble hook and wrapped with thread or fine mesh netting around the hook. This is cast out with a two-handed spinning rod anywhere from 7 to 9 feet long. Conventional revolving spool reels and rods can also be used. The rod is propped up on the bank or shore, and you wait for a bite. Add a tiny bell at the rod tip to signal a bite.

Even when you go after fresh-water monsters such as muskellunge, you can catch them by still fishing. Almost any big minnow or small fish such as a chub, fallfish, yellow perch, bullhead, or shiner can be used for them. But suckers are usually preferred for bait. Suckers from 6 to 12 inches long can be used. Hook the live sucker through the back with a strong hook, add a float a few feet above the bait, and then let it out from a slow-drifting boat in a current or when a light breeze is blowing. Naturally, you have to drift in spots where muskies are known to be present. These are usually along dropoffs, edges or ends of rock bars or reefs, over weed beds, along the edges of lily pads, and in similar favored spots.

Muskies are often slow about taking and swallowing a sucker or other fish. They will often hold it in their jaws or mouths for long periods of time without actually swallowing it. So you should allow plenty of slack line and time for the fish to do this before trying to set the hook.

Another fresh-water monster that can be caught by still fishing is the sturgeon. Along the Pacific Coast from California to Alaska, fishermen catch big white sturgeon weighing several hundred pounds. The Snake River in Idaho is well known for its sturgeon fishing. So are the Columbia and Willamette rivers

in Oregon and Washington. They can also be caught in some
Florida rivers such as the Apalachicola.

Nails driven into sinker to
make it hold bottom better
when still fishing in strong
currents.

You need husky salt-water-type rods such as surf spinning
rods or conventional-type surf or boat fishing rods. Lines should
test 20 to 30 pounds for spinning and up to 50 or 60 pounds
on revolving-spool reels. Heavy sinkers up to a pound may be
needed in some rivers to hold bottom in rivers with strong currents. Hooks should run in sizes from 7/0 to 10/0. Various
baits are used for sturgeon, depending on the river you are
fishing. Along the Pacific Coast, fishermen favor smelt, worms,
shrimp, and pieces of fish. Lamprey eels are very good in
waters where they are found naturally. Florida anglers have
used a ball of moss or algae, which is scraped off the rocks.

Sturgeon fishing, like carp fishing, requires a lot of patience.
It is a waiting game. You can cast out your rig from shore or
lower it from a boat and then let it lie still on the bottom. A
sturgeon will toy with the bait a long time before he finally
swallows it. Once the line tightens, you set the hook and then
brace yourself for a tough battle. The boat angler can raise
his anchor and follow a big sturgeon down the river while he
fights it. But the shore angler has to follow the sturgeon along
the shore, often for long distances, before he finally beaches

it. So it's a good idea to choose a spot where this can be done safely before you even start fishing.

So as you can see, still fishing can be tough and rugged, as in the case of sturgeon fishing, or it can be a lazy, relaxed way of catching a mess of panfish or gamefish from shore or boat without exerting yourself too much. It is a type of fishing preferred by millions of fresh-water anglers.

2

Spinning and Spin Casting

There are so many spinning and spin-casting rods and reels on the market today made by American and foreign companies that it's not too much of a problem to find exactly what you want. Of course, most beginners do not know what they want or need. It may take months or even years before they find out what kind of fishing they like, what kind of fish they want to catch, and where they will be doing most of their fishing.

We can simplify matters by first recommending a "basic" or "all around" spinning or spin-casting outfit that can be used for most fresh-water fishing. Spinning tackle itself is so versatile that even one outfit can be used to catch most of the fish found in this country.

Such a spinning rod for use with an open-face spinning reel can be from 6 to 7 feet long. If it has a medium action, it can handle lures weighing from about one-eighth to one-half ounce. Make sure it has a light aluminum fixed-type reel seat that holds the reel firmly in place. With such a rod, you get an open-face spinning reel that holds 150 or 200 yards of 6-pound-test monofilament line. But when casting lighter lures, you can use 4-pound-test line with such a rod. When using heavier lures, you can go to 8-pound-test. That is why it's always a good idea to buy two extra spools to hold the different-strength lines for quick changing to meet fishing conditions. You'll also have two spare spools of line in case you lose a lot of time from the spool already on the reel.

The "all around" open-face spinning outfit mentioned above is suitable for fishing streams, rivers, lakes, and ponds for trout, bass, pickerel, bullheads, small catfish, carp, and panfish. In most places where there is plenty of open water to fight a fish, such an outfit is practical.

If you plan to fish a lot for small trout, small bass, and panfish in small streams and ponds, an ultralight spinning outfit will cast lighter lures from one-sixteenth to one-quarter ounce. The rod will run anywhere from 4½ to 5½ feet in length, and a matching ultralight or small open-face spinning reel goes with this rod. Lines testing from 2 to 6 pounds can be used with this rod and reel.

For big bass, walleyes, pike, catfish, big carp, and muskellunge, a somewhat heavier spinning rod from 6½ to 8 feet long with a larger open-face spinning reel filled with 8-to-15-pound-test lines is more practical. Some of the shorter, lighter rods in this class can be cast with one hand and lures weighing from three-eighths to three-quarters ounce. The heavier, longer rods with longer butts or handles can be cast with two hands and handle lures from five-eighths ounce to 1½ ounces.

Still longer and heavier spinning rods and bigger reels are used in some areas for Pacific salmon, steelhead, big catfish, and sturgeon. But the three outfits mentioned above will take care of most of your fresh-water fishing needs.

The other basic or "all around" outfit that is especially suited for beginners but that also has found favor with many expert fresh-water anglers is the so-called spin-casting outfit. The other names for the spin-casting reel used with this outfit are "closed face" and "push button" reel. This reel also has a stationary or nonrevolving reel spool, but instead of releasing the line with your finger, as in the case of the open-faced spinning reel, you press down on a button to hold the line, then let up on it to release the line during the cast. And instead of an open face, the reel is enclosed in a cone-shaped cover with a hole in front through which the line runs out. Most of these reels come with the line already on the spool, and these usually test from 6 to 15 pounds. Some closed-faced reels are mounted below the rod like open-faced reels, but the majority of the closed-face reels are mounted on top like a bait-casting reel.

In fact, with such a spin-casting reel you can use almost any rod made for bait casting, but there are rods especially designed for spin-casting reels. These are usually about 6 or 6½ feet in length and should be able to cast lures from one-quarter to five-eighths ounce.

Such an outfit is best for the beginner or angler who doesn't fish too often, because it is easier to cast with and use and will give less trouble than an open-face reel. It is also favored by many expert anglers for night fishing. If you buy a good spin-casting rod and reel, you will have the nearest thing to an "all around" fresh-water fishing outfit that can be used for most fish.

Besides the rod, reel, and line, you'll need a good assortment of lures to use with the spinning or spin-casting outfit. These will usually range from one-eighth to five-eighths ounce. Occasionally heavier and bigger lures may be needed for big bass, pike, lake trout, and muskellunge.

You can divide most spinning lures into three classes: those that float or stay on top of the water during the retrieve, usually called surface lures; those that dive or travel at below the surface up to a few feet; and those that dive to great depths or sink all the way to the bottom. To be fully equipped for all kinds of waters, fishing conditions, and depths, you should have some lures from all the above classes in your tackle box.

However, just owning a spinning or spin-casting outfit and a good assortment of lures won't help you to catch more fish. You have to learn how to use these effectively so that they attract fish and make them hit.

Take the ordinary spoon, a lure that has been around for centuries. They come in various sizes, shapes, weights, and finishes, with the silver or chrome, brass, copper, and painted finishes in different colors the most effective. Their flash, wobble, and darting action work on all kinds of gamefish. When fishing shallow water for trout, use the smaller, lighter spoons. For deeper water, faster currents, use the heavier spoons. The biggest spoons, up to 3 or 4 inches long, are used for pike, lake trout, muskellunge, and salmon in fresh water.

When fishing with spoons for trout or small-mouth bass in streams or rivers, you have to contend with a current. Here the best procedure is to cast across stream and then reel in fast enough to bring out the action of the spoon. If the water is shallow, you can hold your rod tip high and then reel somewhat faster. If the water is deep or you want to work a hole, hold your rod tip down and then reel slower. Casting upstream will also help to get the lure down near the bottom.

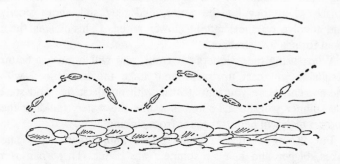

Spoons should be retrieved with rod action so that they rise, then flutter and sink.

When retrieving the spoon across the stream or river, let it pause and flutter at intervals in likely spots such as pockets, behind rocks, logs, under rapids or falls, and in the deeper holes. When the spoon reaches a point below you downstream, you can work it against the current very slowly, often holding it in one spot as long as it is suspended in the water and has action. In fact, you can let it drop a foot or two to imitate a crippled minnow unable to make headway against the current.

When fishing the deeper and quieter pools or in lakes where there are no currents, a spoon will draw more strikes if you cast it out and then reel it back with rod action, such as raising the rod tip quickly and then letting it drop back. This makes the spoon rise, then dive and flutter. You can fish various depths until the fish are located. When they are near the bottom, cast out the spoon and let it sink to the bottom, then start your retrieve.

Spinners are also deadly lures when used with a spinning or

spin-casting outfit. They are similar to spoons in that they depend on flash to attract fish and are made of metal. They come in different sizes, shapes, weights, and finishes. The silver or chrome finish is most popular, but gold, brass, copper, and painted finishes also produce.

When fishing for trout in shallow streams, use the lightest spinners you can get. This is where an ultralight spinning outfit is really effective. With it you can cast the tiny spinners weighing from one-tenth to one-eighth ounce. They make less of a splash when they hit the water, and they sink more slowly and revolve on the shaft at slower speeds. This makes them ideal for shallow streams.

When using the spinners for trout, you will often get better results if you cast upstream and make the lure travel with the current. Here you have to fish with no slack line and start the spinner working as soon as it hits the water. Holding the rod tip high will help to keep it from sinking.

For fishing in deeper runs, pools, and larger rivers and lakes, bigger and heavier spinners are better. These can run from one-sixth to one-quarter ounce. Here you can cast across or upstream in a river and let the spinner swing into holes, pockets, and pools, and around rocks and boulders. Both trout and small-mouth bass go for these spinners in streams and rivers if they are reeled through water where the fish are lying.

Tiny spinners are also very effective when used for panfish such as bluegills, yellow perch, white perch, white bass, and crappies. These should be cast alongside lily pads, hyacinths, and brush close to shore around logs, rocks, and weed beds. For these fish, reel the spinner as slowly as possible and try different depths right to the bottom until you find where the fish are feeding.

With a spinning or spin-casting outfit you can also use plugs of different types, sizes, weights, and finishes. Surface plugs are very effective when used in shallow lakes or near shore, especially early in the morning and evening and when the water is calm. Most surface plugs are made with cupped heads, big metal lips, wings, propellers, or other devices that create a disturbance on top of the water. Some are just plain cigar- or torpedo-shaped and create mostly a wake or ripple.

Surface plugs should be cast close to shore near lily pads, stumps, logs, brush, reeds, and other cover where a bass may be lurking. After the plug is cast, let it lie still until the ripples have disappeared. Then twitch it a bit so it moves barely an inch or two, and let it lie still again. Then twitch it again and let it rest. Remember, you are trying to imitate a crippled minnow, frog, or other creature. They do not swim steadily without stopping for a rest. Try to simulate this action with your lure.

However, there are times when fish such as bass will be chasing minnows on top. Then a faster-moving surface lure will be more effective. You can also work a larger surface plug fairly fast when going after pike or muskellunge.

Underwater plugs or diving plugs are better when fishing later in the day or along dropoffs, over reefs or bars, or over underwater weed beds in deeper water. Here you can cast out and reel fairly fast to make your plug dive and work down below the surface. Although most of the plugs of this type have a built-in action or wriggle, you can add some rod action by jerking the rod tip every few seconds to make the plug dart forward, then pause to give it a more crippled action.

Sinking plugs are good for working the deeper parts of a lake to catch bass and walleyes. Here you wait until the plug hits bottom, then reel and work it very, very slowly so that it travels along the bottom.

But for working deep in rivers or lakes, you can't beat the jig. This old favorite of the salt-water angler has really hit the big time in fresh-water fishing too, and no angler should go on a fishing trip without bringing along jigs in various sizes, weights, and colors. Those that weigh only one-thirty-second to one-eighth ounce are good for trout and panfish.

Jigs sink quickly, even in a fast current, and are ideal for bottom bouncing in streams and rivers for trout, small-mouth bass, and walleyes. Here you can cast slightly upstream, and when the jig sinks and swings with the current and reaches bottom, you start working it back. Jigs have no built-in action, so you have to raise and lower your rod tip to make them dart, rise, sink, and look alive.

Jigs can be made even more attractive by adding a small

minnow, worm, strip of fish, or pork rind to the hook. Or you can cut a short length off the end of a plastic worm and put that on the hook. You can buy such jig head-plastic worm combinations now, and they are killers for trout, bass, panfish, and walleyes.

Plastic worms themselves, of course, have proven to be deadly lures for bass, especially the large-mouth bass in lakes and ponds. The plastic worms now come in various lengths and colors, with the black, purple, blue, green, and red or natural worm color the most effective in most waters. Worms with weedless hooks are best when fishing in heavy growths of lily pads, hyacinths, sawgrass, reeds, or weeds.

There are many ways to use a plastic worm and let it sink slowly to the depth where the fish are supposed to be. Then you reel it back very slowly with an occasional short jerk of the rod tip. If you want to work the worm along the bottom, you let it sink until the line goes slack, indicating it has reached bottom. Then you raise it a few inches with the rod tip and let it settle to the bottom again. Keep doing this during the entire retrieve. You can try striking immediately if you feel a fish grab the plastic worm. If you miss too many fish this way, try letting the fish run with the worm for a few seconds before setting the hook.

There are times and places when working a plastic worm on top is more effective. This is especially true when fishing for bass in heavy cover among lily pads or hyacinths or grass. Here you reel fast enough to keep the worm moving on top so it creates a ripple or wake. Bass will hit such a surface worm hard, and you can set the hook immediately.

In streams when fishing for trout or small-mouth bass, you can let a plastic worm drift naturally with the current. Here you cast upstream so that the worm will sink deeper. Adding a split shot or two a foot or so above the worm will help it to go down deeper.

Spinning and spin-fishing tackle can even be used to cast small panfish fly-rod bugs and even trout flies. One way to use a small popping bug is to get a regular popping plug about one-quarter or three-eighths ounce in weight. Then remove the hooks from this plug and tie on a monofilament leader of about 10- or 12-pound-test and about 14 inches long to the eye at the tail of the plug. Finally, tie the small panfish bug to the end of the monofilament. You can cast this out along shore and work it slowly so that the plug pops and the trailing bug creates a ripple. This rig is especially effective for bluegills, but it will also take the small bass.

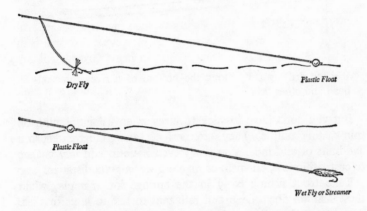

Dry Fly   *Plastic Float*

Plastic Float   *Wet Fly or Streamer*

Using plastic floats to fish flies with a spinning outfit.

If you want to catch trout or bass or panfish on flies with a spinning or spin-casting outfit, get some of the clear plastic floats or bubbles that are usually filled with water or oil to provide casting weight. If you want to fish with dry flies, attach the plastic float on the end of your line and add the dry fly on a 1-foot dropper about 4 or 5 feet above the float. This can be cast across stream, and by holding the rod high, your dry fly will float on top. You can even give the dry fly additional action by pulling it lightly so that it skitters on top. You can also cast upstream, then reel in the slack quickly so your line will be off the water and only the fly and plastic bubble will float on top.

For fishing wet flies, nymphs, and streamers, tie the plastic float or bubble about 4 feet above the fly and fill the float or bubble with water so that it sinks. This will take the fly down to deep water where trout, bass, and other fish lie.

Still another way to fish a fly down deep right on the bottom is to tie a snap swivel on the end of your line. Then attach a dipsey sinker to the snap. Then tie a 3- or 4-foot leader to the eye of the swivel, and on the end of this tie your fly. With this rig you can fish all the deep holes and even fast runs and pockets for trout, bass, and steelhead.

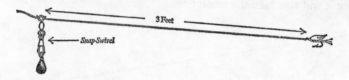

Rig for drifting a fly along the bottom of a river for steelhead and other fish.

But you don't have to stick to lures when using spinning or spin-casting outfits. They are perfect for casting and using live baits of all kinds. You don't even have to add any weight to cast a minnow, crayfish, or nightcrawler a good distance.

Take trout fishing early in the spring, for example, when these fish are down deep and reluctant to rise to lures or flies. A worm drifted into a hole or along an undercut bank or rocky ledge will appeal to both small and large trout. Use a No. 8 or No. 10 hook and run it through the middle of the worm. In quiet waters you can fish the worm without any weight, but to get it down in fast currents, you may have to add some split-shot sinkers above the hook.

The worm should drift with the current naturally, and this will mean that you'll have to let out slack line at times or reel it in at other times. The important thing is to cast well above where you think a fish is lying and let the worm drift into its hiding place at the right level.

Minnows, both alive and dead, can be fished for trout in the same way with a spinning or spin-casting outfit. The minnows can be drifted naturally with the current and tumbled into likely spots in a stream or river. Or you can rig a dead minnow so that the hook comes out near the tail or head and then add 3 or 4 split shot about 18 or 20 inches above the bait.

The best way to fish such a dead rigged minnow is to cast across stream and let it sink, then pull up with the rod to make the minnow rise; then pause, and the shot will pull the minnow down again. This gives the minnow a crippled, twisting action, which appeals to big trout.

You can use many other natural baits for trout, bass, panfish, and other fish with a spinning or spin-casting outfit. Frogs, crayfish, salamanders, grasshoppers, crickets, and other insects can all be fished with deadly results to take the wisest fish in fresh water.

3

Bait Casting

Before spinning reels were introduced into this country, most anglers who fished in fresh water used bait-casting reels. These reels had been around since the early 1800s, when a Kentucky watchmaker named George Snyder invented the first multiplying reel. Also called "plug casting" reels, this revolving-spool reel reigned supreme for casting all kinds of lures, both in fresh-water and salt-water fishing.

When spinning became popular, many anglers turned from bait casting to this new reel, while others who just took up fishing for the first time started off with spinning tackle. Most of these anglers still don't own bait-casting tackle. Many of them never will try bait casting but will continue to stay with spinning or spin-casting outfits for the rest of their lives.

This is all well and good for the casual fisherman who goes out only once in a while, fishes a couple of ponds or rivers, and never plans to travel to more distant waters or experiment and try other kinds of fishing. He'll probably never need a bait-casting outfit.

However, most expert anglers and serious fishermen who fish many waters, different parts of the country, or zero in on big fish in waters where spinning or spin-casting tackle is handicapped, swear by the bait-casting outfit. You will find that most of the anglers who catch the record fish or win fishing contests in various parts of the country use bait-casting outfits.

The reasons why they prefer bait-casting outfits to other kinds of tackle are as follows: First, in the hands of a skilled caster, a bait-casting outfit provides pinpoint accuracy. The caster can drop his lure into a tiny spot near lily pads or hyacinths, alongside logs or stumps, next to shore, or under overhanging trees without hanging up.

You use stronger lines so even if you do get hung up in a pad, weeds, reeds, or bush, you can usually break loose without losing your lure. This also saves you fishing time, since you don't have to row or paddle over to shore to get free, as you usually have to do with a spinning outfit.

If you hook a big fish near lily pads, hyacinths, logs, or stumps, or when you hook a steelhead in a fast current, you can use a bait-casting outfit to stop his run and either turn him or make him go into open water. You have more authority with a bait-casting outfit, whereas in a similar situation with a spinning outfit, you feel helpless as the fish takes line and you can't stop him.

You will also be able to cast and use heavier lures with a bait-casting outfit. This is the second reason why experts prefer bait-casting outfits. The lines are stronger, the rods are stiffer, and the reel is sturdier, making it easy to cast lures up to an ounce or even more with most bait-casting outfits. And when using these bigger and heavier lures, you can set the hook better in the jaws of a big fish with a bait-casting outfit.

If you like to fish deep with bottom-bouncing lures such as jigs, spinners, and flies, weighted plastic worms, and diving or sinking plugs, you'll find that a bait-casting outfit is better, which is another good reason for using it. You'll have fewer breakoffs, save more lures, and hook more fish.

A bait-casting outfit is also better for trolling or fishing on the bottom with bait. These methods tend to strain the rod and line, and unless you use a pretty heavy spinning outfit, you'll find that most fresh-water spinning outfits are too light for such fishing.

So if bait-casting tackle is so good in so many ways, why don't more anglers use it? Well, as mentioned earlier, most fresh-water anglers aren't serious enough about their fishing to care about the differences. And bait-casting tackle is somewhat more expensive and harder to use in the beginning. You have to practice casting and using the rod and reel longer to become good at it. Spinning or spin casting is much easier to master.

But if you plan to broaden your horizon, travel to many fishing spots, or go after big fish in fresh water, then I would recommend investing in a good bait-casting outfit and learning how to use it.

For "all around" bait casting, get a rod that is 5, 5½, or 6 feet long. It should have a "medium" action but still have plenty of backbone. The so-called fast taper rod with a light tip for casting light lures with a stiffer, more powerful midsection for handling heavier lures is a good choice for the angler who wants to start off with just one rod. Such a rod should be able to handle lures from about three-eighths to 1 ounce in weight. This will make it ideal for most bass, big trout, steelhead, walleye, pike, and the smaller muskies.

If you plan to fish for big pike and muskies, steelhead, catfish, lake trout, and coho salmon, you get a still heavier rod capable of casting and handling lures up to 1½ ounces or so. There are also light bait-casting outfits for casting lighter lures, but most anglers prefer to use spinning or spin-casting outfits for casting such lures.

More important than the rod itself and the key to good bait casting is the reel. A modern bait-casting reel is light, casts smoothly, and is a big improvement over earlier reels. The spool is made of aluminum, magnesium, or plastic, so that it starts turning quickly and easily and stops quickly. This helps prevent "birdsnest" or "backlashes," which bothered anglers of former years. Not that you cannot backlash a modern bait-casting reel. It still happens, but not as often as formerly.

A bait-casting reel has a level-winding device that winds the line back on the reel evenly. Most bait-casting reels made today have an antibacklash device that slows down the spool toward the end of the cast. This is a big help for beginners learning how to cast with such a reel. Later on, when they get an educated thumb, they can cast with the antibacklash device turned off completely.

More and more bait-casting reels are being manufactured with free-spool levers or buttons, which allows the spool to revolve during a cast without turning the handle. Still other bait-casting reels have star drags like most salt-water reels, which enable the angler to adjust the tension needed to pull line off the reel.

This is a big help when fighting a fast or large fish and you want to slow down his run.

Bait-casting reels are usually made in two or three sizes, more often in a light, narrow-type reel for light rods and lures and a heavier model with a regular spool to hold more line in the heavier tests. Whichever reel you get, make sure it is not a cheap model costing only a few dollars. It pays to spend somewhere between $25 and $60 to get a first-rate bait-casting reel. It will cast better, perform better, and last longer.

Earlier anglers used mostly braided silk or nylon lines on their bait-casting reels. Braided lines are still good and are recommended for beginners or those who do not fish too often. But more and more expert anglers are using monofilament lines on their reels because they are strong, take more of a beating, cast smoothly, and are almost invisible. For most fresh-water fishing you can use a line testing from 15 to 20 pounds on a bait-casting reel. Occasionally you may need 25- or even 30-pound-test for really big fish or when fishing in heavy obstructions or trolling with heavy weights or bottom fishing for big catfish.

You can use many of the lures mentioned in the previous chapter on spinning and spin casting with a bait-casting outfit also. But they will generally run somewhat bigger and heavier than spinning-type lures. Spoons, for example, used for big bass, pike, muskies, and coho salmon, will be much bigger and heavier than the small ones used for spinning.

The same is true with the plugs you use. For most of the big fish you will seek with a bait-casting outfit, use the larger, heavier plugs. These also have heavier, stronger hooks to hold the bigger fish. Surface plugs, underwater plugs, and deep-diving and sinking plugs will usually weigh from one-half ounce to 1½ ounces.

The same goes for the other lures used with a bait-casting outfit. The spinners, jigs, plastic worms, and pork chunks will usually run somewhat bigger and heavier than those made for spinning.

But once again, you can buy the best bait-casting outfit made and the best assortment of lures to go with it and still have trouble catching fish. It's how you use this tackle and these lures to fool the big ones that counts. To catch more fish and bigger fish you have to learn how to retrieve and manipulate the various lures to attract fish and make them hit.

Take the fishing waters where a bait-casting outfit really is effective: lakes or ponds filled with lily pads or hyacinths, logs, stumps, sawgrass, weeds, and reeds. This is where the big large-mouth bass like to hang out, and this is where you have to know your stuff to get them. One of the best lures to use to draw bass out from under such cover and make them hit is a surface popping plug. Cast as close as you can to the pads, log, weeds, or stump, and let the plug rest for about a minute. Then pop it and let it rest once again. Pop it and let it rest. Sometimes mild pops work best, while at other times a loud pop will attract fish.

Still another surface plug that draws out the large bass from under cover and makes them hit is the type called the "jump" or "nodding" plug. It is usually long and slender and torpedo- or cigar-shaped, with either a pointed or angled head. There is a small propeller at the tail. This plug, when cast and allowed to rest, sits in the water at an angle, with most of the body underwater and just the head showing.

In the hands of an expert, this plug is deadly, and like most surface lures, it works best when fished very slowly. Actually, you can nod, dip, and twitch this plug so it bobs in one spot and keep it there for long periods. The idea is to make it look like a crippled minnow that is disabled and cannot swim.

A deep-running plug that has a wide lip or long lip and dives very deep is lethal when used with a bait-casting outfit. This plug is especially effective in deep pools of rivers or when trying to reach a deep spot in a lake or reservoir. You have to reel fast to get it down to the best depth and even hit bottom every so often to get the best results from it.

Sinking-type plugs are also best handled with a bait-casting outfit. These are the plugs that sink either slowly or fast toward the bottom. They can be worked at almost any depth, depending on how far you let them sink and how fast you reel them in. For best results, try various depths, from a few feet down to the bottom. And instead of reeling them in straight, give them some rod action by making them rise and then sink again in an erratic movement. Use small, sinking plugs for small-mouth bass in rivers, and larger plugs in lakes for large-mouth bass, walleyes, and pike.

The bait-casting outfit is ideal for working with weedless lures in heavy growth where you have to set a hook hard and lead a bass out of the weeds or lose him. For such fishing, one of the best lures you can use is a weedless spoon, with a strip of pork rind or a pork frog on the hook. Silver spoons are best on some days and in some waters, while black spoons are deadly on other occasions and in other waters. Such a weedless spoon can be cast right into the heaviest pads, hyacinths, or weeds, and you can reel the spoon across the top of the water fast over the weeds, then slow down when you reach an open pocket of water.

The same thing can be done with weedless plastic worms or snakes. You can handle the heavier, longer ones with a bait-casting rod and reel, and cast these into the heaviest growth. Then reel the plastic worms or snakes fairly fast on top of the water so that they look like real worms or snakes trying to escape. Or when you come to an open pocket of water, let the worm sink down toward the bottom. Many a time a bass will be following the worm under the pads, then take it when it slides off a pad and starts to sink.

Rig for fishing plastic worms along the bottom.

When bass are down deep, you can fish a plastic worm along the bottom over rocks, weeds, sunken logs, brush, or in any other place where the big ones hang out. Such a worm should be a floater rigged with a single hook at the head and attached to an 18- or 20-inch leader and a barrel swivel. Then add a one-eighth- or one-quarter-ounce slip or egg sinker on the line above the swivel. This will get the worm down in a hurry, and you can work it slowly just off the bottom.

You can use a similar rig for steelhead in rivers, only instead of a plastic worm, you use a spoon or fly or salmon eggs, and the sinker or weight can be heavier if the current is strong. This rig can be cast up and across stream and allowed to bounce along the bottom. You'll find that bait-casting outfit will save more rigs that are bound to get hung up on the bottom and also handle a big steelhead better in the fast currents of the rivers. You will land more fish with the bait-casting outfit.

And when you use jigs, or the jig and plastic worm combinations for bass or walleyes, you'll find a bait-casting outfit best for such fishing. Such jigs come in different sizes, weights, and colors, and can be worked along the bottom so that they bounce along and kick up some sand, mud, or debris. Fish them slowly and with plenty of rod action. If the plain jig doesn't produce, try adding a strip of pork rind, a plastic worm, a real worm, or a small minnow on the hook. You can also try fishing two jigs at the same time.

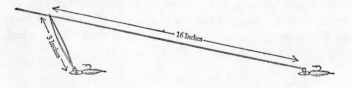

Rig for fishing two jigs at the same time.

A bait-casting outfit is also more practical when fishing for pike, especially when going after them in weeds and around stumps, sunken trees, or other cover. You'll hook and land more pike in such waters. You'll also be able to set the hooks better in the tough jaws of the pike with the stiffer bait-casting rods. And cast the heavier and bigger spoons and plugs usually used for these fish.

When fishing shallow waters for pike, try using a surface plug that kicks up a fuss on top. You can work such a plug fairly fast and jerk it hard to make a big splash. When using spoons in shallow water, cast them out and reel them back with plenty of rod action to make them look like crippled fish. In deeper water, cast out the spoon and let it sink. Often you'll get a strike as the spoon settles toward the bottom. When it reaches bottom, raise it off the bottom, then let it settle back again. Keep doing this all the way in.

Most anglers seeking big muskies also depend on bait-casting tackle to do the trick. Even larger lures are used for muskies than for pike, and they also have tough jaws, so a stiff bait-casting rod is needed. You can also use a bait-casting reel filled with 18- or 20-pound-test line to cast the lures and then hook the fish and boat it safely.

Muskies will also go for a surface plug on many occasions, and the plug can also be worked fairly fast to draw more strikes. These fish have a habit of following a lure without hitting it. Speeding up the retrieve often makes them hit. If you see a good spot that you think harbors a muskie, make many casts there. Or come back later and try it again.

You can also try casting the big spinner and bucktail combinations, spoons, underwater plugs, and any other muskie lures. You can also troll with various lures or your bait-casting outfit not only for muskies but also for bass, pike, walleyes, coho salmon, and lake trout. Trolling for these and other fish will be covered in Chapter 5 of this book.

4

Fly Fishing

Despite the popularity of spinning, spin casting, and bait casting, this fishing tackle hasn't replaced fly-casting tackle. In fact, there has been a renewed interest in fly fishing, and the sale of fly rods, reels, and lines continues strong.

But that isn't the reason why you should take up fly fishing or continue doing it if you already have tried it. If you would like to catch more trout when they are feeding on insects, you can't beat fly-fishing tackle. It is also a deadly way to take black bass, both the large-mouth and small-mouth species. On most streams and rivers fishing for Atlantic salmon, it is the only type of tackle allowed. And even if you are only interested in catching panfish, you will find a fly rod not only a good way to catch these fish, but also a good way to have more fun and sport.

Actually, if you zero in on why most fly fishermen prefer fly fishing to other methods, you will find that they get more satisfaction out of casting, using, and catching fish on the long rod. They find it more relaxing, more fun, more sport, and more of a challenge than, say, spinning, spin casting, or bait casting. There is something about a fly-fishing outfit that makes you feel it is a part of you—sort of an extension of your arm, very close and very personal.

At any rate, as the old saying goes, you shouldn't knock it until you try it. I feel that every fresh-water angler should try fly fishing before he decides it's not for him.

If you haven't got a fly-fishing outfit, how do you go about choosing the right one? Well, here again, just as in choosing other fishing tackle, you have to know what you plan to catch, where you will be fishing, and how many different places you plan to fish. If you are going to spend the rest of your days fishing one stream or one lake for one kind of fish, you can get by with one outfit. However, if you plan to fish various waters for different kinds of fish, you will need two or three outfits.

We can break it down to three basic outfits, which will take care of most fly-fishing situations, most waters, and most fish. First, there's the light outfit, which will be a fly rod of from about 7 to 7½ feet long to cast a double-tapered fly line. Such a rod would handle a DT-5-F fly line. It would be used with a smaller-type, light fly reel. Such a rod is best if you plan to fish mostly with dry flies on the smaller streams, tiny flies, and light leaders for small trout and panfish.

Second, there's the medium fly outfit, which would be 8 or 8½ feet long and would handle a double-tapered line of DT-6-F or DT-7-F. For casting bigger flies and bass bugs you could use a WF-6-F or WF-7-F fly line. This is a weight-forward line. A medium-sized fly reel is used with this rod. This is the closest thing to an "all around" fly-fishing outfit that can be used for panfish, trout in most waters, and bass in open waters. If you can get only one fly outfit, this is the one to get.

The third fly outfit is the heavy one, which would be around 9 feet long and would be used with DT-8-F or DT-9-F or WF-8-F or WF-9-F fly lines. The larger fly reels are used with this rod and line. This is the rod you want if you plan to fish for most bass, steelhead, Atlantic salmon, pike, and any other fairly large fresh-water fish. It can also be used for light salt-water fishing. This outfit can cast the larger flies, bass bugs, and similar bulky lures.

Most of the fly lines specified above are the floating type, but you can also get a sinking line or two to use on a separate spool or fly reel when you want to fish a fly deep.

It is difficult to match the correct fly line to a fly rod unless you know exactly which rod you will be using, and even then, you may have to try casting with the line to see if it matches the rod. If you buy a rod made by a well-known company, it will usually recommend the correct weight line for its rod. This may be listed in the catalog or on the rod itself, or the dealer you buy the rod from will specify the correct fly line.

But nowadays you won't have much of a problem buying a good fly rod, reel, and line that will cast beautifully and deliver the fly to the fish. The difficult part in fly fishing is selecting the flies and learning how to present them to the fish so that they take them.

Let's take dry flies, for example, which can present many problems in fishing, but which are actually one of the easiest flies to use for trout. Unlike the wet flies, which sink and usually cannot be seen, dry flies float on top, and you can follow their drift and see how they are working.

A well-tied dry fly has long, stiff, glossy hackles and tails, which support it high on the water. It is also tied on a light wire hook and is daubed with fly dressing, which helps it to stay afloat.

Dry flies are tied to represent various adult insects that are just leaving the water, hatching, or laying their eggs or have fallen on the water. There are many different kinds or types of dry flies, such as the divided wing, hackle, fan wing, spent wing, variant, bi-visible, and spider.

When it comes to choosing different patterns to carry with you, local preferences and insect life that is prevalent on the waters you will be fishing must be taken into consideration. Most tackle dealers in your area or expert fly fishermen can tell you which ones produce best year after year. You can't go wrong by carrying some of the following patterns: Light Cahill, Quill Gordon, Adams, Henrickson, Fanwing Royal Coachman, Gray Wulff, Royal Wulff, Brown Spider, Red Variant, Black Bi-visible, Brown Bi-visible, Black Gnat, and Black Midge. Dry flies in sizes Nos. 10, 12, 14, and 16 will cover most fishing situations. But in the midges and other tiny flies, you may have to go to those tied on No. 18 and No. 22 hooks.

Dry fly fishing is most effective in the late spring, during the summer, and in early fall. This is when insects are most abundant, and trout will be feeding on them. Dry flies are deadliest when the trout are seen rising and feeding on hatching flies, and you can imitate the flies they are taking. But finding the right fly isn't enough—you also have to make it float or drift naturally with the current without drag. Casting upstream helps, and also mending the line, so that the belly or curve of the fly line is thrown upstream and there is no pull on the fly.

However, that does not mean that you never cast across stream or even downstream. You can cast across stream and get a natural drift of the fly if you cast a series of "S" curves into the fly line, which will create plenty of slack line.

Trout can also be caught by casting a dry fly downstream if you cast plenty of slack into the line and then let out more line from the reel to allow the fly to float without drag at least a short distance.

That is the key to catching trout on dry flies—to make that fly float naturally in the spot where the trout sees it. Sooner or later most flies will drag, especially in broken water. But if the trout takes the fly before the fly starts dragging, then it doesn't matter much. In fact, in fast, broken water, it is harder to keep a dry fly afloat or to prevent drag, but then a trout has to make up its mind faster if it wants the fly. So the trout tends to hit faster and harder in such water. And the turbulence tends to camouflage some of the drag, which may be more noticeable on a flat, unbroken surface.

It's the angler who makes his first cast count who fools and catches the most trout. So it pays to approach quietly, study the water, the currents, the obstacles, the position of the trout —all before you even make the first cast.

That doesn't mean you have to see the trout or know where they are lying to catch them on dry flies. You can cast blindly, wading upstream slowly, reading the water, and casting into pockets, runs, glides, currents, and around rocks and boulders. If you do this carefully, making each cast count and keeping as much as possible of the line and leader from being seen by the trout, you'll get many rises from trout and hook many of them without seeing them at all.

If you do see a trout rise or know where one is lying, never cast directly to that spot. Instead, cast anywhere from a foot or two to several feet above the fish. Float the dry fly to the fish naturally and avoid disturbance from the cast, fly line, or leader.

Although a dry fly is usually allowed to float without drag

most of the time, there are times when "walking" or "skating" a fly on top of the water across the current will draw a smashing strike. Spider flies are good for this and work best with a light fly rod, light fly line and long, fine leader. You cast quartering upstream and hold the rod high to keep as much line and leader off the water as possible. Then pull the fly lightly across the top of the water so that it hops or jumps or skips or glides like a living insect.

If the trout are feeding and striking short or swirling at your fly, the chances are that the fly is too big. Change to a smaller size in the same pattern. Or if they are rising regularly in a sort of a roll in the water, showing their backs or tails and open mouths and refuse to take your regular-sized fly, they may be feeding on midges. Then you have to use these tiny flies to catch fish.

When the hot summer months arrive, trout often start feeding on land insects, called "terrestrials," such as caterpillars, grasshoppers, beetles, and ants. Then you should have some flies tied to imitate these insects. The flies work best when cast close to the shore or overhanging banks where insects are always dropping in, hopping in, or being blown in by the wind.

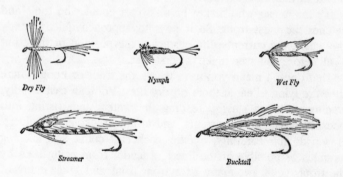

Dry Fly   *Nymph*   *Wet Fly*

Streamer   *Bucktail*

Flies used in fly fishing.

There are many times when wet flies are more effective than dry flies. In fact, trout feed more often underwater than they do on top, so you increase your chances of catching more fish by using lures that move below the surface. Wet flies are tied on heavier-wire hooks than dry flies, so that they sink fast and also have softer hackles, which pulse or breathe in the water. And they should be sparsely tied with a minimum of hackles or feathers.

Some of the most effective wet flies for many parts of the country include the Cahill, Light Cahill, Quill Gordon, Iron Blue Dun, Gold Ribbed Hare's Ear, Royal Coachman, Leadwing Coachman, Professor, Brown Hackle, March Brown, Black Gnat, McGinty, Cowdung, Ginger Quill, and Wooly Worm. If you get these in sizes Nos. 8, 10, 12, and 14, you will have a good assortment for most trout fishing conditions and streams.

The way a wet fly is usually fished is to cast upstream and across stream. Let the wet fly move with the current for most of the drift. When the fly is below you, start to retrieve it in short jerks. Most anglers usually move downstream when fishing a wet fly, but an upstream approach is often better, because you move up on the trout from behind, since the trout normally face upstream when resting or feeding.

Actually, wet fly fishing is more difficult than dry fly fishing because you usually don't see the trout rise and take the fly. And you can't see the fly to know how it is working. You have to guess or imagine where it is and how it is acting. And a fish can examine a wet fly carefully and closely before it takes it.

The fact that you can fish a wet fly at various depths, however, makes it more versatile than a dry fly. One effective way to work a wet fly is to retrieve it very fast by stripping in line by hand in 2- or 3-foot spurts without any pauses in between. While stripping in line with one hand, you lift the rod quickly with the other. The wet fly should travel just below the surface without skipping or causing any disturbance on top.

On the quieter stretches and deeper pools you can cast straight across stream and let the fly sink toward the bottom. On faster stretches you may have to cast almost directly upstream to get the fly down deep. You can even feed some slack line to get it deeper. A sinking fly line will also enable you to get the fly down deeper than when using a floating fly line.

And fishing with two or three wet flies at the same time is often more effective than with just one fly. Wet flies are especially deadly in slow, shallow streams, in smooth runs of big rivers, in quiet pools, and in lakes. And while they will take fish if allowed to drift naturally with the current, they are even better if you twitch the flies while they drift and also when retrieving them after they have drifted below you.

In fast water, use three flies, and cast them across stream, then lift the rod quickly and start retrieving them fast so that they leap and skitter across the top of the water. This will often drive a big trout crazy and draw a smashing strike.

In lakes and ponds there is no current, and here you usually have to give the fly some action to make it look alive. This doesn't have to be violent or fast, but just gathering in the fly line with one hand and slight twitches with the rod tip will suffice. If you can see trout cruising by in a lake or pond, cast the wet fly about 30 to 35 feet ahead of the fish and let it sink toward the bottom. Then as the fish approaches, start bringing the fly in so it rises toward the surface and has some movement.

Nymphs are even more difficult to fish than wet flies. They represent the larvae of various forms of aquatic insects such as stone flies, mayflies, dragonflies, and damsel flies. They are smaller, more drab in color, and even harder to see in the water than wet flies. But since trout feed more on the larvae than on adult flies, nymphs are one of the deadliest flies you can use for trout most of the season.

A good assortment of nymphs would include the stone fly, mayfly, caddis, March brown, Hendrickson, ginger quill, breadcrust, olive nymph, black nymph, dragonfly nymph, and damsel nymph.

Nymphs are fished somewhat like wet flies in that they are cast quartering or upstream and allowed to drift naturally with the current. When the line straightens out, you can retrieve the nymphs in short, quick jerks so that they rise toward the surface. Like a wet fly, a nymph can be worked at different levels, from just below the surface down to the very bottom.

When trout are "bulging" or feeding on nymphs just below the surface, a floating fly line is best, since the nymph shouldn't sink or travel too deep at this time. However, for most nymph fishing, you will find a sinking fly line better, since it permits you to work the fly deeper, especially in fast currents and deep pools.

You can also cast a nymph downstream in strong currents and

Still fishing can be done alone or in groups. Popular spots are often lined with anglers along the shore or with families fishing together. (South Carolina Department of Parks, Recreation, and Tourism)

Although fly fishing is done mostly in streams and rivers, it is also effective in many lakes, like these placid Canadian waters of Patricia Lake, Alberta. (Alberta Government Department of Industry and Commerce Photo)

Spinning is not only for small fish but also for big ones, like this Coho salmon. The light lines used fool more fish and land them too! (Ohio Department of Natural Resources)

A spin-casting outfit is one of the best fishing outfits you can recommend for kids, beginners, and those who fish only a few times a year. (Nebraska Game and Parks Department Photo)

Many expert anglers still use bait-casting tackle to catch big bass, especially in southern waters like Lake Jackson, Florida. (Florida News Bureau Photo by Johnson)

Extra-long fly rods are often used by fishermen, like this one at Riviere Matane, Quebec, to catch big Atlantic salmon in Canadian and European waters. Most modern anglers, though, prefer to use shorter rods. (Quebec Government Photo)

Lake trout like this one caught in Grist Lake, Alberta, are usually taken trolling deep with spoons, using weights and wire lines with light salt-water rods and reels. (Alberta Government Bureau of Public Affairs Photo)

Although trout, like those in this gorge near Shohola Pike, Pennsylvania, can be caught on other fishing tackle, most confirmed trout anglers feel that the only way to take these fish is on a fly rod and an artificial fly. (Pennsylvania Fish Commission Photo)

Black bass go for bass bugs used with a fly rod in a big way, as this specimen reveals. This is obviously a large-mouth bass. (Pennsylvania Fish Commission Photo)

These anglers going after muskies or pike in North Caribou Lake, Ontario, find the bait-casting outfit best for casting the heavier lures and playing and boating big fish. (Ontario Ministry of Industry and Tourism)

Electric motors like this one are becoming increasingly popular for slow trolling. They are quieter than regular outboard motors and are especially effective in shallow water. (Tempo Products Co. Photo)

allow plenty of slack line so that the nymph sinks deep below you. Then work it toward the surface for a few feet before lifting it out of the water.

In deep pools you can cast the nymph out, let it sink slowly and let it lie on the bottom. The same thing can be done in lakes and ponds. Trout may hit the nymph while it is sinking or grab it on the way up when it is being retrieved.

It is not easy to detect a strike when fishing a nymph, and you have to develop a sort of a sixth sense when to react. Sometimes you can see the flash of the fish or see the line or leader move, and you can set the hook. It also helps to hold the line between the fingers of the hand that is holding the rod.

The other flies that are very effective for trout and other fish are the streamers and bucktails. Actually, the word "flies" is incorrect when used to describe these lures. They are tied to resemble minnows or small fish more than any insect. The name "bucktail" is given to the flies that have wings of hair. The name "streamer" is applied to those having long feather wings.

Some of the most popular bucktail and streamer patterns include the Mickey Finn, Edson Tiger Light, Edson Tiger Dark, Professor, Silvery Doctor, Black-nosed Dace, Brown and White, Black and White, Yellow and White, Black Ghost, Gray Ghost, Green Ghost, Montreal, Supervisor, White Marabou, Black Marabou, Yellow Marabou, and the Muddler.

Streamers and bucktails are usually tied on long-shanked hooks in sizes from about 2/0 down to No. 12. The smaller ones are best for small streams and small and low-water trout, while the bigger ones are used on big waters for big trout, bass, pike, and landlocked salmon.

Streamers and bucktails are most effective when fish are chasing minnows or small fish. They are very good early in the year and later on in the summer, when insects become scarce, and at any time of the year for big trout. Use them early in the morning, in the evening, and at night. They are especially deadly after a recent rain that causes the stream to rise or become slightly discolored. That is when big trout often come out to feed.

The usual way to fish streamers or bucktails is to cast across stream and quartering downstream. The line should be taut, and you have to experiment with the retrieve to find out what the trout want. Sometimes a slow retrieve is best; at other times a medium retrieve is needed; while on still other occasions, a fast retrieve is preferred.

The same thing is true in the rod action you give the streamer or bucktail: Sometimes it should be retrieved in short jerks or spurts, while on other occasions long sweeps of the rod or pulls on the line do the trick.

And you have to find out which level the trout are feeding or lying in. There are times when a streamer retrieved fast right on top, so that it looks like a frantic minnow or small fish swimming for its life, draws smashing strikes. At other times the streamer should be retrieved just below the surface, and at still other times the streamer or bucktail should be worked deep, even down along the bottom.

For this a sinking fly is best or a weighted-type streamer or bucktail. And here you can cast across or even upstream a bit and let the lure swing around and sink and even feed more line so that it gets down deep. Then retrieve it slowly right on the bottom.

Streamers and bucktails can also be used in lakes for trout or landlocked salmon. They work best in waters where big trout or landlocked salmon feed on smelt, alewives, herring, or minnows. Casting toward shore or around the mouths of brooks or streams is a good way to take brook trout and land-locked salmon in the spring of the year.

The fly rod is the only fishing tackle you are allowed to use for Atlantic salmon in Maine or Canada. Salmon flies are tied on larger and stronger hooks, and some of the flies are really gaudy and unlike any insect you have ever seen. But year after year they continue to take salmon. Such patterns include the Jock Scott, Silver Doctor, Dusty Miller, Silver Wilkinson, Green Highlander, Blue Charm, March Brown, Black Dose, Lady Amherst, Cosseboom, Teagle Bee, and Mar Lodge in wet flies. These may be tied on hooks from sizes No. 10 to 4/0 or 5/0. The smaller flies are best during the summer when the water is low, while the larger sizes work best early in the season, when the water is high.

Salmon also take dry flies when the water is low and clear. Many standard trout flies tied on larger, stronger hooks can also be used for salmon. Such patterns as the Pink Lady, Rat-faced McDougall, Quill Gordon, Black Gnat, the Wulff flies, and the various spiders and bi-visibles can all be used.

Flies are usually presented the Atlantic salmon, which are seen lying in the river or seen leaping out of the water. A wet fly is cast across stream and slightly downstream. You keep the line straight and avoid any belly or drag, which speeds up the fly. To control this, you may have to take up slack from time to time or let out line if the current is fast, to get the proper drift. The fly should travel just below the surface and not too deep. At the end of the drift you can retrieve the fly slowly. For a change of pace, try retrieving fast, since salmon have been known to strike a fast-moving fly violently on occasion. If you raise a salmon and it misses the fly, keep on casting, since the salmon may rise again and take it.

Dry flies are also cast across or slightly downstream above the fish and allowed to drift toward the salmon. Atlantic salmon will usually take a dry fly early in its drift if they mean business. Toward the end of a drift you will generally get bumps or false strikes. Often a series of casts, letting the fly drift a few seconds, then lifting it off the water, casting a short distance above the first cast, letting it drift a few seconds, and repeating the same procedure, will excite a salmon and make it rise more readily.

Another great fish for the fly rod is the steelhead or seagoing rainbow trout, caught along the Pacific Coast. They can be taken on flies during various times of the year when present in a river, but usually the summer and early fall months are best. This is because the water is low and clear then.

The flies used for steelhead can be specially tied patterns, such as the Silver Demon, Golden Demon, Umpqua, Thor, Shrimp, Lady Godiva, Queen Bess, Harger's Orange, Sky-komish Sunrise, and many others. Many steelhead flies are tied with fluorescent materials. Standard trout flies can also be used both in the wet and dry patterns tied on larger hooks.

However, most steelhead fly fishing is down deep, and a fast, sinking fly line or shooting fly line with monofilament running line are needed. Long casts are usually necessary, and you have to get the fly down near the bottom for best results. Weighted flies can be used to get down deeper.

Bass bugs.

A fly-fishing outfit can also be deadly and very effective when used for black bass. Both the large-mouth and small-mouth bass go for flies or bass bugs during the late spring, summer, and early fall months. Many of the standard trout patterns of wet and dry flies tied on larger hooks will also take bass. The same is true of streamers and bucktails used for trout. They also work well on bass when they are chasing or feeding on minnows.

Then there are the bass bugs specially tied for black bass, and these are made of cork or balsa, or styrofoam or plastic or hair bodies, and with feather or hair wings or tails. They usually imitate moths, beetles, mice, frogs, minnows, or small fish. There are popper bass bugs, hairfrogs, spiders with rubber legs, bullet-shaped minnow bugs, and similar creations that can be used.

The fly rod is most effective on bass when they are in shallow water, so when seeking small-mouth bass in rivers, cast streamers, bucktails, and even dry flies or small bass bugs. The best places to fish are shallow spots, from a few inches to 3 or 4 feet deep. This means casting near shore, in riffles or rapids, shallow pools, and runs along rocks and ledges. The ideal time for this fishing is in the evening during the late summer, when insects are plentiful.

When small-mouth bass are feeding on or chasing minnows in shallow water, a streamer or bucktail skittered across the surface of the water will often tempt the fish to follow the lure and to hit it hard. In a river you can also let a streamer fly float downstream in rapids and then, holding the rod high, retrieve it so that it skips from one spot to another. When fishing streamers or bucktails in pools or lakes, let them sink deep, and then work them with plenty of rod action toward the surface.

When fishing for large-mouth bass, don't fish the bugs too fast. Take your time; it is much better to fish and work a small area thoroughly than to scatter your casts at random all over the lake. Often, casting your bug close to shore or some cover and just letting it lie still will draw a strike. And when you do work it back, do so slowly, and let the bug rest in a spot every so often, like a natural insect, bug, or frog does. Make it struggle, hesitate, and look crippled, and a bass will go for it.

Of course, there are exceptions, such as when using the bullet-shaped bug, which resembles a minnow. This can be worked somewhat faster, to imitate a frantic minnow or small fish trying to escape.

Finally, your fly rod is an ideal weapon for panfish. Bluegills, for example, can often be taken on dry flies or small panfish bugs, such as the rubber spider types. Fish these toward evening; cast a dry fly and let it lie motionless for a while, then twitch it gently and slowly. Rubber spiders can be worked the same way, with short twitches on top, or allowed to sink and retrieved slowly below the surface.

Another panfish that can be caught on a fly rod is the crappie. For these use tiny streamers or bucktails, wet flies, and spinner and fly combinations. Cast them near weed beds or shorelines, and work them very slowly.

White perch also go for tiny streamers, bucktails, wet flies, or spinners. The same goes for white bass, which often chase minnows on the surface. Then a small wet fly, a streamer, or a bucktail cast toward the feeding school will bring a strike.

Once you master casting and fishing with a fly rod, you will find that you'll be using this tackle more often than any other— not only because it is more sport and fun, but also because for many fresh-water fish, it is more effective than other tackle.

5

Fresh-water Trolling

Trolling in lakes or rivers is one of the most effective ways of catching many fresh-water species. In fact, on many days and in many waters, trolling is the best way to catch fish in fresh water. You cover a lot of territory and show your lure to more fish. It is a good way to fish a strange lake or river to locate fish and find the best spots to fish. It is also a good way to catch fish when they are down deep. And trolling is usually a less exerting way to fish than casting a lure, especially with modern electric or outboard motors.

Nevertheless, that doesn't mean that trolling is easy or simple and that all you have to do is drag a lure behind a boat and catch fish. Trolling is more complex than that, and you have to learn and consider many factors before you can become even moderately successful at trolling.

Although in a pinch almost any fresh-water rod and reel can be used for trolling, certain outfits are better than others for certain species of fish and for certain kinds of trolling. One of the best "all around" outfits for trolling is a bait-casting rod and reel filled with about 18- or 20-pound-test monofilament line. The revolving-spool reel makes it easy to let out line or reel it in as the situation demands. The stiffer bait-casting rod and the stronger lines make such an outfit ideal for trolling deep near the bottom, where you often hang up and have to break free. Also, you can handle the bigger fish that hit, and boat them without losing them.

There are also special trolling rods made for fresh water that have longer handles and a foregrip. These are also somewhat stiffer and heavier than bait-casting rods and more suitable for trolling deep and handling the larger lures, trolling weights, and bigger fish. A larger-sized level-wind revolving spool can be used with this rod.

For very deep trolling, many anglers prefer to use the lighter salt-water trolling rods. These can be combined with conventional revolving-spool salt-water reels with star drag. You can load the reel with 20- or 30-pound-test monofilament for shallow trolling or when using trolling weights. For deeper trolling, the reel can be loaded with lead-core or solid Monel wire line.

Both spinning and spin-casting outfits can also be used for many kinds of trolling. They are especially suited for shallow water and near-shore trolling for the smaller species. The thinner lines usually used with the regular spinning or spin-casting outfits make them less visible in clear water. But longer, heavier spinning outfits up to 8 to 9 feet long can also be used when trolling for bigger fish and in somewhat deeper water. With such rods you can use the larger spinning reels filled with 15- or 20-pound-test mono lines.

You can also use fly rods for trolling wet flies, streamer flies, or tiny spoons and spinners for trout, bass, landlocked salmon, and panfish. They are best for trolling close to shore in shallow water where there are few obstructions.

You can use many of the lures mentioned in previous chapters on bait casting and spinning for trolling also. You have to use various kinds of rigs and weights and trolling aids to present your lure or bait at the right level. These will be dealt with later in this chapter for specific fish or fishing.

To catch more fish by trolling, you have to know where to troll, when to troll, which baits or lures to use, how to get them down to the right depth, and how to give them the best fish-appealing action.

There are some general rules about trolling procedures that can be laid down and that will enable you to catch more fish. First, of course, you need a boat and motor of some kind for trolling. And while trolling can be done from any boat, such as a canoe to a big runabout or utility craft, a medium-sized 12- or 14-foot boat with a rather wide beam is best. It is big enough to be stable, and yet one man can handle it. You can also attach rod holders on both corners at the stern to spread two rods and even troll a third rod from the middle of the stern.

Usually the lighter, smaller outboard motors are best for fresh-water trolling. You can troll at slower speeds with them. If you troll in shallow waters a lot, an electric motor is even slower and quieter. In some spots and for some fish, it is even better to row or paddle the boat instead of using a motor.

Before you can catch fish, you have to find out where to troll in a river or lake. Such spots as channels between islands, mouths of streams or rivers entering a lake, points of land, dropoffs from shallow into deep water, sunken islands, trees, brush, rocky bottoms, sand- or gravel bars, weed beds, and edges of lily pads are all good spots to try.

Trolling can be done close to shore or in shallow water early and late in the season, as well as during the summer at day-break, late afternoon, and after dark. During the heat of the day most fish seek the depths, and then they hug the bottom. You have to troll deep to get them.

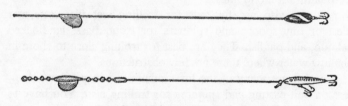

Trolling weight rigs.

The depth at which your lure or bait will travel will depend on how much line you let out, the kind of line you are using and any weight or sinker or rig you are using. When using braided or monofilament lines without any weights, the lure will travel just below the surface. If you add some trolling weights or rigs with sinkers, you can get down deeper and even reach the bottom in moderate depths. For still deeper trolling, you can use lead-core and wire lines and add weights to these.

If you let out a lot of line, your lure will travel deeper. The same is true if you troll very slowly. If you speed up, the lure or bait will rise closer to the surface. When trolling against the current, the lure will be closer to the surface than when moving with the current.

Generally speaking, you should troll at the speed that will bring out the best action of the lure being used. Before you let the lure out all the way, hold it in the water alongside the boat as you move along and watch its action. Then you can speed up or slow down until the lure is working in the most enticing manner.

Usually it pays to start trolling with two or three lines at different lengths and different depths, and with different lures. When you catch a fish and find out which length of line and depth and lure are best, adjust the rest of the lines to suit.

If straight trolling fails to produce a strike, try a zigzag course. This usually makes the lure rise and then sink in an attractive manner. And instead of just letting the rods rest in rod holders or in your hand, quickly raise and lower your rod tip to give the lure added action.

It is very important while trolling to reel in your lines every so often to see if the lures are not fouled or some weeds or debris haven't caught onto the lure. Fish will not hit a lure covered by such material. You can usually tell if the lure is working properly by watching the rod tip or feeling the vibrations by holding the rod.

Trolling procedures and tactics also vary according to the kind of fish you are seeking. Many species of trout can be caught by trolling in lakes and rivers. Some of the biggest trout are taken this way, such as the big brook trout in some of the larger lakes and rivers in Maine and Canada. Trolling with fly rods is one of the best ways to take these big brook trout in northern waters. They will hit streamers and bucktails, which resemble smelt, alewives, minnows, or small fish. The streamers and bucktails are let out behind the boat and trolled along close to shore and around the mouths of brooks or rivers entering lakes.

You can also troll wet flies with a fly rod for brook trout and other trout. Here, a leader holding two or three wet flies is usually best. Make sure your fly line and leader sink so that they don't leave a wake or ripple on top of the water when trolled. When the water is rough, troll into the wind and use short lines of 30 to 35 feet. When the lake is calm and clear, troll longer lines up to 50 to 75 feet.

Rainbow trout can be caught by trolling in lakes or rivers where these fish are found. Here again, a fly rod can be used when trolling close to shore in shallow water. This is best in the spring of the year, when rainbow trout move in close to shore to enter streams and rivers for spawning. Then they will hit streamers and bucktails trolled on a fly rod.

You can also use a spinning rod to troll spinners, spoons, and jigs from just below the surface to several feet down. By adding weights, you can troll still deeper. One of the most effective rigs for trolling deep for rainbows is the "Christmas Tree" or "Cowbells," which is made up of a series of spinners and a lure or bait such as a minnow or worms on the end. This should be trolled slowly and deep, close to the bottom.

Another great fish that can be caught by trolling is the land-locked salmon. When the ice is out in Maine or Canada, these fish provide top sport on a fly rod. They are then found near the surface close to shore and near the mouths of streams where smelt gather. Trolling such bucktails and streamers as the Supervisor, Gray Ghost, Black Ghost, Edson Tiger Dark, or the Nine-Three is highly effective. For best results, trail three streamers or bucktails on the same leader. You can start with three different patterns, and when you find out which they prefer, you can change to that one.

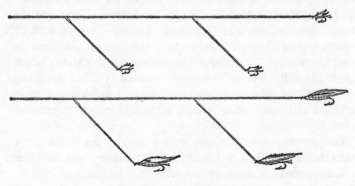

Rigs for trolling three flies.

When trolling for landlocked salmon, follow an S course along a broken shoreline. This will give your flies better action as they sink and then rise on the curves. When trolling a straight course, give the flies some action by raising and lowering your rod tip or grabbing the line near the reel and sawing it back and forth in a quick motion to make the fly look like a live smelt or small fish. Sometimes adding a small smelt or minnow on the hook helps bring more strikes. Trolling close to the boat in the wash is also a good idea.

During the summer months, when landlocked salmon are deep, you can troll with bait-casting rods or trolling rods with wire lines or weights to get the sewed smelt, spoon, or plug down deep.

And instead of using the motor when trolling flies for landlocks, try paddling a canoe as close to shore as possible. This will bring your flies closer to rocky points, rock bars, dropoffs, rivermouths, and areas where smelt and minnows hang out. Salmon follow them into such spots.

During the summer months landlocked salmon are deep, and then you can troll with bait-casting or trolling rods down deep. You can use lead-core and wire lines or weights to get your sewed smelt, minnow, spoon, or plug down to the right depth and temperature.

Similar deep trolling is the best way to take lake trout. Except for brief periods in the spring and fall, when the lake trout rise to the surface and come close to shore, they are usually found down deep, in depths up to 200 or 300 feet. They like to lie over shoals or reefs with deep water nearby.

In moderate depths you can use weighted lines or lead-core lines to get down to the depth where the fish are. But in deeper, larger lakes, you will need a solid-wire line like Monel on a light salt-water trolling outfit and reel to get down deep enough. Usually wire lines testing from 20 to 40 pounds are used, and you can add a 2- or 3-ounce trolling weight between the wire line and your leader so you can bounce bottom with it to know that you are down deep enough. At the end of your leader you can attach a spoon, plug, or multiple spinner rig called the "Christmas Tree" mentioned earlier.

Deep trolling with similar rigs is also the best way to catch

coho salmon. Like lake trout, they will also be found feeding
in shallow water near shore and near the surface early in the
spring. Then trolling with regular monofilament or braided
lines a few feet down will take them. But when they go down
deep later on in the year, deep trolling with weights or wire
lines is the most effective way to get them.

A good way to start trolling for coho is to rig three outfits:
The first can have lures moving from a few feet down to about
15 feet deep; the second line can be down anywhere from
about 15 to 30 or 40 feet; and the third one can be still deeper
down, to 75 or 100 feet.

Coho usually chase and feed on smelt and alewives, so if you
can locate schools of these fish in the depths, you can troll at
that level. An electronic fish locator or depth finder is a big
help in locating such bait and even the salmon themselves.

Trolling speeds for coho salmon will vary from very slow up
to 6 or 7 knots. Usually the speed that will bring out the best
action in the lures is best. The most effective lures are medium-
sized spoons, spinners, and plugs. Minnows or smelt can also
be trolled on a hook. Bright-colored spoons and plugs painted
orange, yellow, and red in fluorescent colors are very effective.

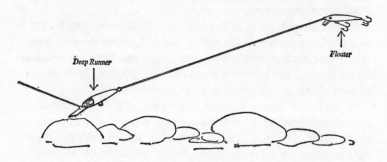

Deep trolling combination.

Trolling is also very effective for black bass, both the small-
mouth and large-mouth varieties. When trolling for large-
mouth bass, you can first try early in the morning and evening
along the shoreline as close as possible to weed beds, lily pads,
and hyacinths. Also try off rocky points, ledges, rocks, and

gravel bars. Shallow-running underwater plugs can be used for this trolling. If that doesn't work, try trolling farther out in the lake along the dropoffs, and over submerged weed beds, using lures such as spinners, spoons, and diving or underwater plugs that travel a few feet down.

During the middle of the day and in the summer, trolling in still deeper water with deep-diving plugs, jigs, and spinners worked slowly along the bottom is recommended. The lure or trolling weight or sinker should bump bottom every so often so you know you are down deep enough.

Small-mouth bass are sometimes caught trolling near the surface close to shore in shallow water on fly rods with streamers or bucktails. Shallow-running plugs, spinners, and spoons will also take them then. Best results are obtained along rocky shores, ledges, or over gravel or rock bars. Most of the time you will catch more small-mouth bass by trolling deep near the bottom, both in rivers and in lakes. In rivers the big pools and eddies can be trolled. In lakes troll spinners, spoons, and deep-running plugs over rocky bottoms, weed beds, and between rocks and boulders.

Another fish usually caught by trolling deep is the walleye. This is especially true during the daytime when the sun is bright. Then the walleyes hang out in the deepest holes and pools, and lures should be worked as close to the bottom as possible. And trolling for walleyes should be done very slowly. They rarely chase or catch a fast-moving lure, so lures worked slowly are best. That is one reason why spinners such as the June-Bug type, with a minnow or worm added to the hooks, is so effective. It spins even when the boat is moving slowly, and it attracts walleyes.

Other good trolling lures for walleyes include spoons, plugs, and jigs, the latter combined with a short length of plastic worm or a minnow on the hook. Jigs also have to be given some rod action by lifting and lowering the rod tip. In any deep trolling for walleyes, it is a good idea to have a sinker or weight below the rig to get the lure or bait down to the bottom and also to bounce along the bottom so that you know you are deep enough.

Trolling is also a good way to catch pike and muskies. Both

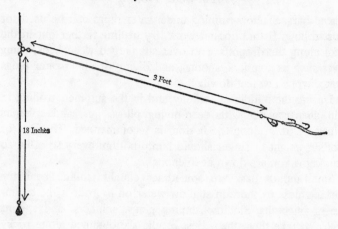

Walleye trolling rig with spinner.

these fish spend a lot of time near shore along weed beds and
lily pads and around sunken logs, trees, brush piles, and gravel
and rock bars. So trolling close to such hangouts with spinners,
spoons, and plugs is best. This shallow-water trolling is usually
best in the spring and fall. During the summer months both
these fish go into deeper water, and then trolling from a few feet
down to depths of 30 or 40 feet produces better.

And finally, trolling works well with many panfish, such as
white bass, which are found in many of our southern impoundments and reservoirs. These fish usually chase gizzard shad or
other baitfish on top and break water. At such times, try trolling a spinner, spoons, tiny plugs, or jigs around the edges of
such schools. You can try trolling near the surface, but if this
doesn't work, try trolling deeper below the feeding schools. If
you don't see any white bass on top, blind trolling around
the mouths of rivers or streams entering the lake or reservoir.
Below dams is another good place to troll. When trolling lures
just below the surface for white bass, you can move pretty fast,
but when they are down deep, slow trolling is better.

Similar trolling can be done for crappies using tiny spoons,
or just plain minnows. A strip of pork rind on a hook will also
catch them. These should be trolled very slowly a few feet down
along weedy shorelines and around bonnets, hyacinths, brush

piles, and sunken trees. You can do the same thing for white perch, yellow perch, and bluegills. If you move too fast with a motor, try shutting it off and rowing the boat. Panfish do not move too fast, and a very slow-moving lure or bait is most preferred.

No matter what fish you troll for, it's a good idea to mark the location so that you can troll over the same spot several times. Most fish tend to school or feed in groups, so repeated trolling over the same spot is wise. One way to mark a spot is to carry a plastic bottle or container with a cord or line wrapped around it and a weight or sinker on the end. Then when you hook a fish, toss this overboard so that the line will unwind until the sinker reaches the bottom. This will serve as a buoy to mark your spot.

6

Drifting, Jigging, Float Fishing, and Night Fishing

One very effective way to fish is from a drifting boat across a lake or pond, using the wind to move the boat at a slow pace along the surface of the water. It is a simple and easy way and a relaxing way to fish, with no boat handling required and no lowering or raising of the anchor every time you want to try a new spot. It doesn't move your lure or bait as fast as when trolling. But neither does the bait or lure stay in one spot or a small area, as when fishing from an anchored boat.

A lure or bait moving behind a boat or along the bottom while drifting has just enough action to make it look alive, yet it doesn't go so fast that some fish can't catch up with it or get discouraged and don't even try. Even the slowest-moving species can catch up with a bait being fished from a drifting boat.

In order for the boat to drift at the right speed, you should have a light breeze or wind, which moves it along at a fairly brisk pace. But it shouldn't move too fast either, because then your bait or lure will be traveling too close to the surface most of the time. If the wind is gentle or too light, you won't move fast enough to give your lure or bait enough action, and you won't cover much territory.

Using your oars or a paddle can help move the boat in spurts for short distances while you drift if the wind is too weak. And if the wind is strong, you can let out a bucket or sea anchor on a line and let it out to slow down the boat. Or tie a light anchor or rock to a line and let it drag along the bottom.

At any rate, the biggest advantage in drift fishing is that you are always presenting your lure or bait to new fish in fresh territory. You will eventually run into individual fish or schools of fish. And a moving bait or lure attracts more fish than one that is lying still on the bottom or gets hidden in the mud, weeds, or between rocks.

You can drift with such lures as streamers, wet flies, plastic worms, spinners, light spoons, plugs, letting out line from the side of the boat as it moves along. When using spinners or spoons or plugs, choose the lighter models, which have a lively action even at slow speeds. The thin spoons are best for this, or spinners that revolve at slow speeds. The best plugs for drifting are the light balsa or plastic underwater types, which wriggle at the slowest speeds. Most of these lures can be given extra action by lifting and lowering your rod tip as you drift along. You can drift in shallow water near shore early in the morning and in the evening with lures that travel just below the surface. Here it is usually best to let out a long line.

When drifting with lures in deeper water, you will have to use a lead-core line to get them down deep, or add weights and sinkers to hold them down near the bottom.

Drifting with live baits is even more effective. Here you simply take a worm or minnow and let it out from the side of the boat and drift along until a fish takes it. You can do this with a plain line or add a float or cork a few feet above the bait. By drifting close to shore you'll catch bass, pickerel, and panfish this way.

When the fish are down deep, you can drift the live baits along the bottom. A simple rig with a sinker on the end and a 2- or 3-foot leader tied a few inches above the sinker with a hook on the end will do the trick. This can be baited with a worm, minnow, frog, insect, or crayfish and lowered to the bottom as the boat moves along. If you raise and lower your rod and bounce the sinker on the bottom occasionally, you'll know if it is deep enough. With such live baits it's a good idea to

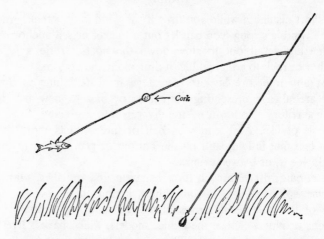

Rig for drifting deep with baits with cork to keep bait
out of weeds.

give some slack line or lower your rod tip when you get a bite
to let the fish mouth and partly swallow the bait before you
try to set the hook. Once you catch some fish in a certain spot,
you can drift over it repeatedly and catch more fish. Take
cross bearings on some landmarks or drop a float and line
with a weight to mark the spot so you can locate it again. You
can also anchor and still-fish or cast lures in that particular
spot.

Drifting is also a good way to locate and catch fish, even if
you are casting a lure toward shore. Here for best results, the
wind should move the boat parallel to the shoreline so that you
can cast your lure toward shore in likely spots.

In recent years anglers have discovered that "jigging" is a
killing way to catch many fresh-water species. Jigging has been
popular in salt-water fishing for many years, but now fresh-
water anglers also know a good thing when they see it and have
adapted it to fresh-water fishing. Actually, a form of jigging
has been done in fresh water for many years, mostly during
the winter months when fishing through the ice. Tiny spoons,
special flies, and jigs are lowered through a hole in the ice and
worked up and down on a short stick or rod. During the winter
months anglers catch yellow perch, pickerel, and occasional
walleyes, pike, and bass this way.

But now anglers have found that jigging also pays off big during the summer months. In fact, when you are trying to reach fish way down deep, it is one of the best methods you can use during the hot summer months.

Basically, jigging is done by merely letting your lure down until you feel it hit bottom, then reel in a foot or two and start working your rod tip up and down so that the lure rises, then sinks or flutters in an enticing manner. This can be done from an anchored boat if you are fishing in a good spot or if you know that a school of fish is present. But most of the time best results are obtained by jigging from a drifting boat.

Almost any spinning or bait-casting rod can be used for jigging, but the rod shouldn't be too flexible or too stiff. Thinner lines are also better for jigging than heavy ones because the lure has better action and sinks quicker to the bottom. There is also less of a belly or curve in your line, and you hook more fish. Of course, the tackle you use will depend on the size of the fish you will be catching. Thus lighter rods and lines can be used for small fish such as panfish in shallow water, while heavier rods and lines will be used for deep jigging for big lake trout.

For most jigging the lead-head "jigs" (also called bucktails) are most effective. They sink fast, the line is tied on top, and the hook rides up, so there's less chance of fouling on the bottom. For fresh-water jigging, white, yellow, brown, black, and combinations of these colors are best in the jigs you use.

Other lures that can be used for jigging include spoons, and these should be on the heavy side so that they get down to the bottom fast and stay there. Jigging is especially effective for lake trout in deep water. Here you can use heavy spoons or jigs up to 2 or 3 ounces to get down to the depths where these fish are found. Some anglers like to use a double-jig rig for these fish. They add a second smaller jig to the hook of the first jig, then add a strip of fish to the hook of this second jig.

In fact, adding a worm, minnow, or short length of plastic worm or pork rind to the hook of any jig will often make it more effective than the plain jig. Such combinations are especially good when jigging for walleyes.

You can also use tiny jigs for panfish such as white bass, white perch, yellow perch, crappies, and sunfish. And jigging

Jig with Strip of Fish

Heavy Spoon

Lures used in jigging for lake trout.

is just as effective when done in fairly shallow water as in deep water. Here instead of using a short spinning rod, use a long cane or glass pole, and tie enough line on it to reach bottom. Then lower it among lily pads, weeds, or other spots where panfish hang out and work it slowly up and down. Here too, adding a small piece of worm, an insect, or a tiny piece of pork rind or fish will make it even more effective.

If jigging straight up and down under a boat doesn't work, try casting the jig away from the boat. Then when it hits bottom, start reeling it back with some rod action so that it bounces along the bottom. This is a good way to catch black bass, both the large-mouth and the small-mouth varieties.

Another method of fishing that is very productive is "float fishing." Here you launch a boat in one part of the river and then float with the current for several miles or more downstream, fishing along the way. In most places it's a two-man job and you need two cars. One car is left at a point where the float trip will end, while the anglers go upriver with the other car to the spot where the boat will be launched.

There are many kinds of boats that can be used for float fishing, such as rubber rafts, canoes, small skiffs, rowboats, and specially built craft for certain areas. But the boat that is usually associated with float fishing is the john boat, originally built specially for float fishing in the Ozarks in Missouri and

Arkansas. Being flat-bottomed and narrow with square ends, it is built to take rough treatment and navigate the mountain streams where it originated. Some of the john boats were as long as 24 feet, but modern versions made from aluminum are shorter and lighter so that they can be handled by two men and carried on top of a car or light trailer.

On any float trip it's a good idea to know your river and all the hazardous spots such as rapids, falls, shallow spots, rocks, and other dangerous obstructions so that you can avoid them or stop before you reach them. Every boat should also have an outboard motor, oars or paddles, and life preservers or jackets that can be worn. It's also a good idea to carry waterproof bags or containers to hold cameras, food, matches, spare clothes, and anything else you want to keep dry from a rain or spray.

Since fishing is the main object in float fishing and not just a boat ride, don't plan on floating for too long a stretch in one day. Plan on only a few miles, and fish this thoroughly. If you want to fish longer stretches, plan on two- or three-day or longer float trips, and camp overnight along the way.

Unless you anchor the boat or fish a quiet pool or beach your boat and fish from shore, the best way to fish on a float trip is to have one man handle the oars or paddle or pole, while the other man casts or fishes. Of course, you can take turns at this so that both of you get a chance to fish. But you need one man always ready to maneuver the boat or keep it out of a dangerous spot or situation.

On some of the big, turbulent rivers such as those found out West in Oregon, Washington, California, and British Columbia, you'll do well to hire a guide who knows the river and how to handle the boat. But there are many safer, quieter rivers in many parts of the country where you can have a relaxing float trip at a leisurely speed and catch fish along the way.

You can catch trout such as brown trout and rainbow trout while float fishing on many mountain streams and rivers. On the White River in Arkansas, trout up to 10 and even 15 pounds are caught in this way. They usually fish the pools and anchor the boat or drift slowly along and fish with baits such as worms, crayfish, and minnows. You can also use a spinning rod with a spinner, spoon, or tiny plug and work these deep and slow.

You can also cast flies such as wet flies, and dry flies for trout on many rivers while float fishing. On many western streams wet flies can be cast toward shore. Here it's a good idea to make the fly drop into the water with a light splash. Since you are moving, your first cast must count, and you have to get the attention of the trout immediately. Larger wet flies therefore work better than small ones.

Fishing with dry flies is somewhat easier, since you can cast toward shore and let the fly and boat move downstream together at about the same speed, and you can give the fly a long float before any drag sets in. The larger dry flies that float well, such as the Wulff flies, are best for this. In August and early September, when grasshoppers are plentiful, use hopper imitations and cast them right up to the bank or shore.

On western rivers in Oregon, Washington, and California, you can catch steelhead on a float fishing trip. Here you need a sturdy drift boat, and it's a good idea to hire a guide if the river is high or treacherous. He'll maneuver the boat so that you can fish the best spots, and, of course, he knows the best spots to fish. He'll also control the boat so that your lure (usually a spoon or spinner or small plug) or your bait (usually salmon or steelhead eggs tied in a cluster) will have the best action or reach the right depth where the steelhead are lying.

In the eastern part of the United States, float fishing is a good way to catch small-mouth bass. Such rivers as the Delaware between New York and Pennsylvania, the Susquehanna in Pennsylvania, the Buffalo River in Arkansas, the Shenandoah and Rappahannock rivers in Virginia, and the Potomac River in Maryland are all noted for such float fishing.

Small-mouth bass will hit small surface plugs, bass bugs, shallow-running underwater plugs, spinners, and spoons in most rivers. Where the water is fairly deep close to shore with overhanging trees, you should place your casts close to shore and even under the overhanging branches for best results. In rocky portions with boulders and holes and pockets, cast around such obstructions. In deeper eddies and pools, let your lure sink, and work it close to the bottom. Or you can anchor and fish with baits such as worms, hellgrammites, crayfish, or stonecats.

So try a float fishing trip and catch more fish. The big advantage in float fishing is that you reach spots and sections of a river that shore anglers or ordinary boat anglers fail to fish. You are always casting to new spots and new fish. You also fish the wilder stretches of rivers rarely seen by shore-bound anglers. And you enjoy some of the best scenery this country has to offer.

If you want to catch more fish, especially during the hot summer months, spend more time fishing at night. On some waters this is almost a must, since bathers, swimmers, water skiers, and speeding boats make fishing difficult and even dangerous. But at night, when things quiet down, the fish usually move close to shore to feed. From dark until daybreak you usually have the lake or river to yourself and can then proceed to catch some of the biggest fish. As a general rule, the fish you catch at night will be bigger than those taken in the daytime.

Take trout, for example, especially the wary brown trout. The big lunkers usually hide under rocks, roots, or undercut banks and in the deep holes during the daytime. But at night they come out to cruise the shallows to search for bugs or unwary minnows or small fish that they can eat. The trout not only emerge from their hiding places, but they are also easier to fool and more inclined to hit a lure or take a bait.

For one thing, the trout can't see you, so you can approach them closer, and you don't have to make long casts. And you don't have to worry about being accurate with your casts or creating too much of a commotion on top of the water. And the fish aren't as choosy when it comes to flies or lures. They can't see the details or colors or size of the flies or lures as they do in the daytime.

You can use a somewhat longer and heavier fly rod and heavier leaders at night. Big wet flies, streamers, or dry flies are more effective than smaller ones, and the hooks in these are stronger and bigger to hold the larger trout. You can even use the smaller bass bugs, since trout feed on larger insects such as moths and big beetles, which fly around at night. In fact, surface lures that are pulled on top to create a small wake or ripple are highly effective because these attract trout to the scene.

You can also use a spinning outfit and tiny plugs, weighted streamers, or live bait for big trout. Worms and minnows can be cast easily with a spinning outfit, and such a rod is especially good when fishing in woods or tree-lined shores where you haven't much room for a backcast with a fly rod. But long casts are rarely needed at night, and you can flip out a bait or roll cast a fly and reach out far enough to take fish.

Even though trout are less wary at night than in the daytime, this doesn't mean that you should wade noisily into the water and make a lot of commotion or waves. Wading quietly is still the best policy. And try to avoid shining a light directly on the water where you will be fishing. A small fountain-pen type of light is best for changing flies or tying knots. Of course, a more powerful light is best for landing a fish or wading in the water to avoid deep spots or rocks. But try not to shine the beam into the spot you will be fishing.

If you want to catch more and bigger bass, try fishing at night. Small-mouth bass, for example, often feed at night—that's the time when crayfish emerge from their daytime hiding places and bass look for them. Big insects also fly at night and fall into the water, and minnows are easier to catch. The quieter nights are usually more productive, especially if you are using bass bugs or surface plugs. Underwater plugs and jigs also produce in the deeper waters.

Large-mouth bass also feed heavily at night, and anglers who know the score make heavy catches of big fish. The best night fishing hours are usually from dusk to about midnight, and then again from about 4 A.M. to daybreak. A spinning rod, spin-casting rod, or bait-casting rod can be used for this fishing. A spin-casting rod is the easiest to use, since you don't have to worry so much about line tangles or loose coils of line. And casting is simpler and almost foolproof.

Surface plugs such as poppers, injured minnow types, and crawlers are good plugs to use at night, especially when casting close to shore in shallow water. Underwater plugs, jigs, and plastic worms are good to use in deeper water.

You can catch bass at night on dark nights or moonlit nights. Dark nights tend to be somewhat better, but on moonlit nights you can wait until the moon is setting or rising, and when it gets high cast into the shadows of trees and bushes. And instead of casting toward shore, bring your boat up to the shoreline and cast parallel to the bank. This way your lure travels through more productive water for longer periods of time. Another trick is to cast to the same spot two or three times. A bass may be attracted to the first cast, but fail to see or catch the plug. When you cast back to the same spot the second or third time, he'll often be waiting for it. And at night, fish your lures much slower than in the daytime. Fast reeling is out—the slower you work your lure the better.

Another fish that feeds a lot at night is the walleye. They come close to shore after dark to feed on minnows, and slow-working underwater plugs are deadly at this time. You can also troll for them with underwater plugs or spinners and worms or minnows. You can also still-fish for them with live minnows.

Still fishing with minnows is also a good way to take white bass, crappies, and white perch at night. All these fish can be caught from shore or piers or bridges or a boat at night. When fishing for these fish, it's a good idea to suspend a light over the water. This attracts minnows and small fish, which in turn attracts the panfish.

Every angler who wants to catch catfish or bullheads knows that fishing for these fish is best at night, when they come out of their daytime hiding places to forage for food. Then almost any catfish bait will take them, but minnows, cut fish, worms, and stink baits are usually used. Best results are obtained by fishing on the bottom with a sinker in a river so that the bait stays on the mud or sand. You can also drift slowly in a boat with your baited rig dragging along the bottom to catch the bigger catfish. Bullheads can be caught still fishing with a cane pole, but here again, make sure your bait is lying on the bottom.

If you do a lot of night fishing, you'll soon develop a sense of "feel" or "touch" that will enable you to work your lures and handle your rod and reel even on the darkest nights. You'll also have to depend more on sound to locate feeding fish and to detect a strike on top. And after you have been fishing for an hour or so, your eyes will adjust to the dark and you'll be surprised how well you can see even on a dark night. And there will be suspense and mystery that are lacking during daytime fishing.

7

Locating
Fresh-water Fish

If there is any one thing that will enable you to catch more fish and make you a better fisherman, it's knowing how to locate the fish you are after. You have to locate fish before you can catch them. You can spend many hours or even days fishing in barren waters or in spots where fish are rarely found. But once you do locate some fish, you can usually make them hit a lure or take a bait.

The easiest way to locate fish is to hire a guide or go out with an expert angler who knows where the fish are in a certain lake or river. Sometimes you will also get good information from a tackle dealer or owner or operator of a fishing camp. These people want you to catch fish and will try to steer you to the right spots.

But most of the time you'll be on your own and will have to find the fish without outside help. This is especially true if you are fishing strange waters. The best way to know where fish hang out is to fish a certain stream, river, or lake as often as possible until you catch fish from certain spots or see them lying on the bottom or cruising around or feeding.

Maps, charts, and lake surveys can be big helps when fishing strange lakes. Such topographical or hydrographic maps, or "sounding" maps, can often be obtained from state conservation departments. Knowing a lake's depths, types of bottom and weed beds, rock and sandbars, sunken islands, deep holes, and dropoffs is a good way to learn where fish hang out.

And one of the best ways to locate fish is to have a thermometer that takes underwater readings at various depths. Fish have certain preferences where they live and feed. They prefer specific water temperature levels, and this is where your lure or bait should be if you want to catch them.

If you are really serious about locating fish in lakes or reservoirs or deep rivers, get yourself one of the light, portable electronic fish locators. It will not only pick up individual and schools of fish, but also will show the depth of the water and type of bottom, which can all be used to locate fish.

If you are a trout fisherman, however, you will have to depend on your own powers of observation and knowledge to locate these fish in a stream. The ability to read a trout stream and know where fish lie and feed will help you to catch more trout. Of course, trout often reveal themselves by leaping or breaking water or dimpling the surface. Or maybe you can see them swimming or lying on the bottom. But most trout remain hidden or are in deep holes or spots where you cannot see them. Then you have to try to figure out where they will be lying and waiting for food.

Trout often hide under the washed-out roots of trees growing alongside streams.

As a general rule, trout want some kind of cover for protection where they can lie away from the direct force of the strong current. Yet they want to be near this flow of water, because it brings food to them. So they will lie near enough to be able to dart out and grab such food as it drifts by. You'll find trout lying in such cover as tree trunks, roots, snags, brush, undercut banks, under rocks, and in similar hideouts. Logjams or piles of driftwood and debris are also favorite haunts for trout.

Trout also prefer certain temperatures and oxygenated water, and you will find most of your brook trout up in the headwaters of a stream, especially if it runs through mountains and forests. During the hot summer months, trout will gather at the mouths of feeder streams and go up these brooks to get away from the warmer water of the main stream. In the main stream they will congregate at spots where springs enter it. They'll also move into the rapids, riffles, and under waterfalls and dams for the same reason: The water is cooler in these places and contains more oxygen.

In fact, many good trout can be caught in surprisingly shallow riffles and rapids. The rainbow trout especially is partial to such fast water and will be found in pockets between rocks and boulders. Spots where such rapids or riffles enter a pool and create white water are very good for all species of trout.

Pools hold trout too, but some pools are better than others. Those that have a barren or smooth bottom and aren't too deep and have no cover are not too good. The deeper, quieter pools that have plenty of rocks, boulders, ledges, roots, and overhanging banks are better. But even here it is difficult to present a fly, lure, or bait to these fish. They have more time to look it over at their leisure, and therefore they are harder to fool. Also, trout in a pool are more likely to be resting than actively feeding.

One good spot to fish in the summer is a grassy bank that is deeply undercut and has fairly deep water alongside it. Trout like to lie there and wait for grasshoppers and other land insects to hop or fall into the water.

When trying to locate trout in lakes, look for the fish close to shore in the spring soon after the ice is out. Brook trout, for example, will be found at the mouths of brooks or streams entering lakes where smelt and minnows gather. Rainbow trout will be gathering at the mouths of such streams to enter them in the spring for spawning purposes. Brown trout will do the same in the fall.

In the summer, trout may also move in close to shore in lakes to feed on insects hatching or being blown into the water. The early morning and evening are good times to be fishing because the water is usually calmer then. You can see the trout breaking or dimpling the surface of the lake.

Trout in many of our western lakes can often be seen cruising below the surface on the prowl for food. In a lake there is no current to wash food down to them, so they are forced to move around to find it. Here the best procedure is to choose a good spot such as a rocky point or anchor in a boat not too far from shore and wait for the trout to swim by. Then you can cast a wet fly, streamer, or nymph ahead of the fish and let it sink.

When trout are deep in a lake, such as during the hot summer months, you have to know the location of spring holes where they gather, or you have to fish deep with lures or bait. Trolling is a good way to locate trout and catch them under such conditions.

If you want big trout, look for them in big waters. Big brook trout favor the larger streams, rivers, and lakes. Big brown trout are also found in the larger rivers and lakes. If a stream or river enters salt water, look for big seagoing brown trout in tidal water at the mouths of such rivers. Rainbow trout also grow biggest in the larger rivers and lakes. However, large rainbow trout will often enter small streams and brooks in the spring when moving up to spawn.

And, of course, the seagoing rainbow trout called the steelhead also enters streams and rivers to spawn after spending time feeding in salt water. The steelhead are even more difficult to locate than rainbow trout or other trout that spend all their lives in the stream or river. The steelhead are almost always on the move and rarely stay in any part of a river for any length of time.

Steelhead runs in specific rivers will depend on the time of year, the weather, water conditions, and other factors. They usually move up the rivers when the rivers are fairly high and after recent rains have raised the water level. But since steelhead move fast, a stretch that was productive one day may be barren the next day. That is the reason why expert steelhead-ers try to know several spots in a river so they can fish as many as possible in one day.

Steelhead are not found in the same spots as trout. The steelhead usually prefer water from about 3 to 8 feet deep. There should be some boulders or obstructions on the bottom. The best runs are generally found between two stretches of fast water. This water should be smooth and not too turbulent or roily.

When the water is low and clear in the rivers, as often occurs during the summer months, wait for a rain or shower to raise the water level or make it a bit cloudy. That is a good time for steelhead. But when the water turns too dirty or muddy from a heavy rain, wait for it to clear before you can expect good fishing. Certain rivers clear faster than others. You can also try fishing the smaller feeder streams rather than the main river itself. The water usually clears faster in these smaller feeder streams.

The time to study a particular steelhead river is during the summer months when the water is low and clear. Then you can note the ledges, depressions, boulders, sunken trees, logs, pockets, and holes where steelhead like to lie or rest. Later on, during the fall and winter months when the water is high and murky, you will know where to fish.

But you can't catch steelhead unless they are in a river. So it pays to read the local fishing columns in newspapers, and ask tackle dealers and local inhabitants if the fish are in a certain stretch of river. You can also ride around to see if any anglers are fishing or if they are catching any fish. Usually when steelhead are running, you will see cars parked by the river or anglers fishing it.

Somewhat similar to steelhead is the Atlantic salmon, which also enters fresh-water rivers after spending time in salt water. Here again, the runs of these fish vary from river to river. Usually the best fishing occurs in the spring and fall months, when the rivers are high and the water is cool.

When fishing some salmon waters, you have to hire a guide, and this is a good policy if you are fishing a strange river for the first time. A guide knows where the salmon lie, which flies are taking fish, and how to present them to the fish in each spot. He can save you a lot of time and help you to locate and catch more fish.

If you are on your own on a salmon river, look for fish lying on the bottom or rolling on the surface. Salmon usually lie in a current but avoid the fastest water and stay along the edges of the main current. They like the tails of pools and can often be found in the shallow water here.

A good time to fish for Atlantic salmon is right after a heavy rain raises the water level of the river. Then new salmon will often move into stretches of the river that may have been barren earlier. And salmon will use the same spots year after year as long as the bottom has not changed radically. So the angler who fishes the same river and stretches year after year has an advantage over the man who always fishes a new river or strange river.

Locating small-mouth bass in a river can also be difficult for the angler who is fishing it for the first time. These fish shun bright daylight during the middle of the day and usually remain well hidden under a rock, roots, overhanging bank or tree, or in a deep pool at such times.

Reading a river containing small-mouth bass helps to find the spots where they are hiding or lying. Look for currents that are usually marked by a line of bubbles or froth at the head of a pool. If there are big rocks and boulders, the small-mouth bass will be found lying below such obstructions.

Most of the time the small-mouth bass will be feeding below the surface and will rarely show. But there are times, usually in the summer and early in the morning and evening, when small-mouth bass can be seen breaking or dimpling the surface of the water to feed on insects or chase minnows in the shallows.

In lakes look for small-mouth bass in the rocky sections where there are big boulders below the surface or even showing above the surface. Then bass will also be found feeding on crayfish and minnows over rocky reefs, gravel bars, along rocky shorelines and cliffs, along dropoffs, and in bays and coves. You will also find them feeding around the edges of islands. In the evening they'll move into shallow water near shore. But during the hot summer months you may have to fish in water up to 20 or 30 feet deep to catch them.

The easiest time to locate small-mouth bass in some lakes is during the spawning season when they come close to shore to build their nests. You can see these nests and often the fish themselves. In some states such as Maine when fishing is allowed during this period, fantastic catches can be made in late May and in early June.

While small-mouth bass are often found around rocks and in fairly swift rivers, large-mouth bass prefer lakes or slow-moving rivers and with some kind of vegetation. Shorelines with plenty of cover such as weeds, duckweed, algae, logs, stumps, overhanging trees, lily pads, and hyacinths attract these bass, and this is where you have to fish. You often have to cast your lure right into the middle of such weeds and pads.

Such lily pads and vegetation and other covers not only provide protection but also harbor insects, snakes, minnows, frogs, and other foods for the bass. They also provide shade and the cooler water. So look for bass in such shady spots, especially during the middle of the day when the sun is bright. Cast around boat docks, piers, anchored or moored boats and rafts, or anything else that provides shade.

In lakes where weeds or other growth are scarce, large-mouth bass will also be found around boulders or rocks. They also congregate over gravel or rock bars that jut out into the lake or reservoir. If there is deep water in front of or alongside these bars, so much the better for large-mouth bass.

But while large-mouth bass prefer the shallow water near shore for food and over much of the time, they don't stay in such spots when the water gets too warm. So during the summer months they may come close to shore in the evening, during the night, and in the early morning. Then as the sun gets high and warm, they move off into deeper water. Here they can often be found along the dropoffs, over the higher ridges surrounded by deep water, and over underwater weed beds.

In man-made reservoirs and impoundments, try to locate old farms, buildings, stone fences, trees, and brush that have been covered by water when the reservoir was filled. These are good spots to fish, since bass hang out there.

Fishing with live baits or trolling deep near the bottom is a good way to catch and locate these large-mouth bass in deep water. So is casting plastic worms, jigs, and underwater and sinking plugs. One point to remember when fishing deep for these large-mouth bass is that they won't chase a lure too far or hit it if it is moving too far away or too fast. Work your lure as slowly as possible, yet with plenty of action for best results.

Large-mouth bass can sometimes be seen chasing minnows or frogs in the shallow water near shore, or you see schools of bass chasing a school of minnows or other baitfish. This is more common in our southern waters on the larger rivers, lakes, and reservoirs. Also in southern waters, especially in Florida, you'll find big bass "bedding" or "spawning" near shore. Then you can see the big female bass over their nests.

Also in Florida, the bass that are in the Everglades and southern Florida conservation areas spread out in the shallow sawgrass areas during the winter months. Then if rain has been scarce during the winter, the water recedes, and many of these shallow areas dry up. You will find the bass concentrated in the potholes, channels, and canals. Fishing around the spillways, locks, and bridges is especially good at such times.

One fish that is often difficult to locate but that provides excellent sport once found is the walleye. They are school fish, and if you catch one or two, you can be sure there are others present. Walleyes are essentially deep-water fish, but they will come into rivers and close to shore in the spring during their spawning runs. If the river has rocks or boulders, try to cast your lure such as a jig, spoon, or underwater plug behind such boulders.

Other good spots in rivers are rock ledges, channels, undercut banks, gravel bars, dropoffs, below rapids and dams, and in the deeper pools and eddies.

In lakes they will be found feeding on gravel and sandbars and on rocky reefs and ledges. Look also for shoals, sandbars, points of land, outcroppings, and dropoffs. During the summer months they will often be in deep water up to 50 or 60 feet deep. But in the spring and fall and early in the morning, in the evening and during the night, they will often come into shallow water to feed on minnows or small fish, their favorite food.

Muskellunge and pike are similar in that both prefer to hang out in lakes where there are weeds, lily pads, sunken trees, stumps, brush piles, logs, rock and sandbars, points of land or islands, and overhanging trees alongshore. Coves are also good spots for these fish. Anywhere that there are big minnows, suckers, yellow perch, sunfish, and other small fish also attracts these predators.

In rivers both the pike and muskie are found in the deeper, quieter pools, eddies, channels, coves, and around sunken trees and logs, as well as below dams, falls, and around big rocks and boulders.

Both the pike and muskellunge tend to break up into lone fish or into pairs and small groups, and they rarely congregate in big schools, except for certain coves or pools in wilderness areas such as in Canada. In the United States they tend to be scattered, and trolling is a good way to run into them; or you can try casting in different fishy-looking spots. Both pike and muskies tend to follow lures right up to the boat, and in this way at least they give away their location. On strange water or in big lakes and rivers, it pays to hire a guide who knows many good pike or muskie spots and can take you there without wasting time fishing barren areas.

The lake trout is another fish that tends to spend much of its time in deep water. But in the spring soon after ice is out, they come close to shore and rise to the surface to feed on smelt, minnows, and small fish near shore. In the Far North of Canada it is possible to take lake trout near the surface, even during the summer months. Even if they do go down in these cold waters, they do not go down as deep as in lakes found farther south.

However, in most waters in the United States during the summer months, lake trout go deep, where the temperature of the water is between 40 and 45 degrees F. This means that you will have to go down to at least 50 or 60 feet in some lakes and down to 200 feet or more in other lakes. Even at these depths, the lake trout prefer reefs, rock bars, boulders, or other uneven bottoms.

When it comes to panfish, you can locate shellcrackers, a species of sunfish, by smelling them, according to southern anglers. They claim that they smell these beds when in the area and fish there. Most sunfish scoop out tiny depressions along-shore, and these depressions can be spotted by their lighter color.

Bluegills tend to stay near shore in weed beds, around lily pads, hyacinths, submerged logs, sunken trees or brush, rocks, and docks. However, during the summer months they do go into deeper water, up to 20 or 30 feet deep, in the middle of the day. A good way to locate and catch these fish is to drift in a boat slowly, close to shore, and drop your bait into likely spots.

Yellow perch are easiest to locate in the spring, when they congregate at the mouths of streams and rivers to enter them for spawning. Then they are close to shore and can be caught from the banks, docks, and bridges. During the hot months they go into deeper water and can be caught over weed beds and in coves, bays, channels, and dropoffs in lakes. In rivers look for them in the quieter pools and eddies, below dams and falls, and near sunken trees and stumps.

White perch can often be spotted swimming in compact schools on the surface. When feeding on insects the perch will dimple the surface in the evening. And on some of our larger lakes the perch will chase minnows or small smelt to the surface, and you will see seagulls swooping and diving over them.

White bass do much the same thing on our larger lakes, reservoirs, and impoundments. They chase and feed on gizzard shad and other small fish, creating a disturbance on top of the water. This usually occurs early in the morning and in the evening. In the spring they move up rivers to spawn and can be located in the quieter pools and eddies and below boulders, rocks, and dams.

Crappies also come close to shore during the spawning season and can be caught in water from 5 to 10 feet deep. This usually occurs in Florida during the winter months. Farther north, they move in to spawn in the spring. Crappies like cover when near shore and will be found under lily pads, hyacinths, sunken brush and trees, and overhanging trees. In the summer months the crappies may go out into the deeper parts of a river or lake. When crappie fishing, it's a good idea to move around and try different spots until you get some bites or a

Crappie like to hang around sunken trees.

fish. Then anchor and fish there. They are school fish, and you will usually get many fish in one spot.

The most successful anglers are usually those who have fished a stream, river, or lake a long time and know where the fish hang out at different times of the year. The more such spots you know, the better your chances of finding some fish on a given day. That is why more and more of these anglers are investing in bigger outboard boats and motors so they can speed from one spot to another and fish as many as possible in one day.

8

Popular Fresh-water Fishes
WHERE, WHEN, AND
HOW TO CATCH THEM

Small-mouth Bass

NAMES AND SPECIES: The small-mouth bass (*Micropterus dolomieui*) is also called the bronzeback, yellow bass, brown bass, redeye, and tiger bass.

RANGE: At one time the small-mouth bass ranged only from southern Canada to Alabama and Georgia, but it has since been introduced throughout New England, along most of the East Coast, and along the West Coast from British Columbia to California.

FISHING METHODS: Bait casting, spinning, spin casting, fly casting, trolling, and still fishing.

LURES: Surface and underwater plugs, spoons, spinners, spinner-fly combinations, bass bugs, wet and dry flies, streamers and bucktails, pork-rind lures, plastic worms, and other imitations and jigs.

NATURAL BAITS: Worms, minnows, stonecats, lamprey eels, hellgrammites, crayfish, frogs, leeches, salamanders, grasshoppers, crickets, and other insects.

WHERE TO CATCH THEM: Small-mouth bass prefer colder, faster, cleaner, and deeper water than large-mouth bass. Small-mouth bass like lakes with sand, gravel, or rock bottoms. Look for these fish in deep water along rocky shores, among sunken and exposed boulders, and near shores with abrupt dropoffs and deep water, rock and gravel bars, and points. In rivers they are usually found in the deeper pools and eddies, under falls, and in the rapids and riffles and shallow heads and tails of eddies. Here they like to lie behind, below, and alongside rocks.

WHEN TO CATCH THEM: Fish early in the morning just before and around daybreak, as well as in the evening and during the night. Dark, overcast, and cloudy or rainy days are better than bright, sunny ones. Fishing is better in the early spring and fall than during the summer months. In states like Maine where the season is open during the spawning season, the fishing is especially good during June. In the summer, fish for them in deeper water during the middle of the day.

HOW TO CATCH THEM: Small-mouth bass will hit surface plugs and bass bugs when spawning, early in the morning or in the evening near shore, or when they are chasing minnows or feeding on insects. Most of the time, however, you have to go down for them with spoons, spinners, and underwater plugs. In rivers, cast across stream and upstream so that these lures sink toward the bottom. Float fishing is a good way to fish rivers. Here casting toward shore under trees or around rocks, boulders, or logs, or below rapids, is often effective.

In deeper waters, underwater plugs, lead jigs, spinners, and spoons can be fished in the deeper holes, over sunken weed beds or rock bars, and along dropoffs. Trolling with plugs, spinners, spoons, and streamer flies can be deadly at times.

Live baits such as hellgrammites, crayfish, worms, and frogs take a lot of small-mouth bass in river pools, eddies, rapids, and in deep holes between rocks in lakes. Live insects are good during the later summer and early fall months. These can be fished on top so they kick up a fuss, or they can be allowed to sink below the surface.

Fly-rod lures such as bass bugs, dry flies, wet flies, streamers, and bucktails are also effective, especially in the late summer, early fall, and toward evening.

Large-mouth Bass

NAMES AND SPECIES: Although there are several species and subspecies of the large-mouth bass, we'll deal here with the most common one (*Micropterus salmoides*). It is also called the big-mouth bass, grass bass, green bass, straw bass, bayou bass, slough bass, lake bass, marsh bass, linesides, and green trout.

RANGE: At one time the large-mouth bass was found mostly throughout the Mississippi Valley and in the eastern part of the United States. But through stocking it is now found in almost every state.

FISHING METHODS: Bait casting, spinning, spin casting, fly casting, trolling, and still fishing.

LURES: Surface and underwater plugs, spoons, spinners, spinner-fly combinations, bass bugs, pork chunks, plastic worms, and jigs.

NATURAL BAITS: Minnows, small fish, frogs, mice, salamanders, grasshoppers, crickets, and other insects as well as worms.

WHERE TO CATCH THEM: Large-mouth bass are found mostly in the warmer lakes and sluggish rivers. They prefer lakes with mud bottoms and weeds or lily pads, hyacinths, sawgrass, and other vegetation. They lurk close to shore around sunken ledges, stumps, sunken trees, overhanging trees, rocky points, underwater reefs or bars, docks, and shady spots. In rivers look for them in the quieter sections, such as the backwaters, pools, eddies, coves, and spots filled with sunken trees, logjams, or other debris. In deeper water they like dropoffs, underwater weed beds, and submerged points.

WHEN TO CATCH THEM: In shallow water early in the morning around daybreak and before the sun gets too high, late in the afternoon, in the evening, and during the night. Early in the spring and during the fall months are peak fishing seasons. Fish during the middle of the day in deep water. Cloudy, rainy days are often good. Fish the first few days of the opening of the bass season in heavily fished waters. In our southern states and especially in Florida, they can be caught the year 'round.

HOW TO CATCH THEM: Use surface lures early in the morning, late in the afternoon, in the evening, and at night, as well as when you see bass breaking water feeding on minnows or insects. Surface lures work best in calm, shallow water near shore. Fish them slowly, allowing the bait to rest often. Do this with bass bugs also.

Underwater plugs are best in deeper water along the drop-offs, and in the midday resting places of the bass. Plastic worms and jigs are also best when bass are down deep. Fish these underwater plugs slowly but with plenty of rod action along the bottom. Spoons and spinners should also be retrieved erratically. Trolling these lures is highly effective when they are down in deeper water.

Natural baits are always good in shallow or deep water. Use lively baits, and let them swim around or kick around to attract the fish. Give the bass plenty of time to swallow the bait before setting the hook.

Atlantic Salmon

NAMES AND SPECIES: The Atlantic salmon (*Salmo salar*) is also called the Kennebec salmon and the leaper.

RANGE: Originally the Atlantic salmon was found from southern New England to Newfoundland and Labrador and Greenland. Now it's rare in the United States except for small runs in some rivers in Maine. There are still good runs of salmon in some rivers in Canada and Europe.

FISHING METHODS: Fly fishing is the only accepted way to catch Atlantic salmon in the United States and Canada.

LURES: Wet and dry flies, streamers and bucktails, and special salmon flies tied for these fish.

WHERE TO CATCH THEM: Fishing for Atlantic salmon is done in some rivers in Maine such as the Machias, Narraguagus, Penobscot, Dennys, and Sheepscot. But the best fishing is found in Canada: in Quebec, Nova Scotia, New Brunswick, and Newfoundland. Many of the best stretches on salmon rivers are private or under lease. Others are under the control of fishing camps and resorts. Some salmon waters in New Brunswick and Quebec are open to the public. In Nova Scotia all salmon waters are open to the public. On some waters you have to hire a guide, and it is wise to do so when fishing a strange river. Salmon lie in different parts of a river under different water and weather conditions. In high water after rains, the salmon are more apt to be on the move and will often lie in shallow water at the heads and tails of pools. In low-water conditions they stay in the deeper pools. They prefer to lie in moving currents that are not too strong.

WHEN TO CATCH THEM: Atlantic salmon fishing is good in the late spring and early summer. There should be a good flow of water in the rivers for the best fishing. But this varies from river to river, and on some rivers the best fishing is during the fall months. Right after a heavy rain that raises the level of the river is a good time to fish during the summer months.

HOW TO CATCH THEM: Casting wet flies and salmon flies and letting them drift naturally with the current is the standard procedure. You cast across stream or slightly downstream and let the fly swing in an arc. The fly should travel just below the surface and not too deep. When the drift is completed, you can lift the fly out of the water and cast again, or retrieve the fly in short jerks. Dry flies are also allowed to float toward a salmon and are most effective during the summer months when the water is low and clear.

Landlocked Salmon

NAMES AND SPECIES: The landlocked salmon (*Salmo salar sebago*) is also called the Sebago salmon, Sebago trout, Schoodic salmon, lake salmon, and ouananiche. The latter name is used mostly in Canada.

RANGE: Landlocked salmon are found in Maine, New Hampshire, Vermont, northern New York State, and Canada. They have been introduced in a few other states but are not too plentiful in those waters.

FISHING METHODS: Fly casting, spinning, spin casting, trolling, and still fishing.

LURES: Wet and dry flies, streamers and bucktails, spinners, spoons, and small plugs.

NATURAL BAITS: Landlocked salmon can be caught on live smelt, minnows, and other small fish. They will also take such baits when trolled.

WHERE TO CATCH THEM: Look for landlocked salmon near shore soon after the ice breaks up on a lake. They like to hang around the mouths of streams and rivers entering the lakes. In the summer months they go down deep. They may return to rivers in the fall for spawning.

WHEN TO CATCH THEM: Spring and early-summer fishing is best, usually in late April, May, and often into June. In July and August deep trolling is necessary to catch them. In September there may be runs in certain rivers for spawning purposes. Raw, windy, and cloudy days are usually better than mild, sunny ones. In fact, rough water is usually more productive than calm water. In the late summer and early fall, look for them early in the morning and in the evening, when they may be feeding on insects or fly hatches on the surface.

HOW TO CATCH THEM: Trolling with fly rods and streamer flies near shore is best in the spring. You can also troll with spinners and spoons. Casting flies and lures toward shore is also effective in the spring and again in the fall; or if you see them feeding on insects, try dry flies in lakes or rivers. Deep trolling with lead-core lines, wire lines, and weighted lines using spoons, plugs, or smelt is necessary during the summer months.

Coho Salmon

NAMES AND SPECIES: The coho salmon (*Oncorhynchus kisutch*) is also known as the Pacific salmon, silver salmon, hookbill, and silversides.

RANGE: It was present mostly in Pacific salt waters and fresh-water rivers from Alaska to California in the past. But in recent years it has been introduced in many fresh-water lakes, such as the Great Lakes, notably Lake Michigan.

FISHING METHODS: Bait casting, spinning, spin casting, fly casting, and trolling.

LURES: Streamer and bucktail flies, underwater plugs, spoons, spinners, and other lures.

NATURAL BAITS: Trolling with sewn-on alewives and smelt or other small fish and minnows.

WHERE TO CATCH THEM: Near shore and at moderate depths in the spring. In rivers and streams in the fall, when they go up these tributaries to spawn. In deep water during the summer months.

WHEN TO CATCH THEM: During April, May, and June, fishing is often good in the shallow parts of a lake. Later on in the summer, during July and August, fishing is better in the deeper sections of the lake. During September the coho will often be concentrated at the mouths of streams and rivers, and from then on until winter will be moving up these rivers.

HOW TO CATCH THEM: When they are in shallow water in the spring, casting lures from shore or boats or trolling a few feet down will catch them. Later on, when in deep water, you have to troll anywhere from 50 to 150 or more below the surface to get them. For this you need lead-core, wire, or weighted lines. When the salmon are in the rivers and streams moving up to spawn, casting plugs, spinners, spoons, and streamer flies in the deepest parts of the river, under banks, logs, and brush is effective.

Steelhead

NAMES AND SPECIES: The steelhead (*Salmo gairdneri*) is actually a rainbow trout that goes to sea, lives there a while, then returns to a fresh-water river to spawn. They are also called salmon trout, summer salmon, and hardheads.

RANGE: Steelhead run up many rivers along the Pacific Coast from California to Alaska. They are most plentiful in Oregon, Washington, and British Columbia.

FISHING METHODS: Fly fishing, bait casting, spinning, spin casting, trolling, and still fishing.

LURES: Wet and dry flies, streamers and bucktails, special steelhead flies, spoons, spinners, small plugs, and plastic lures.

NATURAL BAITS: Worms, crayfish, salmon eggs, and steelhead eggs.

WHERE TO CATCH THEM: Almost any river along the Pacific Coast that has runs of these fish. These runs will vary from river to river, and in some streams the fish will appear in the spring, in others during the summer months, and in still other rivers during the fall and winter months. Steelhead will be found lying in spots in a river where the main force of the current is broken or slowed down, such as in front of, behind, and alongside rocks and boulders, below rock ledges, under banks and overhanging trees, or below logs and driftwood. Most of the time the steelhead will be lying down deep on the bottom.

WHEN TO CATCH THEM: The runs of steelhead up any particular river will depend on the season. In some rivers they appear in the spring, in others during the summer and fall, and in still other rivers during the winter months. Fishing is best when the rivers are high but clear. After a heavy rain or storm when the water muddies, wait a few days until it clears, or fish the feeder streams or headwaters.

HOW TO CATCH THEM: The most effective way to catch steelhead is to drift a lure such as a spoon or spinner or a bait such as salmon or steelhead eggs along the bottom of the river. From a boat you can anchor and let the lure or bait drift downstream with the current or activate it as it holds in one spot. Or you can try slow trolling close to the bottom. During the summer and early fall when the rivers are low and clear, fishing with wet flies or dry flies can be productive. In the winter still fishing from a bank with salmon eggs, worms, or crayfish can be tried.

Brown Trout

NAMES AND SPECIES: The brown trout (*Salmo trutta*) is also called the Loch Leven, Von Behr trout, English brown trout, German brown trout, and European trout.

RANGE: The brown trout was originally found mostly in Europe, but was introduced into this country about 1883 and in other parts of the world. Now it is found in most of our northern states and mountain states and in Canada.

FISHING METHODS: Fly casting, spinning, spin casting, still fishing, and trolling.

LURES: Dry flies, wet flies, nymphs, streamers and bucktails, spinners, spoons, and tiny plugs.

NATURAL BAITS: Worms, minnows, crayfish, salamanders, and land and water insects.

WHERE TO CATCH THEM: Brown trout are found in many waters cool enough to support other trout, and they survive better in somewhat warmer waters and near big cities or heavily populated areas than other trout. Brown trout like to hide during the day, so look for them under rocks, overhanging trees, brush, logs, roots, bridges, undercut banks, or anyplace else that has shade and cover. Pools contain some of the biggest brown trout. So do lakes that are cool enough to sustain trout.

WHEN TO CATCH THEM: Brown trout bite best during the spring and early summer in the daytime. Fly hatches will bring them out, and they will be feeding on the insects. During the summer months, fish early in the morning, in the evening, and during the night. They also feed well after a rain or shower that raises the stream and even discolors the water a bit.

HOW TO CATCH THEM: Use nymphs, streamer and bucktail flies, spoons, and spinners early in the season, as well as baits such as worms and minnows. Live minnows are very good in deep pools and lakes. In the late spring and early summer, dry flies floated naturally are very effective. For big trout, use streamers and bucktails toward evening or when you see the fish chasing minnows or small fish. Wet flies and nymphs can be good throughout the season if presented deep where the fish are lying or feeding.

Rainbow Trout

NAMES AND SPECIES: The rainbow trout (*Salmo gairdneri*) is also called the California trout, Pacific trout, salmon trout, western rainbow, Kamloops, and steelhead. The latter names is applied to fish that run to sea and then return to rivers to spawn.

RANGE: Originally rainbow trout were found mostly in our western states, but it has been introduced widely and is now found in most of our northern states and in many foreign countries.

FISHING METHODS: Fly casting, spinning, spin casting, bait casting, trolling, and still fishing.

LURES: Dry flies, wet flies, nymphs, streamers and bucktails, spinners, spoons, and tiny plugs.

NATURAL BAITS: Worms, minnows, crayfish, land and water insects, and salmon eggs.

WHERE TO CATCH THEM: Rainbow trout are fish of the fast water in streams and rivers. They like the riffles, rapids, fast runs, and the white water at the heads of pools and under falls. In lakes they congregate at the mouths of brooks and streams or rivers feeding into the lake. In clear, mountain lakes they can often be seen cruising along near shore. In warmer lakes they head for deeper water during the summer months.

WHEN TO CATCH THEM: Early in the spring when big rainbow trout enter streams and rivers to spawn, usually in April or May. Soon after the ice is out in lakes is a good time. The fall months are also very good. When insects are hatching on a stream or lake is also a good time to fish with flies. In the summer early in the morning and evening in streams, rivers, or lakes.

HOW TO CATCH THEM: Wet flies and nymphs are good early in the spring and in cold-water lakes throughout the year. Streamers and bucktails are also very effective for big rainbows feeding on minnows or small fish. Rainbow trout also take spinners, spoons, and small plugs in rivers and lakes. Trolling such lures at various depths is also productive on the larger rivers and lakes. Bait fishing with worms, minnows, or salmon eggs drifted with the current in streams or still fished on the bottom in lakes can also be done.

Brook Trout

NAMES AND SPECIES: The brook trout (*Salvelinus fontinalis*) is also called the speckled trout, native trout, mountain trout, brookies, and squaretail.

RANGE: Originally the brook trout was found in the East from Labrador west to Saskatchewan in Canada and south through the Alleghenies to northern Georgia. Since then it has been introduced to many of our western states. But it has dwindled or disappeared in other states.

FISHING METHODS: Fly casting, spinning, trolling, and still fishing.

LURES: Wet flies, nymphs, dry flies, streamers and bucktails, spinners, and spoons.

NATURAL BAITS: Worms, minnows, and land and water insects.

WHERE TO CATCH THEM: Brook trout are fish of the high altitudes and will be found in the headwaters and mountain streams and lakes where the water is clean and cool, or in our northern states and Canada, where the waters remain cool most of the year. In brooks and rivers look for them in shady spots, deeper holes, and under banks, logs, overhanging trees, roots, logjams, rocks, and waterfalls. In lakes the bigger trout cruise close to shore and hang around mouths of streams in the spring and fall to feed on insects, minnows, and smelt.

WHEN TO CATCH THEM: Spring is always a good time in brooks or rivers and lakes. Soon after the ice is out on our northern lakes is a good time to fish for them. In the summer look for the cooler brooks, feeder streams, spring holes, and other cold waters.

HOW TO CATCH THEM: Although brook trout will take a dry fly when they are feeding on floating insects, they tend to do more underwater feeding than other trout. So wet flies and small streamers and bucktails are usually better than surface lures. For big trout the larger streamers and bucktails, spinners, and spoons are good when cast or trolled. Bait fishing with worms, natural insects, and live minnows in lakes can also be done.

Muskellunge

NAMES AND SPECIES: The muskellunge (*Esox masquinongy*) is also known as the great muskellunge, great pike, musky, and by various spellings of the name muskellunge.

RANGE: Muskellunge are found in the Great Lakes region north to Canada. They are also found in the St. Lawrence

River, western New York State, and in the Ohio River and Tennessee River systems and as far south as Kentucky and North Carolina. They are also present in many waters in Pennsylvania.

FISHING METHODS: Bait casting, spinning, spin casting, trolling, and still fishing.

LURES: Surface and underwater plugs, spoons, spinners, and pork-rind lures.

NATURAL BAITS: Big minnows, suckers, sunfish, yellow perch, other panfish, frogs, mice, and other small animals.

WHERE TO CATCH THEM: Look for muskies near shore in weedy coves and around sunken trees, logs, brush, rock and sandbars, points or islands, and overhanging trees. In rivers they like the quieter portions such as pools, eddies, and backwaters, and along shores with sunken trees, logs, or rocks.

WHEN TO CATCH THEM: Try different times of the day. Usually the best fishing is from late morning until evening. In some waters they can also be caught at night. Best fishing is usually in the spring and fall. Cloudy, stormy, and choppy water is usually better than bright, sunny days with calm water.

HOW TO CATCH THEM: Musky fishing means many hours of casting or trolling to get even one strike or catch a single fish. Casting around lily pads, weeds, sunken trees, logs, or other hangouts can be done with surface or underwater plugs. Spoons can also be cast. Most lures can be reeled fairly fast for muskies. Trolling is also effective, especially when the fish move into deeper water in the summer months. Then trolling plugs, spinners, or spoons can be highly effective. Still fishing with live suckers or other small fish or casting a dead sucker can also be tried.

Pike

NAMES AND SPECIES: The pike (*Esox lucius*) is also called the northern pike, American pike, common pike, grass pike, jackfish, jack, and snake.

RANGE: The pike is found in many of our northern states from

Long John boats like this one are often used for float fishing trips, especially in the Ozarks. This one is on the Buffalo River in Arkansas. (National Park Service Photo)

Big strings of panfish such as white bass, crappies, and white perch can be caught at night. Hanging a lantern or other light near the water helps to attract the fish. (Georgia Department of Natural Resources Photo)

Big brown trout like this one from Nebraska's Snake River often feed at night and can be caught on bait or various lures such as wet flies, streamers, and bucktail flies or floating lures. (Nebraska Game and Parks Commission Photo)

Casting weedless lures is a good way to catch large-mouth bass among lily pads, like these in Florida's Lake Jackson. (Florida News Bureau Photo)

Fish often congregate under waterfalls like these on Little Stony River in Virginia. (Virginia State Travel Service Photo)

Casting around the stumps and bases of cypress and other trees in waters like Virginia's Dismal Swamp is a good way to locate black bass, which often hang around such places. (Virginia State Travel Service)

Rainbow trout like fast water and are often found in rapids and riffles, like here in Nebraska's Otter Creek. (Nebraska Game and Parks Commission Photo)

The small-mouth bass is a top gamefish found in our rivers and lakes. They usually prefer rocky bottoms or gravel bars where cray-fish are present. (Wisconsin Natural Resources Department Photo)

There are many kinds of catfish found in our waters. This is a channel catfish, which is found in many of our rivers and lakes. (Idaho Fish and Game Department)

These big brook trout were caught in Gods River in northeastern Manitoba, Canada. Most brook trout are found in our northern states and Canada. (Manitoba, Canada Photo)

The bluegill is one of our largest sunfish and provides sport and fun for millions of anglers. They'll take natural baits, rubber spiders, or panfish bugs. (Nebraska Game and Parks Commission Photo)

Drifting lazily along on a lake is a good way to locate and catch fish. This is Patricia Lake, with Pyramid Mountain in the background, Jasper National Park, Alberta, Canada. You can use bait moved along at various depths or cast lures from the boat. (Canada Government Travel Bureau Photo)

Where rapids enter a pool or lake is a good spot to fish for trout, small-mouth bass, pike, and walleyes. These fishermen are at Hanson Lake Road in northern Saskatchewan. (Canadian Government Travel Bureau Photo)

New York and New England to the Great Lakes and Canada, and has been introduced as far south as the Carolinas. But it is mostly a fish of the colder northern rivers and lakes.

FISHING METHODS: Bait casting, spinning, trolling, and still fishing.

LURES: Surface and underwater plugs, spoons, spinners, bass bugs, streamer and bucktail flies, and pork-rind lures.

NATURAL BAITS: Minnows, small fish such as yellow perch, sunfish, and suckers, and frogs.

WHERE TO CATCH THEM: Look for them in lakes in or near weed beds, lily pads, stumps, logs, sunken trees, coves, reefs, points of land, and around islands and mouths of rivers and streams. In rivers they like the deeper pools, quieter stretches, backwaters, coves, and below obstructions such as dams, falls, logjams, rocks, and boulders.

WHEN TO CATCH THEM: Pike bite best early in the spring and late in the fall in the United States. Farther north, in Canada, they may feed well during the summer months. Early-morning and evening hours are good on many waters. During hot weather, pike may move into deeper water along dropoffs and submerged bars and reefs.

HOW TO CATCH THEM: Casting a plug or spoon into likely spots is effective. So is trolling these lures close to pike hangouts. When in deep water, troll a few feet down. Fishing with live minnows or small fish or frogs can also be done near shore or in deeper waters. Fly casting a big streamer or bucktail or bass bug will raise many fish.

Lake Trout

NAMES AND SPECIES: The lake trout (*Salvelinus namaycush*) is technically a char, but most anglers call it a trout. Other names include Great Lake trout, Mackinaw trout, salmon trout, namaycush, forktail trout, laker, and togue.

RANGE: The lake trout is found in northern New York State, north and west to the Great Lakes, and in Canada and Alaska.

FISHING METHODS: Spinning, bait casting, fly casting, trolling, and jigging.

LURES: Underwater plugs, spoons, spinners, jigs, and bucktail and streamer flies.

NATURAL BAITS: Smelt, ciscoes, whitefish, suckers, alewives, and other minnows or small fish.

WHERE TO CATCH THEM: They are found close to shore in the spring in the United States and may be near the surface and shore in the colder Canadian waters. But most of the time they are down deep, anywhere from 50 to 300 feet or more. They prefer temperatures between 40 and 45 degrees F. They also like to lie or feed over submerged reefs, rocks, shoals, and the deeper holes in shallow lakes.

WHEN TO CATCH THEM: Soon after the ice is out in the spring on most lakes. Also during the fall months, when they often return to the shallows or surface again. Look for them around the mouths of tributary streams and rivers where smelt, alewives, whitefish, and other small fish and minnows gather. Stormy, windy, and overcast days are usually better for fishing than bright ones.

HOW TO CATCH THEM: Casting or trolling with streamer flies or spoons or spinners or plugs near shore in the spring and fall. Deep trolling with lures or sewed-on smelt or other fish baits with wire lines or weights is best during the summer months. Deep jigging with heavy spoons, other metal lures, or jigs is also good during the hot months.

Pickerel

NAMES AND SPECIES: There are three kinds of pickerel found in United States waters, but two of them—the grass or mud pickerel and the barrel pickerel—are too small and too limited in range to be important. The one usually caught and sought is the chain pickerel (*Esox niger*), also called the banded pickerel, eastern pickerel, grass pike, green pike, jack, jackfish, and snake.

RANGE: The chain pickerel is found from eastern Canada south to Florida and in the Mississippi Valley to Missouri and Texas.

FISHING METHODS: Bait casting, spinning, spin casting, fly casting, trolling, and still fishing.

LURES: Surface and underwater plugs, spoons, spinners, bass bugs, streamers and bucktails, and pork-rind lures.

NATURAL BAITS: Minnows, frogs, nightcrawlers, and small fish.

WHERE TO CATCH THEM: Pickerel are usually found in the shallow parts of a lake near shore among lily pads, weeds, and grass, in coves, and around logs, stumps, sunken trees, and rocks. In rivers look for them in the quieter, slower sections, pools, eddies, backwaters, and coves, and along shorelines with weeds, logs, brush, rocks, and other obstructions.

WHEN TO CATCH THEM: Pickerel bite well throughout the day, but early morning and late afternoon and evening are a bit better. They also bite well throughout the year, but spring and fall see them more active. They can also be caught through the ice in the winter.

HOW TO CATCH THEM: Cast surface plugs around lily pads, logs, and weeds, and along the shoreline. Spoons are also good, and so are spinners, but these should be weedless when fishing in heavy vegetation. Streamers and bucktails used with a fly rod are excellent. Work all lures right up to shore or the boat. Live minnows fished a few feet below a float will take many pickerel. So will a strip of perch belly or a pork-rind strip skittered among the weeds and pads on a short line and long cane or glass pole.

Walleye

NAMES AND SPECIES: The walleye (*Stizostedion vitreum*) is also called the walleyed pike, pike-perch, blue pike, yellow pike, dore, glasseye, and jack salmon.

RANGE: Walleyes are found in Canada, the Great Lakes region, and south throughout the Mississippi Valley, as well as along the Atlantic slope to the Carolinas.

FISHING METHODS: Bait casting, spinning, spin casting, trolling, and still fishing.

LURES: Underwater plugs, spoons, spinners, spinner and worm or minnow combinations, jigs, and plastic worms.

NATURAL BAITS: Minnows and small fish are best. Lamprey

eels are also good in rivers. The walleye will also take worms, crayfish, and frogs at times.

WHERE TO CATCH THEM: Walleyes like lakes or rivers with deep water and gravel, sand or rock bottoms. In rivers look for them in the deeper pools, eddies, below dams, falls, and rapids, and around rocks, boulders, and undercut banks. In lakes they frequent rock and gravel bars, and rocky ledges and points that drop off into deep water. They also hang out along rocky shores with cliffs that border deep water. And they also gather at the mouths of streams and rivers entering a lake.

WHEN TO CATCH THEM: The best fishing usually takes place in the spring, when walleyes enter feeder streams and tributaries for spawning purposes. They also feed closer to shore in shallow water in the spring and fall. During the summer, fish at dusk, early in the morning, and during the night. In the middle of the day, fish the deeper parts of a lake or river.

HOW TO CATCH THEM: Walleyes are essentially deep-water fish, and most of the time you have to fish for them near the bottom. In rivers, casting spoons, spinners, sinking plugs, and jigs across stream and upstream so that they swing into deep holes and into undercut banks and pools near the bottom is effective. Trolling deep with such lures is also productive at night or in the daytime. Jigging with jigs or heavy spoons or metal lures can also be tried. Still fishing with live minnows on the bottom is a good way to reach them and catch them.

Bluegill

NAMES AND SPECIES: The bluegill (*Lepomis macrochirus*) is the largest member of the sunfish family and is also called the bream, blue bream, blue-mouthed sunfish, blue sunfish, copper-nosed bream, sun perch, and dollardee.

RANGE: The bluegill has been introduced to so many waters and states that it is now common in most of our warm waters.

FISHING METHODS: Spinning, spin casting, fly casting, and still fishing.

LURES: Panfish bugs, rubber spiders, flies, tiny spinners, spoons, and jigs.

NATURAL BAITS: Worms, crickets, roaches, grubs, grasshoppers, caterpillars, and tiny minnows.

WHERE TO CATCH THEM: Bluegills are mostly found close to shore. During the spawning season you can see them forming nests or guarding these nests near shore. At other times look for them around weed beds, lily pads, hyacinths, rocks, brush, sunken trees, logs, pilings, and docks. The bigger fish like somewhat deeper water along dropoffs.

WHEN TO CATCH THEM: Almost any time of the day you can have good fishing for bluegills, especially with natural baits a few feet down. For fly fishing with panfish bugs or flies, the late afternoon and evening hours when insects are active is somewhat better.

HOW TO CATCH THEM: Still fishing a few feet down with natural baits under a float or cork is the most productive method. But the fly-rod angler can have a lot of fun and sport and catch big bluegills by slowly moving a dry fly, panfish bug, or rubber spider along the surface or below the surface. Another good way to catch them is to add a sinker to the end of your line, then tie a short leader with a hook a few inches above the bait. This can be still fished from shore by casting it out or from a boat by lowering it to the bottom.

Yellow Perch

NAMES AND SPECIES: The yellow perch (*Perca flavescens*) is also called the red perch, ringed perch, raccoon perch, zebra perch, lake perch, striped perch, and convict.

RANGE: Yellow perch are found in the Hudson Bay drainage of eastern Canada south to Kansas. Along the Atlantic Coast they are found from Nova Scotia to the Carolinas. But they have also been introduced in many of our western states.

FISHING METHODS: Bait casting, spinning, spin casting, fly casting, and still fishing.

LURES: Tiny spoons, spinners, flies, and jigs.

NATURAL BAITS: Worms, small minnows, insects, and pieces of fish.

WHERE TO CATCH THEM: Yellow perch are found in many lakes, ponds, and sluggish rivers. They are also fairly common in tidal rivers, estuaries, and brackish bays. They prefer weedy bottoms or weedy shores, but will frequent sandy and gravel or rocky bottoms. Smaller fish will be in shallow water, while the bigger perch prefer deeper water.

WHEN TO CATCH THEM: Best fishing usually takes place in the spring soon after the ice is out when the perch enter streams to spawn. But they bite well all year 'round if you find a school. They move around quite a bit, and you either have to wait until a school comes by or look for the schools. They are active during the winter months and are caught through the ice.

HOW TO CATCH THEM: Most yellow perch are caught still fishing with worms, tiny minnows, or insects, usually with a float a few feet above the hook. But they will also hit tiny flies, spinners, spoons, or jigs if they are retrieved slowly a few feet down. Tiny strips of fish belly are also good for yellow perch when fished from a drifting boat or cast out and allowed to sink, then retrieved very slowly.

Crappies

NAMES AND SPECIES: There are two kinds of crappies: the black crappie (*Pomoxis nigro-maculatus*) and the white crappie (*Pomoxis annularis*). The black crappie has also been called the Calico bass, strawberry bass, grass bass, papermouth, tinmouth, and just plain crappie. The white crappie has been called some of the same names as the black crappie and also sac-a-lait, strawberry perch, suckley perch, bachelor, newlight, campbellite, lamplighter, and many other names.

RANGE: The black crappie is most numerous in northern waters in Canada, the Great Lakes to New Jersey and south to Texas. It has also been introduced along the Pacific Coast. The white crappie is found from the Great Lakes and Ontario to the Gulf Coast.

FISHING METHODS: Spinning, spin casting, fly casting and still fishing.

LURES: Tiny spinners, spoons, wet flies, small streamers, and jigs.

NATURAL BAITS: Tiny minnows make the best bait, but they will also take worms, grasshoppers, mealworms, crickets, nymphs, and other insects.

WHERE TO CATCH THEM: Crappies like cover and will be found around lily pads or bonnets, hyacinths, weeds, brush, sunken trees, old stumps, logs, and other shady spots such as rafts, houseboats, rowboats, piers, and docks. Anglers in some lakes sink or weigh down trees and brush to attract them.

WHEN TO CATCH THEM: In the spring they come in close to shore to spawn, and then fishing is good around the spots mentioned above. In the summer they go into deeper water, and then you may have to fish in water up to 20 or even 30 feet deep. In the fall they return to the shallow-water spots.

HOW TO CATCH THEM: Still fishing with a tiny live minnow a few feet down is the most common and dependable method. But they will also hit tiny spoons, spinners, flies, and jigs if these are cast or trolled slowly at various depths. Jigging with special crappie jigs or regular jigs up and down is also a good way to catch them. They can also be caught at night on minnows from bridges, piers, or a boat. A light suspended over the water helps to attract them to a spot.

White Bass

NAMES AND SPECIES: The white bass (*Roccus chrysops*) is also called the silver bass, barfish, gray bass, sand bass, silversides, striper, and striped bass.

RANGE: Originally the white bass was found throughout the Great Lakes and the Mississippi River drainage. But it has been stocked in other areas and is now very plentiful in our southern states in the reservoirs and impoundments.

FISHING METHODS: Bait casting, spinning, spin casting, fly casting, trolling, and still fishing.

LURES: White bass will hit tiny plugs, spinners, spoons, streamer and bucktail flies, jigs, and most tiny artificial lures.

NATURAL BAITS: Small minnows make the best bait, but the white bass will also take crayfish tails, worms, and insects.

WHERE TO CATCH THEM: White bass like big waters and are usually found in wide rivers, big lakes, and reservoirs. Here they come in close to shore in the spring and fall and in the evening and during the night. At other times they cruise in big schools looking for minnows or other small fish, even in the middle of a lake. They also like feeder streams or rivers entering a lake for feeding and for spawning.

WHEN TO CATCH THEM: White bass are easiest to locate and catch when they are actually chasing shad minnows or other baitfish and can be seen breaking water. In some waters this will attract gulls, and you can look for such birds wheeling and diving over the fish. When they enter streams in the spring is a good time to fish for them. At other times look for them alongshore in the morning and evening and in deeper water during the day.

HOW TO CATCH THEM: Casting small surface or underwater plugs, bass bugs, streamer flies, jigs, spoons, or spinners into feeding schools seen on top. Trolling with many of these lures around the feeding schools is also effective. At other times cast deep-working spoons, spinners, or jigs and reel them in slowly along the bottom. Still fishing with live minnows down deep is also highly effective, either during the day or at night.

White Perch

NAMES AND SPECIES: The white perch (*Roccus americanus*) is also called the silver perch and sea perch.

RANGE: White perch are found mostly along the eastern seaboard from Nova Scotia to the Carolinas, but they have been introduced into other waters too.

FISHING METHODS: Bait casting, spinning, spin casting, fly casting, trolling, and still fishing.

LURES: Tiny plugs, spoons, spinners, jigs, and flies.

NATURAL BAITS: Worms, minnows, baby eels, crayfish, grass shrimp, seaworms, pieces of crab, and insects.

WHERE TO CATCH THEM: They are found mostly in our fresh-water and brackish-water rivers, lakes, ponds, bays and estuaries, and in salt water along the East Coast. Look for them in depths from about 6 to 20 feet over mud, clay, sand, or rocky bottoms. They will often chase minnows or be seen feeding on insects around dusk.

WHEN TO CATCH THEM: They bite throughout the day, with a preference for early morning, evening, and night. They may spend the winter in brackish or salt-water bays, but will move up into the rivers in the spring to spawn, and fishing will be good at this time.

HOW TO CATCH THEM: Casting tiny lures and reeling them in slowly close to the bottom. You can also cast small streamer or bucktail flies when they are feeding on minnows, and dry flies and wet flies when they are feeding on insects. Trolling with various lures is also effective at times. Bait fishing with minnows, cut bait, worms, grass shrimp, and pieces of shedder crabs in brackish water or salt water can also be done.

Shad

NAMES AND SPECIES: The shad (*Alosa sapidissima*) is also known as the common shad, white shad, American shad, Atlantic shad, and silver herring.

RANGE: Originally the shad was found on the East Coast from the St. Lawrence River in Canada to the St. John's River in Florida, but it was also introduced on the Pacific Coast, and is now found there from Southern California to Alaska.

FISHING METHODS: Bait casting, spinning, spin casting, fly casting, and trolling.

LURES: Shad will hit flies, spinners, spoons, and tiny jigs or shad darts.

NATURAL BAITS: Shad will occasionally take worms, tiny minnows, and grass shrimp.

WHERE TO CATCH THEM: Shad are caught in the rivers they

enter for spawning purposes. On the East Coast such rivers as the Connecticut, Hudson, Delaware, Susquehanna, Potomac, Rappahannock, Cape Fear, Edisto, Savannah, and St. John's can be fished. Along the West Coast they run up the Russian, Sacramento, Feather, Columbia, Umpqua, Coos, and Willamette rivers.

WHEN TO CATCH THEM: The season will vary according to the location of the river. In Florida the winter months are often good, and farther north April, May, and June are the best months. On the West Coast the spring months are also good. Daytime fishing is best, with early-morning and late-afternoon hours favored.

HOW TO CATCH THEM: Casting with a fly rod or spinning rod while wading a river is a good way to catch shad. They can also be caught while casting from an anchored boat. In some rivers trolling also produces. Shad move up the main channels in rivers and will be found where there are dams and falls, and below rapids and rocks. You can often see them milling around if the water is clear. Cast the lure upstream and let it swing downstream and sink deep. Slow reeling is best and a natural drift is most effective, but at times some rod action helps to bring strikes.

Catfish

NAMES AND SPECIES: There are several kinds of fresh-water catfish usually caught in the United States. The channel catfish (*Ictalurus puctatus*) is one of the gamest and is also called the speckled catfish, fiddler, and silver catfish. The blue catfish (*Ictalurus furcatus*) is our largest catfish, sometimes reaching 150 pounds or more. It is also called the great forktail cat, Mississippi catfish, chucklehead cat, and *poisson bleu*. The flathead catfish (*Pylodictis olivaris*) is also called the mud catfish, yellow catfish, and shovelhead catfish. The white catfish (*Ictalurus catus*) is also called the forktail catfish and white cat of the Potomac.

Then there are the bullheads or horned pouts, which are the smaller members of the catfish family. There are three kinds: the black bullhead, the brown bullhead, and the yellow bullhead.

RANGE: The larger catfish, such as the channel catfish, blue catfish, and flathead catfish, are commonly found throughout the Mississippi Valley and our southern states. The bullheads are found mostly in the states east of the Rockies. But catfish and bullheads have also been introduced in the West, especially in California.

FISHING METHODS: Mostly by still fishing, with bait-casting, spinning, and salt-water tackle.

LURES: Channel catfish will occasionally take a slow-moving artificial lure such as a plug, spinner, or jig.

NATURAL BAITS: Worms, minnows, small fish either whole or cut into chunks, meat from various animals such as poultry, beef, liver, pork, rabbits, small birds, mice, frogs, and salamanders. Various stink baits, and doughballs made from combinations of cheese, meat and flour, or fish that have been aged for days or even weeks. Congealed chicken or other animal blood can also be used. Even fruits, berries, and laundry soap have been used successfully.

WHERE TO CATCH THEM: Catfish are found in many lakes and sluggish parts of streams and rivers. Look for them in pools and eddies and under dams, falls, and rapids. They will hide under overhanging banks and around logs, ledges, tree roots, sunken trees, and brush piles, especially in the daytime. The deeper holes and pools in rivers and streams also attract them, as do muddy bottoms.

WHEN TO CATCH THEM: Fishing for catfish and bullheads is always better in the daytime when the water in a river or stream becomes discolored or muddy after a recent rain. Fishing starts in the spring and continues until the fall months. They are more active at night when the water is clean or low, and that is a good time to fish for them.

HOW TO CATCH THEM: For best results the bait you are using should lie on the bottom in a likely spot. But for channel catfish you can let the bait drift with the current into their hangouts. Drifting with a boat with the wind or current very slowly is also a good way to catch them if the bait rides close to the bottom. If permitted in your state, you can also use set lines, trot lines, and two or three rods at the same time while waiting for a bite.

Carp

NAMES AND SPECIES: The carp (*Cyrinus carpio*) is also called the German carp, European carp, golden carp, silver carp, mud carp, mudhog, waterhog, river hog, and bugle-mouthed bass.

RANGE: Carp are found in many parts of the world, but originally came from Asia, then were introduced to Europe and in this country during the late 1800s. Now they are found in many of our states.

FISHING METHODS: Still fishing, with bait-casting, spinning, or spin-casting tackle.

LURES: Carp will rise occasionally to a fly or hit an artificial lure, but fishing for them is rarely done with lures.

NATURAL BAITS: Doughballs made from various combinations of flour and cornmeal are the most common bait. Various flavors and scents such as sugar, honey, molasses, and anise are added to these. At other times carp will also take parboiled potatoes, carrots, turnips, canned or fresh sweet corn kernels, lima beans, green peas, and other fruits and vegetables. They have also been caught on worms and insect larvae.

WHERE TO CATCH THEM: Good carp waters are fairly easy to locate in most areas where they have been introduced. They like almost any lake, pond, or river that has a muddy bottom and plenty of vegetation or weeds. In rivers look for them in the quieter pools and eddies and backwaters. They come close to shore in late May, June, and during the summer months. They can often be seen lying in schools just below the surface. They also leap and splash on top of the water.

WHEN TO CATCH THEM: The best fishing usually takes place from May to November, with May, June, September, and October the best months. Carp can be caught during the daytime, but bite best early in the morning, in the evening, and during the night.

HOW TO CATCH THEM: Carp baits should lie on the bottom for best results. Two or three fishing lines can be set out alongshore and tied to dock bells, or set the click on the reel. The bait should be cast out anywhere from 20 to 75 feet from shore. Then the angler should sit down and wait quietly for a bite. When a carp first takes a bait he fools around with it, picking it up and dropping it—do not try to set the hook at this time. Wait until he takes it for good and starts moving away with it before you set the hook.

9

Salt-water Bottom Fishing

There are many kinds of salt-water fishing, and each devotee raves about his particular favorite method of fishing. Surf anglers will tell you that their fishing is tops for sports and thrills. Other ocean anglers boost trolling, or boat casting or fly fishing, spinning or big-game fishing. In fact, some of these anglers who seek the more glamorous and publicized gamefish make you feel that the type of fishing they do and the species they seek are the only ones worthwhile. They tend to look down on bottom fishermen who seek the so-called bottom fish.

Yet if you made a count or survey of the number of salt-water fishermen out on the water on a given day, I'm certain the bottom fishermen would outnumber all the other salt-water anglers combined. So there must be a reason why bottom fishing is so popular. Actually, there are several reasons why bottom fishing attracts so many people from all walks of life and continues to attract them year after year.

First, like most kinds of fishing, it offers the same fresh air and sunshine, exercise and sport, fun and relaxation. Next, it is a relatively inexpensive form of salt-water fishing. Once you buy your rod, reel, line, and obtain some bait, you are all set to go. It is also convenient—you can do some kind of bottom fishing almost anywhere along our coasts. There is bottom fishing from party boats, private boats, rental skiffs, bridges, piers, jetties, causeways, bulkheads, rocks, and shores. And the seasons are long in most areas. You can fish all year 'round and catch some kind of bottom fish.

Bottom fishing is also one of the best ways to catch some fish for eating purposes. Your chances of catching some kind of bottom fish during a day's fishing are better than if you go after more glamorous species by other methods of fishing. This also makes bottom fishing somewhat easier, and almost anybody can learn to catch bottom fish without learning too many trolling or casting skills, or ways of using lures, as is required in other kinds of fishing.

Don't let this obvious simplicity fool you, though. On many days you'll find bottom fishing easy and catching a bagful of fish is no problem at all. But there will be other days when you will need all the skill and knowledge you possess to catch even a few bottom fish. As with most kinds of fishing, it's the guy who knows all the tricks and who has mastered the various skills who catches the most fish.

Bottom-fishing tackle will vary on where you fish, what kind of fish you are seeking, the size of the fish, the tides, currents, and depths you are fishing, and other conditions. For all-around use and for fishing from most party boats, piers, bridges, and small boats for small and medium-sized bottom fish, the so-called boat or pier rod is most practical. It will range from 5 to 7 feet in over-all length and is used with a conventional reel holding anywhere from 150 to 300 yards of line, testing from 20 to 50 pounds.

For fishing in very deep water for big fish and where heavy sinkers or weights are needed, a somewhat heavier trolling-type rod with a bigger reel in the 4/0 or 6/0 size may be needed, since these are often filled with lines testing up to 80 or even 100 pounds.

And for light fishing in bays, inlets, sounds, and other shallow waters for small fish and with light sinkers, a so-called bay type of rod can be used with a small salt-water reel filled with 15- or 20-pound-test line.

Light spinning rods can also be used for this bay fishing for small fish. But you can't use too heavy a sinker with such rods because the tip is limber and the lines that are used are very light. The longer spinning and conventional surf-type rods are also used for bottom fishing mostly from boats, piers, bridges, or jetties, where casting a good distance may be required.

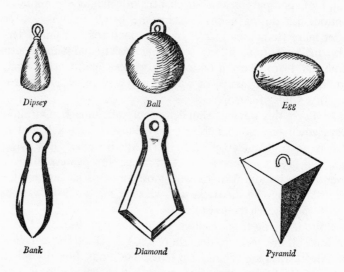

Dipsey   *Ball*   *Egg*

Bank   *Diamond*   *Pyramid*

Sinkers used for salt-water bottom fishing.

A bottom fisherman will need an assortment of swivels, snaps, spreaders, hooks, sinkers, and nylon or monofilament leader or line for tying rigs in different strengths from about 15 to 60 pounds. The hooks usually used for salt-water fishing are the Sproat, O'Shaughnessy, Eagle Claw, Chestertown, Carlisle, and Virginia. The sinkers usually are the egg or oval sinker, the bank sinker, diamond sinker, round sinker, and pyramid sinker. The type and weight of the sinker you use will depend on the strength of the tide or current, the strength of your line, the depth being fished, and the kind of bottom being fished. It is a good idea to carry several kinds and in different weights to take care of most conditions.

A bottom fisherman should know how to tie a rig for the fish he is seeking and the place he is fishing. These vary from area to area, and you can buy ready-made rigs in most tackle stores. But if you do a lot of bottom fishing, you can expect to lose a lot of rigs, so it is cheaper and more convenient if you tie your own.

Basic bottom rigs include the sliding sinker rig. Here a leader with hook anywhere from 20 inches to 3 feet is tied to a barrel swivel. Then an egg or oval sinker is slipped on the fishing line, and the end of the line is tied to the other eye on the swivel.

Another basic bottom rig has one hook on a snell or short leader tied to a three-way swivel or cross-line swivel on the line. This hook can be tied just above the sinker or up to 3 or 4 feet above it, depending on the fish sought and level you want to fish. A variation of the one-hook rig is the two-hook bottom rig. Here you tie the first hook near the sinker and a second hook high enough to clear the first one. You can also tie three-, four-, or even five-hook rigs.

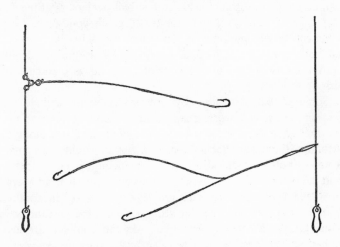

Two basic bottom-fishing rigs.

Still another handy bottom rig that can be tied in no time and dispenses with snaps, swivels, spreaders, or other hardware is made with a length of about 4 to 5 feet of monofilament leader or line. On one end of this line tie a loop to which the fishing line will be attached. Then on the other end tie another, bigger loop, to which the sinker will be added. To complete the rig, tie a couple of still longer loops between the two loops on each end. To these you add the hooks. This rig is especially useful in rocky areas or other spots with obstructions on the bottom. If you lose it, you only lose two hooks and a sinker.

There are many other kinds of rigs used in our coastal waters, and you can easily learn to tie these when the need for them arises. It's a good idea when tying these rigs for a fishing trip to make up several of them in advance and place each one in a paper or plastic bag and label it for the fish or fishing you plan to do. Then you won't waste valuable time tying these rigs on the fishing grounds when you lose a rig and have to replace it in a hurry.

Bottom fishing is done with some kind of natural bait, which can be bought at fishing tackle stores, bait dealers, boat liveries, and fish markets. You can also try to catch your own. Many baits can be obtained during low tides by looking under rocks, among seaweed, and in tidal pools, or by wading in shallow water and using a scoop net or seine. You can also catch small fish on tiny hooks.

Some of the baits used by bottom fishermen include sea-worms such as clamworms, sand worms, blood worms, and pile-worms. Then there are the many kinds of clams found along the Atlantic, Gulf, and Pacific coasts. Strips of squid catch many kinds of bottom fish, and so do crabs, including the hard-shell, soft-shell, and shedder varieties. Shrimp, both live and dead, are used for many fish and are especially good in southern waters. Baitfish such as spearing or silversides, sand eels, killifish, herring, anchovies, pilchards, and mullet are used either alive or dead. Larger fish can be cut into chunks, steaks, or strips for bait.

To catch bottom fish, you have to locate them, and this can be easy in some spots. Just look for a fleet of boats anchored or drifting over a certain spot and join them. Of course, if you go out on a party boat, the captain will take you to the best spots; or if you rent a boat or buy bait from some boat livery or marina, the owner or manager of the place will often direct you to the best fishing spot.

When you are on your own, it's important to remember that

most bottom fish will congregate along bottoms, where they can hide and find food. This usually means that the best fishing will be over broken or rocky bottoms, over coral reefs, or over seaweed or kelp beds. This is where the bottom fish will find worms, clams, oysters, mussels, shrimp, and small fish to feed on. The so-called banks or plateaus, which tend to be higher than the surroundings, are good spots to fish; so are sunken wrecks and artificial reefs created by sinking various materials to the bottom. Many of these are marked by buoys. Bottom fish also hang out under piers, bridges, and causeways, and around jetties and breakwaters.

Bottom fishing is often done from party boats (also called "head boats" and "drift boats" in many areas). They sail from the larger cities and towns and ports along the Atlantic, Gulf, and Pacific coasts and charge a few dollars for a day's fishing. In some spots where the fishing grounds are close by, they make half-day trips. In other places they must travel long distances, and here it's usually a full day. In still other spots they make two- or three-day trips to distant grounds. In some ports you can go out at night. On most of these boats they supply the bait, often the rod and reel too, or you can rent one and the mate or crew will tell you how to fish.

Bottom anglers are often called "bottom bouncers," "sinker bouncers," and "line jerkers," sometimes with contempt by those who fish with lures. But there's a reason for this bottom bouncing with the sinker. The smart bottom fisherman knows that his bait should be on or near the bottom at all times. So by raising his rod and then quickly lowering it, he can feel the sinker hit bottom, and he knows he is deep enough. If he can't feel bottom, he lets out more line.

This bottom bouncing also serves another purpose. It gives the bait movement and action as it rises and then sinks again, and this attracts fish to the scene. At the same time you can "walk" your rig and bait along the bottom away from the boat with the tide and current, and fish at varying distances from the boat or pier or bridge. For this you should use a sinker just heavy enough to hold bottom in the tide or current but light enough to move a few feet when you lift it off the bottom. You may have to change to a lighter sinker or a heavier one, depending on the strength of the tide.

Setting the hook in a bottom fish requires a certain knack, which comes with experience and practice. Certain fish will grab the bait, swallow it, and run and hook themselves, or you just lift the rod to set the hook. But still other fish will play with a bait, suck it in, and lie still or nibble nervously. Here a slow lift of the rod will often indicate that the fish has swallowed the bait. With other fish you have to let them nibble, and then when you feel a solid tug or pull, you set the hook.

Bottom anglers are often troubled by bait stealers or small fish that nibble at the bait and mangle it or steal it off the hooks. Here it is usually a waste of time to try to hook them. Instead, change to bigger baits so that it will take them longer to clean the hook; or you can try tougher baits, which aren't stolen so readily. Baits such as crabs, squid, sea snails, whelks, conchs, and strips of fresh fish are tough and stay on the hook for a long time. Another trick is to use the softer and more attractive baits in combination with the tougher baits. Thus, if the softer bait is stolen, you still have some bait left on the hook and don't have to reel in your rig as often.

Speaking of baits, it's a good idea to change your baits often if the fish aren't biting too fast. A fresh bait is more attractive and gives off a stronger scent, which draws more fish. And bring along plenty of bait when going bottom fishing. Using tiny pieces to conserve bait is a poor policy when bigger pieces will attract more fish and last longer.

One exciting thing about bottom fishing is the suspense and uncertainty about the species you will catch when you drop your rig overboard and let it plummet to the depths. Mixed bags are common in bottom fishing, and you usually wind up with at least two or three different kinds of fish, sometimes more. As in most types of fishing, however, you'll do better if you aim at catching a single species and take the others as they come. Naturally, the fish you will catch will depend on where you fish, the time of year, the bait, and the methods used.

The flounder is one of the fish caught by bottom fishermen. There are many kinds of flounders along our coasts, but the one most sought is the so-called winter flounder, which is found along the Atlantic Coast. They frequent bays, sounds, inlets, and similar inland waters. A piece of sand worm or blood worm about 1½ inches long will take them, as will clams and mussels. The bigger "snowshoe" flounders are caught around Block Island, Rhode Island, and here heavier tackle is in order.

Another member of the flounder family often caught by bottom anglers is the "summer" flounder, or "fluke," which runs up to 12 to 15 pounds and is caught from Rhode Island to Virginia and the Carolinas, and also in the Gulf of Mexico. They are most plentiful in bays, sounds, inlets, tidal rivers, and close to the beaches in the ocean. Drifting with small whole fish and strips of squid and fish is the way to catch them.

An even larger member of the flounder family is the halibut. They may run up to 150 or 200 pounds in weight, and they are caught at times by bottom fishermen. Atlantic halibut are only caught on rare occasions by sports fishermen, usually from party boats in the deep water off Massachusetts, Maine, and Canada. But the Pacific halibut is fished for more often in Oregon, Washington, British Columbia, and Alaska. Even more plentiful is the California halibut, a somewhat smaller species running up to 60 or 70 pounds in weight. Most halibut are caught by still fishing or drifting with small fish or strips of fish for bait.

Two popular bottom species in Atlantic waters are the sea bass and porgies. Sea bass and porgies are caught in much the same waters, such as bays, sounds, and inlets, at offshore wrecks and banks, and in shellfish beds. For porgies you can use Nos. 1/0 or 2/0 hooks, and also this same size for the smaller sea bass. For larger sea bass a 4/0 or 5/0 hook is better. Both fish will take seaworms, clams, squid, and shrimp.

Another popular bottom fish caught from the spring to late fall months is the blackfish or tautog. They are most plentiful from Massachusetts to Virginia, and they like rocky bottoms, mussel and clam beds, rocky shorelines, reefs, and sunken wrecks. They will take a clam or seaworm bait or a fiddler crab or green crab.

During the late fall, winter, and early spring months, cod are sought by many bottom fishermen in North Atlantic waters from Canada to Delaware. They are taken mostly from party boats and private boats on banks, rocky bottoms, and in shellfish beds. Nos. 7/0 or 8/0 hooks baited with clams, squid, or small fish will catch them. The haddock and pollock that are found in the same waters as cod are also caught on the same baits and hooks.

Another popular winter fish is the silver hake or whiting, caught also in North Atlantic waters both offshore and close to shore from piers and jetties, especially at night. But boats fishing in deeper water get them in the daytime also on Nos. 4/0 or 5/0 hooks baited with small baitfish, clams, or squid.

Farther south along the Atlantic Coast, bottom fishermen go after croakers and spot. Small hooks baited with seaworms, clams, shrimp, or shedder crab will catch these fish from boats, bridges, and piers in bays, rivers, sounds, and inlets.

Also caught in southern waters are the numerous grunts, excellent panfish that literally pave the bottom. They like reefs and rocky bottoms, and are numerous under piers and bridges and in most bays, inlets, and ocean waters. Tiny hooks baited with pieces of shrimp, shedder crab, or cut fish will catch them.

Somewhat bigger in size and more sport and fun on rod and reel are the snappers. There are many species in southern waters, such as the red, gray, mangrove, dog, and lane snappers. They are found offshore over reefs and banks and around docks, bridges, and mangroves. They bite best on live shrimp, but they will also take dead shrimp, cut mullet, and small baitfish.

The groupers are another large family, such as the red, black, yellow, and Nassau groupers. They also run big in size, with some members such as the Warsaw grouper and Jewfish. They like rocks, coral, reefs, banks, and similar hangouts. Smaller groupers can be caught on live shrimp, crabs, cut mullet, and small fish. Larger groupers are caught on bigger fish up to several pounds in weight on big 10/0 or 12/0 hooks.

Another big fish often taken by bottom fishermen is the black drum. They run up to 100 pounds or more and can be caught from New Jersey to Florida and in the Gulf of Mexico. Of course, most of the fish will run small in weight, especially in the bays and inlets. But in some areas they run bigger in size, and it is common to get fish running from 30 to 60 pounds in weight. They can be caught on big 6/0 to 9/0 hooks baited with clams, cut fish, crabs, or shrimp.

Along the Pacific Coast there are many kinds of bottom fishes that can be caught. One very large family of fishes are the so-called rockfishes. There are at least sixty species along the Pacific Coast, and they look somewhat similar. Some of the more popular ones are the bocaccio, chilipepper, yellowtail rockfish, black rockfish, orange rockfish, vermilion rockfish, and the sculpin. The rockfishes are found from Alaska to the Gulf of California, depending on the species. Some are plentiful only in certain local areas. But you will find some kind of rockfishing in California, Oregon, or Washington. For the smaller kinds, a No. 1 or 1/0 hook is best. For the larger ones, hooks up to 7/0 or even 8/0 may be needed. The best baits for them include small live or dead fish such as herring, sardines, and anchovies. Others prefer mussels, clams, shrimp, or squid. As their name implies, these fish like rocky areas and also kelp beds. Some are found close to shore, while others can be taken from boats in deeper water. They can usually be caught the year 'round in most spots.

Another large family of bottom fishes are the surf perches and sea perches. They are found from Alaska to Baja California. They are fairly small fishes, rarely reaching more than 1½ feet in length, but they are numerous and number many species. Small No. 4 or No. 6 hooks baited with bits of clam, mussel, seaworm, or shrimp can be used for them. The surf perches are found along sandy beaches, while the sea perches prefer rocky shores or deep water. These fish can also be sought throughout the year in many waters.

The lingcod is another popular bottom fish found from Alaska to Baja California. They are found from shallow water to deep water around rocky reefs and kelp beds. They can be caught on 4/0 or 5/0 hooks with small live or cut herring, sardines or anchovies, shrimp, and squid.

The cabezon is another fish often caught by bottom bouncers in California, Oregon, and Washington. They bite best on clams, mussels, shrimp, seaworms, and small live or cut bait-fish. Use Nos. 1, 1/0, or 2/0 hooks for them. They are found along rocky shores and offshore, where boat anglers catch them.

The greenlings such as the kelp greenling, white-spotted greenling, and rock greenling are often caught by Pacific bottom anglers. They are found from Point Conception to Alaska. Small No. 2 or No. 4 hooks baited with clams, mussels, shrimp, seaworms, and small crabs can be used for these fish.

One of the larger fish caught by bottom fishermen at times is the white sea bass, which runs up to 80 pounds or more in weight. They hang around kelp beds and reefs along the Pacific Coast. They will take a sardine, anchovy, or mackerel on a 4/0 to 6/0 hook. One of the best baits is a whole live squid lowered to the bottom.

An even bigger fish caught in bottom fishing is the California black sea bass, which may reach 500 or 600 pounds. They are found from San Francisco to the Gulf of California. Heavy tackle, and big hooks in sizes 12/0 or 14/0 baited with small whole fish such as barracuda, mackerel, sardine, tomcod, bonito, or squid are required to catch them.

Other fish caught by Pacific bottom anglers include the queenfish, ocean-whitefish, opaleye, sheepshead, Pacific hake, and Pacific tomcod.

So bottom fishermen never have to worry about running out of fish to catch. If one species is scarce or not biting, there is always another kind they can go after.

10

Pier and Bridge Fishing

Many anglers who have never fished from a pier or bridge feel that such fishing is fine for old men, women, and kids, but not for them. They tend to believe that pier and bridge fishermen don't catch too many fish, and those that they do get are small or not real gamefish. Many believe that pier and bridge fishing is too easy and not much of a challenge.

But anyone who has done much pier and bridge fishing knows that fishing from such structures can be a real challenge and demands plenty of skill and know-how. They also know that when you go pier or bridge fishing, you never know what you will catch. It may be a 14-foot shark or 6-foot tarpon, or a tasty bluefish or pompano. It could even be a sailfish or a 50-pound striped bass or channel bass. All of these fish and many others have been caught by pier and bridge fishermen.

The great thing about pier and bridge fishing is the economy —many piers and bridges are free, or there may be a small charge of $.50 or $1.00 for an entire day's fishing. This, of course, appeals to many elderly, retired people or others who have limited incomes, as well as to families where three or four people want to go out fishing. There are many who also like the safety and convenience of pier and bridge fishing. Boat fishing has its dangers, and many people are uncomfortable on boats or become seasick.

The convenience of pier and bridge fishing cannot be beat. You don't have to worry about chartering or renting a boat days or weeks in advance. You don't waste any time running out to the fishing grounds and then making the long trip back. A pier or bridge fisherman can arrive or leave whenever he wants. There are many piers and bridges that are open to fishing twenty-four hours a day.

Today's modern fishing piers are a far cry from earlier ones built years ago. Then you had a few narrow, rickety wooden piers, which were usually too short, and they did not offer much in the way of accommodations. Nowadays there are many solid wooden or steel and concrete piers that run several hundred feet out into the ocean; some are over 1,000 feet in length. Most of them have a T shape on the end to accommodate more anglers. Many of them have rest rooms, benches, snack bars, live-bait wells, running water, and tables for cleaning fish or for washing up. There is usually a tackle shop where you can buy bait, rigs, sinkers, and other tackle, and even rent a rod and reel. It all adds up to safe, comfortable fishing, which appeals to people of all ages and both sexes.

When it comes to bridges, there are many such structures crossing salt-water bays, sounds, rivers, and inlets that can be fished. But others may be closed to fishing because of heavy auto traffic or lack of space for anglers to stand. Still other bridges are too high or over channels where boat traffic is heavy. In Florida, bridge fishing is a way of life, and there are hundreds of them open to fishing. There are often special catwalks or walkways along the sides of some bridges for anglers so that they can fish in comfort and safety. Still other bridges have wide sidewalks where you can fish without worrying about being hit by an auto.

The fishing tackle you will need for pier and bridge fishing will vary according to the spot you fish, how far you have to cast, and the size of the fish running. The nearest thing to an "all round" pier or bridge rod would be what is usually called a salt-water pier or boat rod from 6 to 8 feet in over-all length. It would be on the stiff side, and it would be used with a conventional salt-water reel filled with about 150 or 200 yards of 20-, 25-, or 30-pound-test monofilament line. The lighter lines are best if the fish are running small. Heavier lines are better if you expect bigger fish or if you have to lift fish weighing several pounds from the water to the pier.

Pier and bridge anglers also use long rods similar to surf

rods in spots where fish run big and you have to make long casts to reach the best fishing spots. A spinning surf rod from 9 to 11 feet long with a big salt-water or surf spinning reel holding anywhere from 250 to 400 yards of 15- or 20-pound-test line is a good outfit for such fishing. Anglers also use conventional-type surf rods from 8½ to 10 feet long with a conventional revolving-spool surf reel filled with 30- or 36-pound-test line.

For catching small fish and for working light lures, a handy and versatile rod is the one-handed spinning rod about 6½ or 7 feet in over-all length, and a light salt-water spinning reel holding about 200 yards of 8- or 10-pound-test line. Such an outfit is good for casting jigs, small spoons, plugs, and other lures. It can also be used to catch small fish for bait.

Lighter or heavier outfits than those mentioned above are used at times for pier or bridge fishing, for special conditions, and for certain kinds of fishing. If the bridge or pier is low, you can use a fly rod at times. When going after big fish weighing 100 pounds or more, big-game or trolling rods with 4/0, 6/0, or even 9/0 reels filled with lines testing from 60 to 130 pounds may be needed. But the average pier or bridge angler will use one of the first three outfits mentioned above most of the time and fish for smaller species.

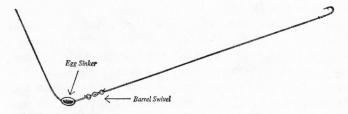

Bottom rig used for pier and bridge fishing in Florida and other southern waters.

The terminal rigs used for most pier and bridge fishing are similar to the bottom rigs described in the previous chapter. You can usually buy a ready-made rig from a tackle shop or on the pier itself. But most pier and bridge "regulars" tie their own rigs either in advance or bring along nylon line or leader material, hooks, swivels, snaps, and sinkers for tying rigs on the fishing spot.

For fishing live baitfish from a pier or bridge, no sinker is used. The hook is attached to the end of the line or leader, and the baitfish is allowed to swim around under the pier. Or you can add a cork or plastic float or a balloon a few feet above the hook, impale a live fish on the hook, and then let the float carry the bait out a good distance from the pier.

In fact, if you want to catch big fish, you'll do best if you use live baits as often as possible. You can buy live baitfish such as killifish, mullet, pilchards, shiners, or other local baitfish or small fish on many piers. If it is not available, you can often catch your own bait. This can be done with a light spinning rod. You can tie on several tiny gold-plated hooks on your line. Often the small fish will go for the bare hooks alone if you jig them up and down. Or you can bait the hooks with small pieces of clam, worm, or shrimp. Baitfish can also be caught in special wire rings, which trap them in the gills when they try to swim through. If there are small fish swimming in compact schools near the pier or bridge, you can try casting a rig with a series of treble hooks or lures and try to snag a few baitfish. Some of the larger fish used for bait such as snappers, grunt, bluefish, blue runners, and pinfish can be caught on baited hooks or tiny lures.

Many piers or tackle shops or bait dealers sell various baits that can be used for pier or bridge fishing. These include live, dead, or frozen sand worms or blood worms, shrimp, squid, clams, mullet, anchovies, sardines, and various crabs.

Not all piers or bridges are alike or offer equally good fishing. Some are better than others, and it depends on their location. Some piers are noted for a variety of species, while others are noted for a certain species. It also depends on the season and what kind of fish are found in the area. The spring and fall months are usually good at most piers and many bridges because fish are more actively feeding then or schooling or migrating. But other piers and bridges offer good fishing during the summer months, and some even have runs of fish in the winter. In Florida, for example, there is often year-'round fishing for some kind of fish on most piers and bridges.

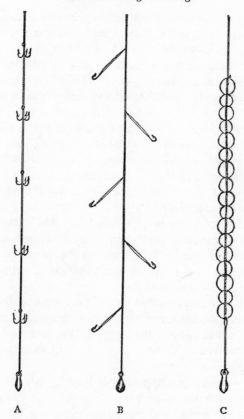

A   B   C

Bait-catching Rigs

The three bait-catching rigs shown here can be used to catch bait-fish and small fish from piers and bridges.

(A) This consists of several treble hooks tied a few inches apart and a sinker on the end. It can be cast or lowered among the bait-fish and then yanked to snag them.

(B) Here you tie several tiny Nos. 8, 10, or 12 gold-plated hooks on short dropper loops, and a sinker on the end. Baitfish often bite on the bare hooks, but you can also add pieces of shrimp on the hooks.

(C) This is called a pilchard ring and has a series of connected wire loops and a red string or cord tied across the rings. A sinker is attached to the end. The ring is lowered under a pier or bridge where pilchards are numerous, and when they try to swim through a ring they get trapped.

Bridges, of course, are not specifically built for fishing but for spanning inlets, rivers, or bays. But fortunately most bridges are built in spots where the river or inlet is narrow and there are strong currents where baitfish, shrimp, crabs, and other marine creatures get swept along with the tides and currents. So gamefish and other fish usually hang around under the bridges.

But even though a pier or bridge may be noted for its good fishing, you still have to know the best spots to fish. The entire length of a pier or bridge is not equally productive. Certain fish such as king mackerel, sharks, bonito, cobia, and other big fish prefer the deeper water, and you'll catch more of them near the end of the pier.

Other fish such as porgies, blackfish, sea bass, croakers, sheepshead, snappers, grunt, and grouper will often be found right under the pier or bridge among the piles and supports. They come to feed on the mussels, barnacles, worms, crabs, and other marine life found there.

And still other fish such as striped bass, channel bass or redfish, bluefish, weakfish, sea trout, snook, pompano, and whiting will move up and down the length of the pier or bridge and often venture into shallow water and even the rough surf itself.

If you see fish breaking or bait leaping, you can fish that spot. This often happens when certain winds or storms or high seas drive the baitfish under or near the pier, or when a school of mullet or other baitfish comes swimming down with the current or tide under a bridge. Then gamefish follow such bait or lie in wait for them under a bridge.

In certain areas where the water is clear, you can often see fish swimming or lying on the bottom or feeding under a pier or bridge. In Florida or the Bahamas and other tropical waters, you can often see the fish take your bait or hit your lure.

And when fishing from a pier or bridge, try to locate the channels, dropoffs, holes, reefs, rocky areas, mussel or oyster beds, and grassy bottoms, and cast your bait or lure toward such spots.

Finally, you can often tell if the fish are running at a certain pier or bridge by reading about it in your local outdoors or rod and gun column; or you can ask the local fishing tackle or bait dealers if there are fish running there. The operator or owner of a pier will usually tell you what fish are biting on his pier. You can also talk to anglers leaving the pier or go out on it and see if they are catching any fish.

One of the great things about pier or bridge fishing is that most of them are open all night and you can go out in the evening right after work or get up and try fishing early in the morning for an hour or two. Night fishing is often better on a pier or bridge than in the daytime, since baitfish are attracted by the lights, and gamefish follow the baitfish in. Or the gamefish lie in the shadows waiting for small fish, shrimp, or crabs to swim by. Try to choose a spot near a light, and cast your bait or lure in the dark area just outside the circle of light. Some anglers even bring their own lights and suspend them over the water to draw baitfish and the larger gamefish.

Tides play an important part in both pier and bridge fishing. The fishing may be good on one side on the incoming tide, and then when the tide changes and starts to go out, you may have to shift operations to the other side. Some fish are more active near slack water, while others bite better when the tide is running stronger. The change of tide is a good time to fish for most gamefish and bottom fish. At inlets or rivermouths the outgoing tide is usually better than the incoming tide because baitfish, crabs, shrimp, and other foods are carried out of the bays at that time.

The pier and bridge "regulars" who fish often soon learn all the tricks of the game and the best techniques and methods for each fish. If you watch them closely and see how they fish, you can soon pick up these tricks and techniques and do likewise. One such trick is to chum under a pier or bridge to draw fish to your spot. This can be done by scattering or dropping some ground fish, crushed clams, mussels, or crabs in the water below you. Or you can fill up a "chum pot" or "chum bag" with similar food and lower it on a string into the water. In deep water or a strong tide or current you may have to add a rock or other weight to the chum pot or bag to get it down deep enough.

Another trick is to get your baited rig away from the rest of the crowd on the pier. This can be done by casting where allowed so that you fish some distance from the pier or bridge where there is less competition from other baits in the water. When fishing in a strong tide or current you can let the rig and sinker move out quite a distance by letting the sinker bounce and then drift out a few feet by raising and lowering your rod tip. The lighter sinkers are best for this.

If the wind is blowing from shore out into the ocean, use a balloon a few feet above your bait to carry it out away from the pier into deeper water. This technique works best for tarpon, king mackerel, sharks, and barracuda in southern waters with live fish but can also be used for other species with other live or dead baits.

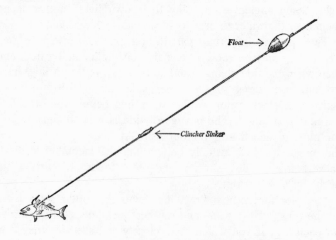

Pier and bridge rig for live-bait fishing.

Bridge anglers can do much the same thing with a cork or plastic float attached a few feet above the bait; only instead of letting the wind carry your bait out, you use the current or tide to do the same thing.

When there is little or no current or tide, you can cast your rig out and when you feel the sinker hit bottom, you can reel in slowly and lift and lower your rod tip as you bring the bait in. This moving bait attracts halibut and fluke or summer flounders. When fishing for porgies, sea bass, snappers, or pompano, you can do the same thing, but let your bait stay in one spot for a few seconds before moving it to another one.

It's also a good idea to bring along two or three rods and then fish with all of them at the same time if it is allowed on the pier and if the pier or bridge isn't crowded. In that way you can try different rigs and baits and cast them out in different spots and increase your chances of catching more fish.

Most fish bite best from a pier or bridge when the water is clear and free from such debris as seaweed. Water that is too dirty or brown and that has too much floating kelp, rockweed, sea lettuce, or other debris usually slows down the fishing. If the pier is long you may find cleaner water at the end; or when fishing from a bridge, wait for changes in tide, especially incoming water, which may clear up the water.

Certain fish such as striped bass, channel bass, snook, bluefish, and pompano often come in closer to shore when the water is rough and there is plenty of surf. If the water is only slightly discolored it is easier to fool such fish as striped bass and snook. Striped bass and snook also feed better during cloudy, stormy weather and at night than on bright, sunny days.

Most anglers use natural baits from piers and bridges, but you can also catch plenty of fish with lures, especially when you see such gamefish as striped bass, channel bass, snook, bluefish, mackerel, bonito, or weakfish chasing baitfish or breaking water. But you can also cast a plug, jig, metal squid, bait tail, or spoon around the pier piles or bridge supports and work it past spots where fish are lying. You can also cast your lure a good distance away from the pier or bridge and work it on the surface, below the surface, or down deep. Most bucktail or nylon or feather jigs or bait tails are best for such casting.

When going after tarpon from bridges, cast your plug or other lure upcurrent and reel it with the current fast enough to bring out the action of the lure. On other nights they may be on the other side of the bridge and you have to cast and work your lure against the tide. At night you will often hear the tarpon or snook or striped bass splashing as they feed below the bridge.

You can also try a bridge trolling technique for tarpon, snook, or striped bass. You drop your lure over the side of the bridge where the tide is moving away from it and start walking while trailing the lure in the water alongside the structure. But make sure you have strong tackle, because when a big tarpon or snook or striper grabs your lure on a short line, you'll have your hands full. In the case of the tarpon you'll lose most of the big fish on the first jump or two anyway, but even a big snook or striper will run your line around a bridge support and cut it. Anglers who specialize in such bridge trolling use heavy poles and short lines of wire leader material and don't give the fish much chance to run or fight. They strong-arm them in if they can be lifted out of the water.

That's one of the biggest drawbacks in pier or bridge fishing: You lose a lot of big fish that insist on running under these structures; or the line breaks when you try to lift the fish out of the water. If you hook a big fish, try to let it run away from the pier or bridge into deeper water and fight it at a distance until it tires. Then slowly work it toward you, and when it turns over on its side or gives up, you can try to bring it up.

With small fish there isn't too much of a problem. If the rod and line are heavy enough, you can reel the fish right in and lift it over the rail. With a lighter rod and fairly strong line, you can grab the line and hoist the fish up.

With bigger fish you can sometimes walk along the pier or bridge and beach them on shore. Some piers close to the water have long-handled gaffs that can be used to gaff the fish. Or you can make a three-pronged gaff hook on a strong line that has a big snap that is closed around your fishing line, and this slides down and snags the fish. Most piers will have some kind of drop net attached to a strong line that can be lowered and maneuvered under a fish to lift it out of the water and haul it up to the pier.

Naturally, things can get a bit wild on a crowded fishing pier or bridge when the fish are running and everyone is excited and wanting to get in on the act, or if someone hooks a big fish and has to play it with so many lines in the water. Most anglers fishing nearby will be considerate and try to give the angler with the hooked fish some room to play the fish. They will either lift the rod over or under the angler's line.

To avoid tangles when fishing from a pier or bridge, try to cast straight out. Casting overhead is dangerous and should be avoided if the pier or bridge is crowded. You can learn to cast your sinker or lure a surprising distance by letting it swing under the pier or bridge and then flip it out.

Pier and bridge fishing is a social and friendly type of angling, where you rub shoulders with people from all walks of life and from different parts of the country. You can swap information and stories and have a lot of fun. It is also a very relaxing type of fishing, and you can sit on a bench or bring a folding chair and take it easy. Bring along some drinks or food if you plan to stay awhile and even a portable radio to listen to the ball game, news, or music while you wait for a bite. Pier and bridge fishing appeal to thousands of anglers, and you'll often see the same people fishing there day after day. They know a good thing when they see it.

11

Surf Fishing

Surf fishing is one of the more difficult forms of salt-water fishing, and more people hesitate to try it because they feel that they'll never be good at it; or if they do try fishing the surf a few times with poor results, they get discouraged and quit and turn to easier types of salt-water fishing.

Yet if these anglers kept at it and learned the fundamentals of the sport and acquired the casting skill, know-how, and techniques and tricks of the game, they would soon be catching some fish and enjoying a type of fishing that has much to offer.

Surf fishing is a very convenient type of fishing. You don't need a boat or have to make reservations or charter a boat days or weeks in advance. You can come and go as you please—a drive down to the beach and a quick look around, a few casts, and if things look bad, you can pack up and go home. Many surf fish bite best at night, early in the morning, and in the evening. So you can go down early and fish before you go to work, right after you come back from work, or during the night if you don't mind missing some sleep.

Surf fishing is also very economical. Once you acquire the rod, reel, line, lures, boots or waders, and a few other accessories, you are all set to fish almost anywhere at little cost. No fancy big-game rods and reels, or lavish boats or expensive charters, or costly fuel bills to run a boat all over the ocean looking or trolling for fish. In surf fishing the poor guy is on an equal footing with the rich guy. And the fish in the surf don't care if you're a man, woman, child, or young or old—they'll bite on anyone's line without discrimination.

Finally, surf fishing will keep you occupied for the rest of your life—there is always something new to learn about the weather, winds, tides, beaches, jetties, rocky shores, baits, lures, and the habits of the fish you are seeking. There's always a challenge, and you have to solve the problems yourself with no help from anyone else. So when you do catch a big fish or several small ones from the surf, you know you did it on your own and you get a great feeling of satisfaction and accomplishment.

But if you want to try surf fishing, you have to start with the proper equipment right from the beginning. Many anglers try to use makeshift tackle such as boat or pier rods or fresh-water gear. Or they buy the wrong rod, reel, and lures for their area or the type of surf fishing they plan to do.

Before you can buy the right surf rod, you have to know the area you will fish, the weight of the lures or sinkers you will cast, how far you have to cast, the size of the fish you will catch, and similar conditions. That is why it's a good idea to buy your surf rod in the area you plan to fish. The clerk can usually recommend the right rod for you; or if you know a surf angler who fished your area, you can ask him or find out what kind of rod he uses.

We can simplify matters a bit by breaking down the surf rods and reels into three classes: light, medium, and heavy. Light spinning surf rods will run from about 8 to 9 feet in over-all length and are used with the smaller surf spinning reels filled with 10-to-12-pound-test lines. They are best for casting light lures and sinkers and fishing for small fish where tides, currents, and surf aren't too strong.

A medium-weight surf spinning outfit will run from about 8½ to 10 feet in length and can be used with larger surf spinning reels filled with 15-to-18-pound-test lines. This outfit is the nearest thing to an "all around" surf outfit and is the best one to get if you can afford only one rod and reel. It can be used in most surf fishing areas for medium-sized and occasionally big fish. It can cast fairly heavy lures good distances and can also be used for bottom fishing with sinkers and bait.

The heavy-weight surf spinning outfit will run from 10 to 12 or even 14 feet in over-all length. It can be used with the largest surf spinning reels filled with 20-to-25-pound-test line. It can cast the heaviest lures and sinkers up to 4 or 5 ounces. This is the best outfit for making long casts, handling big fish in rough surf and strong currents.

The surf angler will also need boots or waders, waterproof jacket, web belt, surf bag or pouches, headlight, ice creepers or wading sandals for fishing jetties or rocky shores, fish stringer, sand spike for holding the rod upright, knife, and pliers.

A good assortment of lures is also needed for meeting the changing conditions and fish you're apt to encounter. Lures such as metal squids, Hopkins lure, popping or swimming surface plugs, underwater plugs, jigs, plastic bait tails, and plastic eels are effective in most areas. Get big heavy lures for use with heavy outfits and for big fish and long casts. Get lighter, smaller lures for use with lighter outfits for smaller fish.

Surf anglers also use many kinds of natural baits, depending on the area being fished and the fish being sought. They will use clamworms, sand worms or blood worms, clams of various kinds, shedder, peeler, and hard crabs of different species, shrimp, sand bugs, squid, mullet, menhaden or bunker, herring, anchovies, sardines, mackerel, sand eels, and other small fish or pieces of larger fish.

These natural baits are fished on two kinds of bottom rigs. One is the "standard surf rig," which has a three-way swivel a few inches above the pyramid sinker. The hook on an 18-inch-to-24-inch leader is tied to one eye of the swivel, and the fishing line to the remaining eye.

The other rig used in surf fishing is the "fish finder" rig. This has a special fish finder, which is made with a ring on one end and a snap on the other. The fishing line is threaded through the ring of the fish finder, and a barrel swivel is tied to the end of this line. Then a leader of about 2 feet with the hook is tied to the remaining eye of the barrel swivel. The pyramid sinker is held by the snap on the fish finder.

Getting equipped for surf fishing is the easy part of the sport.

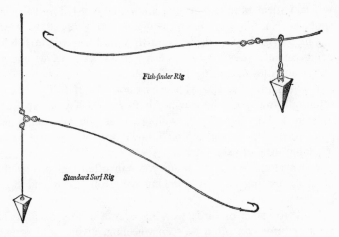

Fish-finder Rig

Standard Surf Rig

Two types of surf bottom rigs.

Now you have to learn how to use this gear and how to make fish take your bait or hit your lures. But before you can do this you have to first locate the fish. This is one of the hardest tasks in surf fishing. The beaches and rocky shores run for miles, and fish come and go with the tides and the time of day. You can waste a lot of time fishing in the wrong places or at the wrong time.

The veteran anglers who have fished a certain area for many years have a big advantage over a beginner or even a skilled surf angler fishing a spot for the first time. The veteran knows when certain fish appear at certain times of the year. He knows which tides and wind and water and weather conditions produced best in different spots. And he usually knows several good spots that have produced in the past that are bound to produce again in the future.

The outdoor writers in local newspapers who tell where the fish are can be big helps in locating fish in the surf. They will often print information about a run of fish or who caught some fish at a certain spot and even name the beach. If you can, try to get down there as soon as possible, and the run may still be on. Even if you get there too late, keep an eye on that stretch of beach or shore because surf fish will feed there again in days to come, and you can get in on some of the action.

Tackle dealers in surf fishing areas can also tell you the best spots to fish. They have surf anglers visiting the store weighing in fish or buying tackle, and they find out where fish are being caught. They may even fish the surf themselves and tell you where they caught them.

If you know a friend who does a lot of surf fishing, he can often tell you where he caught his fish. And if you can find a veteran surf angler who is willing to let you go fishing with him, you have it made. You'll have one of the best guides available for surf fishing trips.

Down at the beach or shore you can often see surf anglers lined up casting or even catching fish. Join them and try to get your share.

Look for gulls or birds working over a school of fish. The gulls or birds can often be seen wheeling, diving, and screaming to feed on baitfish being driven to the surface by the larger gamefish. Even if you just see the gulls sitting on the water, hang around for a while. This often indicates that fish were feeding there earlier and the gulls are waiting for them to return.

Still other times you may see baitfish such as mullet, menhaden, herring, shiners, anchovies, spearing, or smelt skipping or leaping out of the water as bigger fish chase them. Or you may see the gamefish themselves breaking or leaping. Then, of course, you know where they are and can cast lures into the feeding schools. Even if you see fish breaking too far out to be reached with your cast, don't give up and leave. Wait for the school of fish to move in closer to shore. This usually happens at dusk when the baitfish move into shallow water for protection and the gamefish follow them.

The above are all the obvious ways of locating fish in the surf. But how about the days when you don't see any birds working, or fish or bait breaking, or anglers catching any fish. In other words, all you see is miles of beach, jetties, or rocky shores. Where do you start fishing?

This is where the ability to read the beach, the water, the waves, and bottom formations will be valuable. You can often tell by the color of the water just how deep it is. Dark blue, dark green, or green water means that there is a hole, channel, slough, or dropoff—all good spots to fish.

Water that is light green, milky, or brown indicates a shallow spot, usually a sandbar, reef, or flat. When the surf is rough, the water in such shallow spots will usually be white or creamy. Such wave action tosses around the baitfish, crabs, clams, and other marine life, and gamefish come in to feed on them.

The way the waves break on a beach or shore will give you a good clue to the bottom formation and depth also. If the waves crest and break some distance from shore and then roll in creating white water, these indicate a shallow spot or gradually sloping beach. If the waves do not curl and break until they get close to the beach, it indicates a sharply sloping beach with deep water a short cast away. Then fish will often be caught just beyond the breakers.

If a wave crests and breaks creating white water, then reforms again to pass over a darker spot, these indicate a sandbar with a deeper hole or slough inside this outer bar. This deeper water is a good spot to fish, especially along the dropoff from the sandbar to the slough.

Sandbars usually don't run parallel to the beach without a break or cut. Such breaks or cuts have currents or rips as the water enters and leaves; baitfish and other foods get swept back and forth in the turbulence. Such a break or cut is a prime spot to fish.

For the same reason, any inlet or river emptying into the ocean is usually a hot spot. Baitfish enter and leave through such inlets and rivermouths, and on an outgoing tide gamefish will be outside waiting for them.

Rock jetties and breakwaters along sandy beaches built to curb erosion are also good spots to fish. Such structures attract and harbor small fish, crabs, shellfish, and worms, and these in turn attract the larger gamefish. Here casting along the sides of the jetties and around the end or front can be very productive.

Rocky shores also teem with marine life and food for fish and are always good spots to fish. Here you'll find boulders or sunken rocks and deeper holes and pockets where all kinds of surf fish congregate to feed. Rocky points are especially good, since you can often cast into deeper water, and waves break at the front, creating stronger currents and turbulent water. Coves also attract fish, and the best ones will have rocks or boulders either showing or submerged and deeper holes where fish can lie and wait for smaller fish to come by or waves to sweep out other foods.

Tides also play a big part in locating and catching fish in the surf. The time to be out fishing is usually during a change of tide, either the start of the incoming or the start of the outgoing. Some spots will be productive during the low tides, while others are better during the high tides. Usually shallow areas, sandbars, reefs, and mussel beds are best when there is enough water to cover them by at least 2 or 3 feet. Then gamefish will move into such shallow areas to feed. If you are using artificial lures, the lower tides are usually better because then there is more rough water and white water around rocky points, dropoffs, partly submerged rocks, and boulders, and at the ends of jetties. Then fish come in to feed and it is easier to fool them with the lures.

The weather and time of day can also mean a lot when surf fishing. Usually fish come closer to shore to feed when it is stormy, rainy, or cloudy. If the day is bright and sunny, wait until dusk, night, or daybreak to fish. Strong winds onshore create more surf and white water, and this is a good time to fish for striped bass, bluefish, channel bass, and pompano. But if the wind blows too strong or there is a prolonged storm, the water will turn a dark brown or have a lot of weeds, straw, and other debris. Then fishing usually falls off. Wait until the water clears, and then the fish will be hungry and eager to take a bait or lure.

The fish you will catch in the surf will depend on where you fish, the time of year, the baitfish present, the water temperature, and the migrations and movements of the fish themselves. Along the Atlantic Coast, especially from Canada to the Carolinas, the striped bass is king. They are also caught in the surf along the Pacific Coast from Oregon south to central California, with most of the best fishing just north and south of San Francisco. Stripers will hit many lures such as metal squids, Hopkins lures, surface and underwater plugs, jigs, plastic eels, and rigged eels. They can also be caught on baits such as seaworms, clams, squid, shedder crabs, mullet, herring, and other fish. Stripers bite best when the surf is rough, at dusk, during the night, and early in the morning.

Another highly popular surf fish is the channel bass, which is found along the Atlantic Coast from Virginia to Florida and in the Gulf of Mexico. They occasionally hit lures such as metal squids, Hopkins lures, and other metal lures. But most of them are caught on bottom rigs baited with small whole or cut menhaden, mullet, spot, whiting, and similar fish. They'll also take clams, squid, and shrimp in some areas. Channel bass like a moderate surf with some white water to feed in the sloughs and breaks and can be caught in the daytime and at night.

Bluefish appear in the surf in schools from time to time along the Atlantic Coast from Massachusetts to Florida and along our Gulf Coast. They hit many of the same lures as striped bass, with metal lures usually favored. They'll also take small whole fish or cut fish on a bottom rig.

The weakfish, both the northern or common weakfish and the spotted weakfish or sea trout found in southern waters, are often caught in the surf. They'll hit small top-water and underwater plugs, spoons, and jigs. They'll also take small whole fish, or cut fish, shrimp, squid, and seaworms. The northern weakfish runs in the surf from May to October, while the sea trout is caught best in the late fall and winter months.

The whitings (called "kingfish" in northern waters) are often plentiful in the surf along the Atlantic Coast, Florida, and in our Gulf Coast states. They are small but bite avidly on seaworms, clams, shrimp, sand fleas, and strips of squid.

Pollock sometimes appear in the surf, mostly along the coasts of Canada, Maine, Massachusetts, Rhode Island, and Montauk Point, New York. They will hit metal squids, heavy spoons, small plugs, and jigs. They are often caught during the summer months in Canada, but farther south the spring and late fall are best.

Surf anglers along New England, New York, and New Jersey beaches fish from rocky shores and from jetties for blackfish or tautog, which are caught on seaworms, clams, fiddler, and green crabs.

Other fish caught in northern waters from the beaches, rocky shores, or jetties include fluke or summer flounders, sea bass, porgies, and mackerel.

Surf anglers fishing in southern waters are apt to run into such fish as tarpon in the surf at times. They have been caught

as far north as Virginia in the surf, but your chances are better
in Florida and along the Gulf of Mexico. Here they come in
and roll within casting distance or feed in the inlets and rivermouths. They'll hit metal lures, plugs, and jigs, and also take
natural baits such as dead or live mullet, pinfish, catfish, and
crabs. Tarpon are usually more active during the night tides.

Another southern fish that often feeds in the surf is the
snook. They come in when mullet or other baitfish are moving
along the beaches and can be caught by casting plugs, spoons,
jigs, and other lures. They bite best early in the morning, toward evening, and during the night.

A school of jack crevalle, Spanish mackerel, false albacore,
bonito, or cobia may appear along many southern beaches
and hit lures or baits.

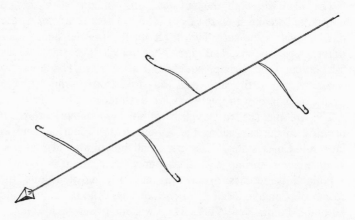

Rig used for pompano when surf fishing.

One of the most highly sought surf fish in the southern
waters is the pompano, which is caught from Florida and Gulf
Coast beaches. They come in when the surf is fairly rough
and can be caught on hooks baited with sand bugs or fleas.

Then there are the many different kinds of sharks and sting-
rays that are often caught from the beaches either by accident
or with deliberate intent. For them you need the heaviest surf
rods if you want to beach them.

Along the Pacific Coast besides the striped bass you're apt

to catch a salmon or a steelhead if you fish around rivermouths and inlets in the surf. These fish enter such waters to spawn, usually during the fall months, and can be caught by casting such lures as plugs or spoons or by fishing with baits such as herring or sardines.

Other fish caught in the surf along the California, Washington, and Oregon coasts include the many sea and surf perches that come in close to feed along sand beaches and rocky shores. They'll hit tiny lures along rocky shores such as spinners, spoons, and jigs, but are more often caught on baits such as clams, shrimp, pile worms, mussels, and sand crabs.

Along rocky parts of the Pacific Coast you're also apt to catch one of the many rockfishes, often called "sea bass" in the state of Washington. They'll also hit spinners and jigs or take baits such as herring, shrimp, clams, worms, and squid.

Also in the same waters where rockfish are found are the lingcod and greenling. These two fish run larger in size, and lingcod will sometimes take lures, but both fish are more often caught on fish strips, baitfish, shrimp, squid, and worms.

The corvina is caught along sandy beaches south of San Francisco and takes seaworms, shrimp, clams, sand crabs, and mussels. Also caught along this stretch are the yellowfin croaker and spotfin croaker. They will take seaworms, sand crabs, mussels, clams, and shrimp on small No. 1 or 1/0 hooks.

Once you become a skilled surf angler you can go to almost any beach, rocky shore, or jetty and catch fish. It may take a while to learn the best spots and which lures and baits and rigs work best in a certain area. But once you get this information, you will be able to catch fish on an equal footing with local inhabitants of the area.

12

Inshore Trolling

One of the most effective ways to catch salt-water gamefish consistently day in and day out in bays, inlets, tidal rivers, along our beaches, rocky shores, and anywhere else not too far from land is by trolling. Such inshore trolling when done by a skilled skipper or angler will usually catch more fish than any other method, and with less effort and work on the part of the angler. The boat does most of the work in activating the lure or bait and presenting it to the fish at the proper level.

Trolling is so effective because it keeps your lure in the water for long periods of time, gives it continuous action or movement, and presents it to new fish all the time. You cover a lot of territory, and sooner or later run into a single fish, several fish, or a big school of fish.

Because trolling looks simple and easy, many anglers feel that all you have to do is run the boat and drag a lure or bait through the water and the fish won't be able to resist the offering. But most anglers who have done any inshore trolling at all soon realize that there is a lot to know, a lot to learn, and many skills and tricks to master before you can catch fish consistently.

The tackle used for inshore trolling will vary with where you troll, the lure or bait you use, how deep you troll, the tides and currents prevailing, the weight and kind of line employed, and the fish you expect to catch. For trolling in shallow-water bays and on flats in tidal rivers and creeks, you can often use the lighter salt-water bait-casting-type rods, pop-

ping rods, or even spinning rods. Here the smaller reels filled
with lines testing from 10 to 25 pounds can often be used.

A good general rod for inshore trolling would be a conventional-type rod in the light or medium class with a tip section from 5 to 6 feet long and a butt section from about 14 to
20 inches long. It can have regular ring guides and tip top or
roller guides and tip top. These should be of hardened steel
such as carboloy to take the wear and tear of trolling, jigging,
and fighting fish, especially if you use wire lines for deep trolling. With such a rod you can use a size 3/0 or 4/0 salt-water
trolling reel with a metal spool. Such an outfit can be used for
many inshore fish running up to 50 to 60 pounds in weight.
It can be used with lines testing from 25 to 60 pounds, but for
most inshore trolling, a 30-pound-test line will be strong
enough.

Some anglers trolling in inshore waters like to use longer surf
fishing-type rods up to 10 to 11 feet in length, either conventional or spinning rods. These are placed in rod holders so
that they spread out off the transom in a "V" and act as sort of
outriggers to keep the lures or baits apart when trolling. Such
long rods can also give the baits a skipping action on top of the
water, which is effective for some inshore fish.

Inshore trollers also use various kinds of sinkers and
weights to make up trolling rigs. Some of these are the regular
bank bottom fishing types, others are round "cannon ball"
weights, and still others are specially designed trolling keels and
weights with bead chains and snaps that are tied to the end of
the line to keep the lure down deeper or to prevent the line
from twisting. Swivels are important when trolling and you
should get the best ones you can. The ball-bearing types are
most dependable and efficient.

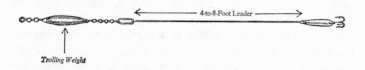

Basic inshore trolling rig.

The line you use for trolling will depend on the area and

fishing you are going to do and how deep you have to go. For surface or near-surface trolling the regular braided nylon, Dacron, or monofilament lines will serve the purpose. For going down deeper, a lead-core line can be used. And for still greater depths and strong current, tides, or rips, you can't beat a Monel single-strand wire line.

The leaders you use at the end of your line will also vary according to the fishing you will do and the fish you expect to catch. For fish with sharp teeth, wire leaders from 2 to 10 feet long are employed. When using braided lines or wire lines, monofilament leaders should be tied to the end of these lines, and these will range from 3 feet up to 25 or 30 feet, depending on the area trolled, the lures used, and the fish you expect to catch. Such leaders will also vary in strength from 30 to 60 pounds.

For most inshore trolling, two or three rods can be held in rod holders and trolled at the same time. For some types of trolling, the anglers hold the rods and even give the lures added action by jigging or snapping the rod back and forth. It also depends on the lure you are using—some have a built-in action and require no additional rod action. But others like jigs come in straight, and here jigging them makes them more appealing to the fish.

Trolling inshore usually requires a man at the helm at all times, while the rest can fish. Handling the boat, keeping it on a straight course or over the best spots, meeting the incoming waves, and avoiding obstacles or other boats are full-time jobs. And when a fish is hooked, you need a man at the wheel to maneuver the boat while the fish is being played.

Where you troll inshore will, of course, be determined by the fish you are seeking, the area you are fishing, the hot spot where fish are running, and other conditions. If you are familiar with the area, you will know which spots attract and hold fish. Inshore trolling is usually best over reefs, sand, and rocks, mussel or shellfish bars, and near breakwaters, jetties, seawalls, inlets, and bridges. Rips and clashing currents and tides and turbulent water are always good spots to try. Landmarks and shorelines have identifying features that often help to locate good spots within sight of shore. And, of course, a depth finder

Party boats or drift boats leave many ports along the Atlantic, Gulf, and Pacific coasts to bottom fish for various species. This one leaves from Destin, Florida. (Florida News Bureau Photo)

Bottom fish aren't supposed to put up much of a fight. But by the bend of this guy's rod, the codfish on the end isn't giving up too easily. (Photo by Vlad Evanoff)

When the fish are on a feeding spree, action on the piers and bridges is fast and furious. (Florida Department of Commerce Photo)

Some bridges, like this one at Marco Island, Florida, have specially constructed catwalks where anglers can fish in safety and comfort.

Pier fishermen often catch big fish, such as this cobia caught along Florida's Miracle Strip. (Florida News Bureau Photo)

The channel bass is sought and caught by many surf anglers from Virginia and the Carolinas to Florida and the Gulf of Mexico. These fishermen are at North Carolina's Core Banks. (Photo by Joel Arrington)

These two surf anglers are toting catches of stripers, a direct result of seeing birds working and then fishing that spot. (Photo by Vlad Evanoff)

If you fish the surf with bait, you can relax and sit and wait for a bite, like these anglers on Padre Island. (National Park Service Photo)

Inshore trolling is often productive for big channel bass, such as this one being gaffed in Oregon Inlet, North Carolina. Large spoons are usually used for such trolling. (Photo by Joel Arrington)

Live baitfish, such as this blue fish, are often used when drifting for king mackerel, tarpon, cobia, and sharks. Other baitfish can also be used for these and other big fish. (Photo by Joel Arrington)

Heavy trolling outfits, such as the one being held by this angler, are used to catch swordfish, blue marlin, black marlin, and giant tuna. (Florida News Bureau Photo)

One of the largest billfish taken by offshore trolling is the blue marlin. This one was hooked off Bimini in the Bahamas. Others are caught from North Carolina to Florida and in the Gulf of Mexico. (Bahamas News Bureau Photo)

More sailfish are caught by offshore trolling than any other billfish. This beauty was taken in Florida waters. (Florida News Bureau Photo)

or fish finder is a big help in determining the depth of the water, the bottom, and even the bait and fish themselves.

When you see fish breaking or birds working, it always pays to troll in that spot. But don't head the boat right through the middle of the school. Maneuver the boat in front of the fish so that your lures swing into their view. Or troll around the edges of the school to avoid putting them down.

If you see other boats trolling in a spot, it's a good idea to move up close enough to see if they are catching any fish. If they are, you can join them and troll with them, but far enough away so that you don't interfere with their lines or the boats themselves.

The length of the line you let out while trolling will depend on the lure being used, the depth you want to reach, the fish you are after, and the water conditions prevalent at the time. In the beginning you can let the lines out to different lengths behind the boat, then when you get a hit or a fish you can adjust all the lines to the same length. Once you discover the proper length of line needed to catch fish, you can mark your line so that you can let out the same length each time.

As a general rule, when trolling in clear and shallow waters you let out longer lines than when fishing dirtier, deeper waters. When the water is rough you can usually troll with shorter lines than when it is calm and flat.

The speed of the boat will also depend on the lure being used, the fish sought, the depth to be reached, and the type of waves and current in a given spot. When trolling in rough water you usually slow down anyway to make the boat ride better. Trolling with the current calls for a faster-moving boat than when trolling against the current. Some fish such as bluefish, bonito, albacore, and tuna will hit a fast-moving lure. Others such as striped bass, weakfish, channel bass, and pollock prefer a slower-moving lure. When trolling near the surface you can move along faster, but when trolling close to the bottom, a slower speed in called for.

The best speed is usually the one that brings out the proper action of the lure being used and obtains the most strikes. Such lures as feathers, jigs, some metal lures, and strip baits must be trolled fairly rapidly for best results. Others such as rigged eels, plastic eels, spoons, plugs, and tube lures are most effective when trolled slowly. It's always a good idea to test your lure on a short line alongside the boat to see that the lure is working properly before you let out the line all the way. Sometimes a change of pace—speeding up and then slowing down—will bring a strike.

It also pays to experiment and try different lures and different speeds and depths. If you have three or four lines out, use a different lure on each line and troll at different depths. After you get a strike or catch a fish, you can put the same lure on every line and troll them at the same depth.

The angler who is alert and on the job at all times is the one who catches the most fish. Either hold your rod or be right near it to grab it if a fish hits the lure. And with some lures such as jigs, jigging is needed to make the lure effective. Here a short, quick, snappy movement of the rod will bring the most strikes.

When trolling always keep an eye on the rod tip and try to feel the lure working. The minute you notice something different or notice the rod tip stop vibrating, reel in your line and check your lure. The chances are that it will be fouled or it is covered with grass, seaweed, straw, or other debris. A fish will not hit a lure covered with such stuff.

One group of anglers who have narrowed inshore trolling down to a science and an art are the striped bass fishermen. They troll day and night in bays, rivers, inlets, along beaches and rocky shores, in dangerous and tricky waters, and often in bad weather. And day in and day out they take more fish, both the smaller schoolies and big cow stripers, than the casters, bait fishermen, and others using different methods.

In shallow-water bays and rivers you can troll such lures as spinners and worms, worms alone, plugs, and spoons just below the surface or down deeper a few feet or even near the bottom. Some anglers fishing in Maine rivers prefer plastic worms or eels, with weighted action heads for trolling. In these waters you usually catch the smaller stripers, so smaller lures are best.

In Pacific waters anglers trolling for striped bass like to use a wire spreader that enables them to troll two lures. One wire arm holds a 3-foot leader, and to this a jig is attached. The other wire arm holds a 6-foot leader, with a plug, spoon, or plastic skirt for the lure.

Anglers along the Atlantic Coast have found the so-called umbrella gig highly effective for striped bass trolling. This has a wire rig with several arms, which enables you to attach anywhere from five to a dozen or more lures, usually plastic tubes, and troll them at the same time. This looks like a small school of bait going by, and you often catch two or three fish at the same time. The red, black, or amber tubes are most effective, but they should have a curve or bend, which gives them action. This is done by bending a long-shanked hook, which holds the tube.

Spoons of various sizes are also very effective lures for striped bass trolling. The smaller ones are best for the school bass, while big "bunker"-type spoons work best on the cow bass. Spoons should be trolled fairly slowly so that they have a side-to-side wobble but never turn over or spin.

Striper anglers also use big underwater plugs for trolling. These can be single- or double-jointed models and have natural fish finishes or red and white, yellow, or silver colors.

Still another deadly striper lure is the jig, either feather, bucktail, or nylon. These are usually used with pork-rind strips, or strips of squid or fish on them.

Rigged eels and plastic eels are also trolled for big stripers, especially at night, daybreak, or dusk. Somewhat similar are the surgical rubber or plastic tube lures. These come in short lengths for the smaller fish and long 18-inch models with two or three hooks for bigger stripers.

Most of the lures above are used on wire lines to get down deep near the bottom. Usually Monel single-strand wire testing from 30 to 60 pounds is used to get down in currents and tides. You can have 100 or 200 yards of this wire line on the end of a monofilament line or braided Dacron backing line. This line should test at about the same strength as the wire line being used. On the end of the wire line you should have a monofilament leader anywhere from several feet to 25 or 30 feet in length. This can test at about 50 to 60 pounds.

Wire lines are also used with a drail or trolling weight added between the line and the leader. Such weights will get your lure down deeper with less line out and also enable you to bounce bottom occasionally to feel if you are deep enough.

Trolling inshore is also done for bluefish. The smaller blues can be trolled on light salt-water outfits, spinning rods, bait-casting rods, and popping rods. But bigger blues should be trolled with the same outfits used for striped bass. These blues will also hit most of the same lures as striped bass. But bluefish often range farther offshore than stripers and are caught up to several miles off the beach. When these fish are near the sur-face, troll fairly fast for best results. But when they are down deep, troll more slowly.

Another fish often caught trolling in northern Atlantic waters is the pollock. They feed over reefs, around points and jetties, and in tidal rips. They'll take spoons, other metal lures, jigs, and plastic tubes.

You can also catch channel bass when trolling inshore waters. For them a large spoon trolled slowly about 150 to 300 feet behind the boat in shallow water is best.

Anglers in southern waters can take tarpon while trolling such inshore waters as rivers, sounds, bays, inlets, and along beaches. The best lures for trolling are spoons, plugs, and jigs, and these should be trolled slowly for best results.

Another fish caught trolling inshore in bays and inlets, over reefs and grassy flats, and in tidal creeks is the barracuda. They like to hit a spoon, plug, jig, or a mullet strip trolled pretty fast. In tidal rivers and creeks, troll close to the man-groves or shore with a mullet strip on a tandem-hook rig.

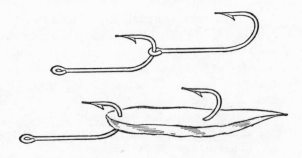

Double-hook rig for inshore trolling fish strips.

Snook can also be caught by trolling in the same spots as the barracuda and tarpon. They also like spoons, underwater plugs, and jigs, but they also hit plastic eels or eelskin lures and rigged eels in some areas. Some anglers in the Everglades region also like to troll a 10- or 12-inch needlefish on a 2- or 3-ounce jig. Snook will be found lying under bridges, along mangrove shores, along dropoffs of sand- and oyster bars, and in deep holes.

Many king mackerel are also caught trolling in southern waters, in the ocean not too far from shore. They'll hit spoons, jigs, feathers, plugs, and other artificial lures at times. But the most effective bait is a ballyhoo rigged on a double-hook rig. If you want to catch a big king mackerel, try slow trolling a live bait such as a blue runner, goggle eye, pinfish, or other small fish.

Spanish mackerel are also found in southern waters and can be caught by trolling tiny spoons, other metal lures, and jigs. And if you troll down deep with wire lines, you're apt to catch a grouper, snapper, amberjack, and many species ordinarily caught bottom fishing.

Along the Pacific Coast a lot of inshore trolling is done for salmon. These fish are found in the ocean off the beaches or shore, at rivermouths and inlets, and in sounds, bays, and the rivers themselves. This fishing is usually best in the spring and summer when salmon gather at the rivermouths and in the sounds to ascend the rivers.

A particular sporting way to troll for coho or silver salmon is close to shore, with fly rods and big streamer flies tied on single or tandem hooks. A tiny spinner is often added just in front of the fly. These flies are trolled fairly fast along the edges of kelp beds or where candlefish are present. The fly should travel just below the surface, and it is best to let out about 100 to 150 feet of line.

You can also troll with long, fairly heavy spinning rods, conventional salt-water rods, and similar gear. Usually lines testing about 15 to 20 pounds are best with the spinning rods, and 30-to-50-pound-test monofilament is used with the regular trolling rods.

Both the king salmon or Chinook and the coho or silver

salmon will hit spoons, plugs, and herring when trolled. The herring are hooked with single or double hooks, and either the whole herring, a plug-cut herring, or a strip of herring is used. The bait should wobble in a slow, crippled fashion for best results. Many anglers also add a "dodger," which is a big flashing metal attractor ahead of the bait or lure. Usually a crescent or keel-shaped trolling weight is added to the line to get the rig down deep enough.

Of course, you have to know where to troll for Pacific salmon. It pays to have knowledge of the tides, currents, bottom, and water depths in the area being trolled. Usually salmon will be where the herring, candlefish, or other baitfish are thick. Salmon like to feed in strong currents and rips and along dropoffs and edges of channels.

Coho or silver salmon are usually closer to the surface, and trolling anywhere from 5 to 25 feet down is often effective. Chinook or king salmon are usually deeper, and trolling from 30 to 100 feet or more is needed. In strong tides and rips you may need weights up to 2 or 3 pounds to get down deep enough. Wire lines can also be used to get down to such depths. The heavy weights are usually attached to sinker release devices, which drop them as soon as a fish is hooked.

The speed of boat trolling for salmon will depend on the salmon sought, the depth, currents, and the lure or bait used. You can troll fairly fast when using plugs, spoons, or other artificial lures. And coho or silver salmon like a faster-moving lure or bait. When you troll for king salmon or Chinook, troll at a slower speed. Herring and sardine or anchovy baits can also be trolled slower than lures.

When trolling with the natural herring, sardines, or anchovies, don't try to set the hook too soon. A salmon may first nip or bump the bait in an attempt to slow it down or cripple it, then return to grab it. So wait until you feel his second "take" or a strong pull before you try to set the hook.

So if you want to catch more fish, master the techniques and skills of inshore trolling and use them often. It takes patience, and a lot of hours must be spent pulling the lures or baits through the water. But it often pays off big in the long run.

13

Offshore Trolling

The previous chapter covered inshore trolling in relatively shallow water near shore or in protected bays, sounds, tidal rivers, and inlets. This chapter will cover offshore trolling, which is usually done in deeper water some distance from shore and often for "big game" fish. But there are spots where deep water is found close to shore, and big fish are also taken there. And not all the fish taken in offshore waters are big—some of them weigh only a few pounds.

The fishing tackle used for offshore trolling usually falls into one of the classes established by the International Game Fish Association, which has separate divisions for 12-, 20-, 30-, 50-, 80-, and 130-pound-test lines. Extra-light rods are used with 12- and 20-pound-test lines. Light rods are used with the 30-pound-test lines, while medium-weight rods are used with 50-pound-test lines. The rod used with 80-pound-test lines is considered heavy, while those used with 130-pound-test lines are in the extra-heavy or very-heavy class.

You don't have to buy the most expensive rod for offshore fishing. But it should be well-made and have sturdy component parts, which will take a beating in offshore trolling. They should have roller tips and guides, a sturdy screw-locking reel seat, and a strong butt. Most offshore rods will have tip sections about 5 feet or a bit longer and butt sections ranging from about 15 to 22 inches.

Offshore fishing reels are precision products built for hard usage for fish that fight long and hard, make fast runs, and give the reel a workout. There are moderate-priced models that stand up well, and more expensive types made of aluminum and stainless steel and anodized in gold finishes to protect them against corrosion. The reels are available in different sizes to match the different rod weights and for different kinds of trolling. Small reels start with numbers 1/0, 2/0, and 3/0 for light rods; 4/0 and 6/0 reels for medium rods; and on up to 9/0, 12/0, and 14/0 reels for heavy and extra-heavy fishing.

The lines used for offshore trolling are usually made of Dacron or monofilament. Monofilament lines are usually used in the lighter tests and up to about 80-pound-test. They are almost invisible and can take a lot of abuse and abrasion. But they have more stretch than a Dacron line. Dacron lines are still popular for heavy fishing when using lines over 100 pounds and are also preferred by some anglers in the lighter tests.

The offshore angler also needs leader material for making up leaders of various strengths and lengths for the different kinds of fishing. For most offshore trolling, the single-strand stainless steel wire material is used to make up leaders. It comes in different diameters and strengths, from the No. 2 or lightest strength, testing 27 pounds, up to No. 15, testing 282 pounds. For trolling lures or small baits for the smaller fish, a leader from 3 to 5 feet is often long enough. For bigger fish, leaders from 5 to 10 feet can be used, while for the largest fish and most billfish, leaders up to 15 feet are employed.

In recent years offshore anglers have also started using heavy monofilament leaders instead of the wire. These are used in the lighter tests of 80 to 150 pounds for smaller fish and up to 200-, 300-, or 400-pound-test for the bigger fish. Monofilament leaders have the big advantage of not being so visible in the water, they are more pliable and won't kink like wire, and they result in more strikes or hits from the fish. But they can't be used for fish with sharp teeth such as sharks or wahoo.

Most offshore trolling is done with various whole natural fish such as mullet, balao or ballyhoo, eels, mackerel, bonito, flying fish, squid, dolphin, needlefish, small barracuda, bonefish, and similar fish. Or strips are cut from the sides or bellies of these fish and used for trolling.

Offshore trollers also use lures of various kinds such as

spoons, feathers, cedar jigs, diamond jigs, feather, bucktail, and nylon jigs, plugs, and pork-rind strips.

There are also many plastic imitation lures that can be used for offshore trolling. These are usually soft and flexible and made to look like the real baitfish, squid, or eel.

Teaser for offshore trolling.

Offshore anglers also use "teasers" of various kinds, which create a commotion on top of the water and attract fish. These are usually made from wood or plastic and look like giant plugs, except that they do not have any hooks.

If you have never done any offshore trolling before, it's a good idea to charter a sport fishing boat that does such trolling, or go out in a friend's boat a few times and see how he does it. If you watch a charter boat skipper or an expert friend handling the boat, the lines, the lures, and the fish after they are hooked, you'll get a much better and quicker idea of how it's done than if you try to learn by "trial and error" on your own.

Offshore trolling requires at least two men to do the job right. One man is at the wheel at all times running the boat, while the other man handles the outriggers, lines, lures, and bait.

Most offshore trolling is done in two ways. First there is "straight" or "flat" trolling, where the line runs directly from the rods to the lure or bait in a straight line from the stern behind the boat. This is usually the best way to troll lures where the fish strike and hook themselves immediately.

The other way to troll offshore is with "outriggers." These are long bamboo, metal, or glass poles that extend outward from the sides of the boat at an angle. Some boats also have an outrigger extending vertically from the center of the boat. Outriggers have a clothespin or some other clip that can be lowered or hoisted on a line to the tip of the outrigger by means of a pulley system. The fishing line from the rod is attached to the clothespin or clip and is raised up to the tip of the outrigger.

Outriggers allow up to four or more lines to be trolled at the same time. They also keep the fishing lines off the water and at an angle that makes the bait skim or skip attractively along the top of the water. They also keep the baits away from the wake of the boat. And they make it possible to hook more fish such as billfish, which tend to slash at a bait, then return to mouth it. The first strike releases the line from the outrigger, throwing slack line on the water. This gives the billfish time to grab and mouth the bait. When the line straightens out, the angler comes back with the rod and sets the hook.

In outrigger trolling you rarely hold the rod in your hands unless you expect a strike or see a fish following the bait. Most of the time the rod stays in the rod holder. You usually have a few seconds to grab the rod before the line straightens out completely.

Flat lines are usually trolled anywhere from 20 to 200 feet behind a boat. Outrigger lines will range from about 75 to 125 feet out. Of course, if you troll flat lines and outrigger lines at the same time, it's a good idea to have the flat lines shorter than the outrigger lines unless the flat lines are weighted and riding deeper, in which case they can be longer.

A good offshore angler will always be experimenting with the length of the lines, different lures, altering the speed of the boat, different maneuvers, different depths, and various other tricks and techniques that could mean the difference between fish and no fish.

Many such skippers will start trolling with a different lure or bait on each line and will keep changing the lure or bait until he catches some fish. Then he'll put that bait on all the lines. Or if a plain bait such as a ballyhoo or mullet doesn't produce, he'll add a Jap feather lure or plastic skirt ahead of the fish.

If a dead baitfish doesn't work, the offshore troller will sometimes change to a live bait. Slow trolling blue runners, pinfish, yellowtail, skipjack, and other small fish hooked through the back can be deadly for many offshore fish. They can be trolled from outriggers or by using a kite that keeps a live bait-fish swimming on the surface in an attractive manner. At other times the live baits can be trolled below the surface from a few feet to 20 or 30 feet down.

A smart offshore angler also varies his course while trolling. Instead of always trolling on a straight line, he tries a zigzag or "S" course, or he runs the boat in wide circles. This causes the lures to sink, then rise, and this often results in strikes from fish than when a lure or bait is traveling straight.

Like the inshore troller, the offshore angler also tries to avoid running through a school of fish or over a lone fish. Instead he maneuvers the boat in front of the fish or school of fish or along the edges of the school so that he doesn't frighten them. You can also circle the school so that your lures or baits swing in toward the fish so that they see it.

It is also very important when approaching a single big fish or a school of fish to keep your boat at the same speed and not increase or decrease the speed too suddenly. If you do have to speed up or slow down, do it very gradually over a period of time. Fish can be alerted or frightened by changes in engine speeds.

Offshore trolling is also governed by the kind of fish you are seeking, and the tactics, techniques, and methods will often vary with each fish. Take the Atlantic sailfish, which is one of the most popular and plentiful billfish taken by offshore trolling. These fish are most plentiful off Florida's east coast during the winter months, but they are caught all year 'round in many tropical waters. They also move up as far north as North Carolina during the summer months.

Trolling for sailfish is best along the edges of the Gulf Stream. They can sometimes be seen leaping out of the water, or several sailfish will surround or "ball" a school of baitfish or small fish. When the water is choppy, the fishing is usually better than when it is calm. In fact, many anglers seeking sailfish will wait until a northwest wind kicks up the water.

If you see a sailfish following a bait on an outrigger but refuses to hit, try pulling the fishing line from the clip and let the bait stop and sink. A sailfish will often grab such a bait when it refuses to hit the bait moving on top of the water.

Most of the time a "dropback" is necessary, either with a flat line or the outrigger line to enable the sailfish to grab and mouth the bait. But there are also occasions when the sailfish grabs the bait and gets hooked immediately; then, of course, no dropback is necessary.

The speed at which you troll for sailfish will vary with the baits used, water conditions, type of waves encountered, and what the fish prefer. Usually the best speed is the one that brings out the best action in the lure or bait—they should skip along the top of the water and at times dip below the surface, but they should return to the top of the water again in a short time.

When trolling for blue marlin, bigger baits are used, such as Spanish mackerel, dolphin, bonito, small barracuda, bonefish, and big mullet and squid. Blue marlin also hang around the Gulf Stream or other currents, and in many spots you have to travel far from shore to locate them. In certain spots where the Gulf Stream or other strong currents and deep water are found close to shore, you don't have to go too far out. In such spots as North Carolina, Florida, the Bahamas, Puerto Rico, and the Virgin Islands, blue marlin are caught fairly close to shore.

Blue marlin like fast-moving currents and seem to surface best when the sea is choppy, during the late afternoon, and on rainy, squally, and dark days. If you see a line of eelgrass or sargassum weed drifting along, try trolling along the weeds—they attract dolphin and other small fish, which in turn draw the marlin; they also catch blue marlin in Pacific waters, especially in the waters around Hawaii. Here many fish are caught on artificial lures made from metal, wood, lucite, and plastic skirts. The Knucklehead is one such lure, manufactured by the Sevenstrand Tackle Company in California; this lure dives, leaps, skips, and skims across the water like a live baitfish or squid, and marlin will often hit them hard and hook themselves.

Another marlin that is more plentiful in Pacific waters is the striped marlin. They run from 100 to 600 pounds and are caught off California, Baja California, Mexico, South America, and Hawaii. They are often sighted cruising on the surface, with their fins and tails showing above the water. Then you can present the fish bait, usually a flying fish, by running the boat so that the bait swings in front of the fish. Sometimes you'll even see several fish on the surface at once; then you can often hook more than one fish. Striped marlin will also hit artificial lures such as the Knucklehead and plastic imitations of fish or squid.

Still another popular marlin found along the Atlantic Coast is the white marlin. It ranges along the East Coast from Florida up to Massachusetts. It is also plentiful in the Gulf of Mexico, the Bahamas, and Puerto Rico. White marlin like to range along an "edge" where the dirty, green inshore waters merge with the clean, blue offshore waters. This may be only a few miles off the beach in some areas or up to 40 or 50 miles out in other spots. The best fishing is usually found from the 20-fathom curve on out to the edge of the deep.

White marlin will take such baits as a whole squid, ballyhoo, mullet, rigged eel, or strip bait trolled at speeds from 4 to 8 knots. White marlin will often follow a bait for long periods of time without hitting it. If this happens, try reeling in all the baits except one. If the fish still doesn't take it, reel it in a few feet. Then drop it back. Keep reeling it in and dropping it back to tease the fish and make it angry enough so that it charges and grabs the bait.

Anglers trolling offshore waters along the Atlantic Coast also catch tuna. The smaller school tuna running from a few pounds up to 100 pounds or so are the ones usually caught trolling. They'll hit such lures as feathers, cedar jigs, nylon jigs, metal lures, spoons, and strip baits trolled at fast speeds, usually from 5 to 10 knots. And they will often hit such lures close to the boat from only 15 to 40 feet astern. In fact, they are attracted by commotion in the water and the boat's wake or whirling propellers. If there are tuna in the area and they refuse to hit the lures, you can try speeding up the boat and circling around. This turbulence and white water often excite the fish and make them hit.

Other tricks that often work on school tuna include hooking one fish and keeping it in the water, while other anglers grab their rods and jig their lures rapidly. This may hook other fish following the first fish. School tuna are often seen swimming on top or leaping out of the water but not feeding. If the water is calm or flat, wait until the wind picks up and makes it choppy. Then fishing for tuna usually improves. If you can't catch the school tuna during the middle of the day, try fishing early in the morning or late in the afternoon.

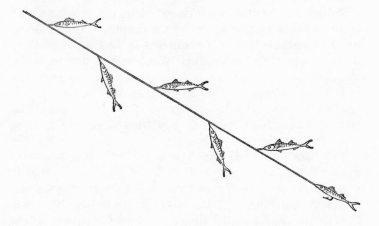

A "daisy chain" of several fish is trolled for giant tuna.

With the bigger giant tuna, different techniques, baits, and tactics are required. Here larger baits such as mackerel, herring, mullet, and squid are trolled for the big fish. Such baits can be trolled singly or in "daisy chains" of several mackerel, herring, or squid rigged on a line. Only one of the baits, usually the last one, will have a hook in it. These baits can be trolled blindly, but in spots where giant tuna are sighted "pushing" on the surface or chasing fish, you can head toward them and troll the chain of baits in front of them. If the tuna show interest and head for the baits, reel fast to tease them into striking.

The smaller members of the tuna family, such as albacore, false albacore, and bonitos, are often taken by offshore anglers while trolling. They'll hit many of the same lures as school tuna, but these can be somewhat smaller for the bonitos. They also like a fast-moving lure, but these are trolled on longer lines than for school tuna.

The dolphin is often caught in offshore waters, especially in tropical waters near the Gulf Stream and other currents. They'll hit lures such as spoons, jigs, feathers, bone squid, and plastic skirts. They'll also take whole rigged mullet, ballyhoo, sardines, and strips cut from fish. To find them, look for schools of flying fish, weedlines, floating objects such as logs, boxes, crates, and sea turtles, and troll near these. If a sargassum weedline stretches for long distances, run your boat alongside it and follow it until you run into fish.

One trick that will enable you to take several fish out of a school of dolphin is to keep the last fish that is hooked in the water until another one is hooked. Keep on doing this and it will hold the fish close to the boat until most of them are caught or they lose interest.

Another great fighter taken trolling offshore is the wahoo. They'll hit lures such as spoons, other metal lures, feathers, jigs, and plastic skirts. You can also get them on whole small fish or strips cut from bonito, dolphin, and mackerel. These are trolled fast from flat lines rather than outriggers because you'll hook more fish that way.

There are many other fish caught by offshore trollers, such as the amberjack, yellowfin tuna, blackfin tuna, roosterfish, barracuda, and sharks, and if you troll deep with wire lines or weights or planers, you can even catch grouper of various kinds.

Offshore trolling is a fascinating game, with many surprises and many encounters with such interesting marine animals as whales, porpoises, sharks, sea turtles, rays, and similar creatures.

14

Drifting

Drifting must have been discovered by some lazy angler a long time ago as one of the easiest ways to catch more fish without knocking yourself out. When trolling you have to have someone at the wheel at all times; but this can be monotonous and boring, and it also takes quite a bit of energy and alertness. Anchoring is not too bad if you stay in one spot all day, but if you have to move around and try several spots, it can be a lot of work lowering and raising the anchor.

But when drifting, you shut off your motor, let out your line, and then just let the boat move along with the tide, current, or wind. Drifting is actually a slow form of trolling without using the motor. It can be done in shallow or deep water and is effective for a wide variety of species, from bottom fish to surface gamefish.

One of the main reasons for the success of drift fishing is that you cover more territory and constantly present your bait to new fish. A moving bait also attracts more fish than one that is lying still on the bottom, where it often gets covered by sand, mud, or weeds, or falls into a hole between rocks. If you are drifting with a bait just below the surface or several feet down, it has a slow, wobbling action, which also attracts fish. A moving bait also seems to attract bigger fish, and when using a bottom rig it scares away such pests as bergalls, skates, crabs, and other bait stealers.

Of course, successful drift fishing depends on favorable conditions, such as a moving tide or some wind. Too weak a tide or too little wind will cause a boat to stay in one place or move very slowly, and that is not too good. On the other hand, too strong a tide or wind is also bad, because then a boat moves too fast and it is difficult to present your bait or rig at the proper level.

The types of bottom you are over also decides the method of fishing you will use. When fishing over rocky bottoms, shellfish beds, reefs, or banks that cover a wide area, drifting is usually best. But when fishing small spots—such as sunken wrecks, holes, rock piles, bridge supports, or other obstructions —anchoring is usually better.

Party boat skippers do a lot of drifting with their boats and get a lot of fish for their customers. In fact, these head boats are called "drift boats" in Florida. On most party boats that specialize in drift fishing, anglers line up on one side of the deck and their lines stream away from the boat. This is best, since you have fewer tangles with other lines and avoid cutting or fouling your line on the bottom of the boat. But on some crowded boats you may be forced to fish with your line running under the hull. Then a longer rod, such as a surf stick, helps to keep the line as far away from the boat as possible.

Most party boat anglers and many private boat fishermen prefer a conventional boat rod and star drag reel holding 200 or 300 yards of 30- or 40-pound-test monofilament line. But when going after bigger fish in deeper water, they may use heavier outfits with bigger reels filled with 60-to-100-pound-test mono or Dacron line.

Fishing from a drifting boat has long been the favorite and most productive way to catch the fluke or summer flounder found along the Atlantic Coast. These fish lie half buried in the sand or mud and dart out to grab a killifish or other small fish. Favorite baits for them are live killies or dead spearing, sand eels or shiners, usually with a strip of squid as an added attraction. These are used on double or tandem hooks in sizes 4/0 or 5/0 for small fluke and up to 6/0 or 7/0 for bigger "doormat" fluke. Larger baits are also used for the bigger fluke such as smelt. You can also cut strips from the first fluke you catch and use these as bait. The rig used for this drifting has a 3-foot leader tied a few inches above the sinker.

On the Pacific Coast, anglers also drift for halibut and in

some areas use leaders up to 8 feet long. Herring and long strips of pork rind or small whole fish make the best baits for them. Drifting is also best for the Atlantic halibut, which are sometimes caught off Maine and Massachusetts.

Party boats and private boats also do a lot of drifting for cod and pollock in northern waters. If both fish are in the same spot, a two-hook rig can be used. The first hook can be tied about 2 feet above the sinker and the second one about 4 feet above the first. The bottom hook can be baited with a clam, while the top hook can be baited with a strip of squid. In rocky areas a cod rig with a single hook tied about 1 foot or 2 feet above the sinker is best. You're almost certain to lose some rigs when drifting and fishing over such broken bottoms, so why lose two hooks when you can lose only one?

Other bottom fish caught in North Atlantic waters while drifting include whiting or silver hake, porgies, and sea bass. For them you can use the regular one- or two-hook bottom rigs with the proper size hooks suited for each fish baited with clams, squid, or strips of fish, depending on the particular fish's preference.

Along the Pacific Coast party boats also drift for many bottom species such as white sea bass, greenling, lingcod, and the various rockfishes. The latter two fish are often taken in very deep water requiring heavy rods, big reels, strong lines, and heavy weights or sinkers. Such baits as live or dead anchovies, pieces of mackerel, bonito, and chunks and fillets cut from other fish are often used. Strips of squid are also good. In such depths you not only need heavy weights but can also use such lines as Monel or bronze wire.

When drifting for bottom fish you have to be constantly alert and hold your rod at all times. Over rocky bottoms you have to lift your sinker to clear the high rocks, then drop it back when the danger of fouling is over. When a fish bites, he may take the bait and swallow it instantly, but most of the time it pays to drop back some slack line and lower your rod tip to give the fish more chance to mouth the bait.

If the current and wind are weak, you can often drift with the rig under the boat, but when the wind or tide is strong, it may be necessary to let out more line so that the rig stays on the bottom.

And as the tide changes or the wind increases or decreases, you may have to change weights or sinkers in order to get your bait down to the bottom. In most shallow or average depths, bank or diamond or ball sinkers from 4 to 16 ounces can be used when drifting. But when drifting is done in greater depths, from 200 to 600 feet, you may need weights up to 2 or 3 pounds.

Party boats and private boats also drift for the more exotic gamefish and surface feeders. Here the lines are usually streamed out from the side of the boat and the baits move closer to the surface. You'll see whole fleets in northern waters off New York and New Jersey drifting and chumming for bluefish during the summer and fall months. Bunker chum is used, and hooks baited with butterfish are let out in the chum slick while the boat is drifting. Besides bluefish they also get school tuna, false albacore,and bonito on these drifting boats.

The same thing is done in Pacific waters on the party boats there. They use live anchovies or sardines for chum, and the same fish are also used for bait to catch yellowtail, tuna, albacore, and barracuda. (Chumming methods and techniques will be covered in more detail in the next chapter.)

Around Florida and in the Gulf of Mexico, the party boats and private boats often drift for king mackerel using pilchards, ballyhoo, or shrimp, often on tandem hooks (king mackerel tend to bite off the tail of a baitfish and get away if you only use one hook). If the drift is really slow and you let out a lot of line and your bait gets close to the bottom, you'll catch snappers, yellowtail, and grouper in southern waters.

Along the Pacific Coast salmon anglers do a lot of drifting for these fish. The technique called "mooching" is really drifting with the tide or current using whole or cut herring for bait so that it spins slowly as the boat moves along. When the sea is rough, the action of the waves or swells will raise and lower the boat, imparting a lifelike injured action to the bait. But when the ocean is smooth, you can "work" your rod up and down to give the bait some action, or you can reel in a few feet, then let the bait drop back again.

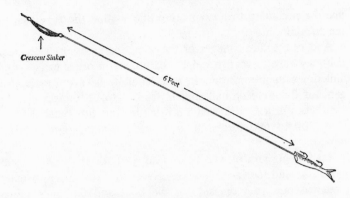

Rig used for Pacific salmon mooching.

The herring baits used for king and coho salmon are pre-pared in three ways. One way is to use a whole herring. The second way is to use a "plug cut" herring, where the head is cut at an angle. And the third way is to cut a "spinner" or fillet from the side of a herring. These baits are usually used on two-hook rigs.

These salmon baits are used on a rig consisting of a 2-to-6-ounce crescent sinker about 6 feet ahead of the bait. When drifting for king salmon, lower this rig to the bottom until you feel the weight bounce. Then reel in several feet and keep it there so that you don't hang up on rocks or weeds, and keep the bait away from bottom fish. Another trick is to lower the rig to the bottom, then reel it in slowly toward the surface to make the bait spin attractively.

Instead of using dead baits, try drifting with live fish if you want some real action. In southern waters this is a good way to catch big king mackerel, amberjack, tarpon, barracuda, grouper, and sharks. Various small live fish such as mullet, pinfish, goggle eyes, squirrel fish, blue runners, grunt, and snappers can be used for bait. These small fish can be hooked through the back or lips and let out from a drifting boat on a line with or without a float. If the fish stays too close to the surface, you can add a sinker a few feet ahead of the live bait-fish.

When using such a live fish for king mackerel or barracuda,

use a double-hook rig on a wire leader. But for most fish, a single hook on a monofilament line or leader is best.

At Boca Grande Pass and Captiva Pass in Florida, anglers drift for tarpon with live fish baits or crabs, but attach the sinker with light line or wire so that it is released when a tarpon gets hooked and leaps out of the water.

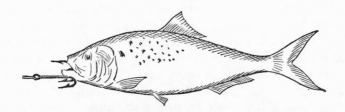

Hooking a menhaden when drifting for big striped bass.

Striped-bass anglers have discovered in recent years that one of the deadliest ways of taking big stripers is by drifting with a live bait. Thus anglers fishing off the New England coast; Long Island, New York; and off New Jersey use live menhaden or bunker for bait while drifting. Bunker are often difficult to obtain and keep alive in a tank or on a hook. So they are usually snagged or bought from a commercial bait man and used almost immediately. Hook the bunker with a small-size No. 2/0 or No. 3/0 treble hook, impaling only one of the hooks through the upper jaw.

The bunker used for stripers should be allowed to go down to the bottom, so you may have to let out up to 100 feet of line. If the tide or wind is strong, you may have to add a trolling weight anywhere from 1 to 3 ounces about 5 or 6 feet ahead of the bait.

If you can't obtain live bunkers, try to catch some live mackerel and use them while drifting for striped bass. Mackerel can usually be caught on tiny metal lures with a spinning rod and transferred to a large tank of water. If this water is kept well aerated and cool, the mackerel will live for some time.

One of the toughest live baits of all for striped bass is an eel anywhere from 10 to 18 inches long, hooked through the jaw, lip, or eyes, and drifted just off the bottom. Although live eels will take stripers in the daytime, they work best at night, especially along rocky shores such as those found in New England. When using live eels, let them head for the bottom, which they usually do, but in rocky areas or where there is weed or kelp on the bottom, don't let them hide in this stuff. As soon as you feel the eel touch bottom, raise your rod to get him away from it, then lower it again.

Striped bass will also take other live fish such as herring, alewives, and small pollock; even blackfish or tautog have been used with good results while drifting. Along the Pacific Coast in the San Francisco area they drift with live fish such as anchovies and shiner perch using sinkers from a few ounces to 2 pounds and long 8- or 9-foot leaders to get the live baitfish down to the bottom in strong currents and tides.

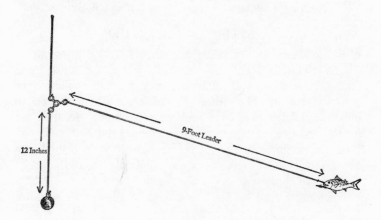

Rig used in drifting for striped bass with shiner perch in Pacific waters.

Drifting with live baits can also be done offshore for billfish too. In Florida many sailfish have been caught on live blue runners drifted just below the surface or deeper. Blue runners can be caught by trolling or casting in inlets and around buoys, piers, rocks, and jetties, and kept alive in a bait well or large container. If you can't get blue runners, you can try using small yellowtail, grunt, snappers, or pinfish.

Hook these baits through the back and let them swim out naturally as the boat drifts lazily along the edges of the Gulf Stream or other waters where sailfish are present. You can fish these baits on a plain line at various depths from several feet down to depths of 30 or 40 feet. Or you can add a cork, styrofoam, or balloon float a few feet above the bait.

You can do much the same thing for other fish such as white marlin, black marlin, blue marlin, swordfish, big-eye tuna, giant bluefin tuna, and sharks. Live baits are best for these fish, but if you can't obtain live ones, use dead menhaden, butterfish, mackerel, herring, whiting, ling, bonito, or almost any other fish of the right size.

In the case of tuna and sharks, it also helps to chum while you are drifting, using ground bunker and chunks of fish ladled over the side as the boat drifts along. Here you can often drift with anywhere from two to four lines at the same time. Two lines can be down deep, even with a small sinker or weight a few feet above the hook to get it down, while the other two lines can be let out with floats to keep the bait closer to the surface.

When using any of the live or dead fish baits for the fish mentioned above, do not try to set the hook as soon as a fish grabs the bait. Instead, let the fish run for a few seconds or even longer until you are pretty sure that it has swallowed the bait. Then come back sharply with the rod tip to set the hook.

Drifting is also a highly effective method when fish are breaking or feeding on top. At such times a boat moving or trolling among the fish or too close to the school can put them down. But if you shut off the motor above the fish and drift slowly toward them, don't alert or scare the school, and they usually stay and feed up on top for longer periods. Then as you drift, you can cast lures toward the fish. And even if you don't see fish, you can drift along the beaches, in the ocean, in inlets, tidal rivers, bays, and creeks and cast lures toward likely spots. In many of these spots the water is shallow and a drifting boat is less likely to frighten the fish than a boat with the engine running and moving along creating a wake or waves. (Such drifting and casting for various fishes will be described in more detail in Chapter 16 on boat casting.)

So drift your way to fish and you'll sneak up on them without alerting or frightening them. They'll often break and feed all around the boat, and a short cast will reach them. And if you catch fish, you can usually repeat the process by drifting in the same area again and again. If the water is fairly shallow, you can throw out a marker buoy (a plastic bottle or big cork float with a line and weight are good for this) and pinpoint the spot where you can make more drifts. You can also take cross bearings by lining up objects onshore so you can return to the same spot for more drifts. If you are not familiar with the waters or best spots for drifting, watch where the other boats such as party boats, drift boats, charter boats, and private boats are drifting and you can drift at a distance alongside or behind them and fish the same spots.

All in all, drifting may not require as much energy or work as other methods of fishing, but it is a highly efficient and deadly way to catch more fish and bigger fish. So give it a try this season and I'm sure you'll agree that drifting often beats trolling or anchoring.

15

Chumming

Nowadays for many fishermen, chumming is almost a must if you want to catch your share of fish or more fish. With so many boats fishing the more popular spots and many of them using chum to attract fish, the boat that doesn't employ such chum is handicapped. The fish will almost invariably congregate around a boat dispensing chum and ignore or pass up a boat that isn't offering such a free handout.

The main idea behind chumming is to encourage fish to eat something with no hook attached in the hope that they will later take something with a hook. Chumming also draws fish to a certain spot. Instead of the angler moving about in search of fish, he waits for the fish to come to him. What you are really trying to do is to fool the fish with free samples and dispel his suspicions so that he will more readily take a baited hook.

There are various methods and techniques used in chumming, and the angler who knows and practices them will often catch fish when ordinary bottom fishing, casting, or trolling methods fail to produce. There are many gamefish and bottom fish that will respond to chumming and gang up at certain spots or near the boat and stay there as long as you continue to feed them.

Anglers seeking giant tuna know that one of the best ways to get these big fish to take a bait with a hook in it is to first attract them up to the boat with chum and make them excited and whet their appetites for more of the same.

The chum usually used for giant tuna is the menhaden or bunker. This flat, deep-bodied, oily fish about 1 foot or so in length is seined commercially. Millions of pounds are caught annually for industrial purposes. But each year more and more of these fish are being diverted for use in chumming. Sports fishermen use tons of the ground bunker for chum.

Menhaden or bunker can now be bought fresh, iced, or frozen, either by the bushel or in cans or blocks. Whole bunker are often sold by the bushel and must be ground by the angler. Those sold in cans or frozen in blocks are already ground and ready for use.

The usual method of chumming is done by getting a big container (a plastic garbage can is good) and filling it with seawater. Then the ground bunker is added and the whole mess is stirred around until it is the consistency of a thick soup. Then you can start ladling the stuff over the side or stern of the boat in order to form a chum slick. A cheap, handy ladle for this can be made from an empty tin can nailed to a wooden handle.

Ladle for dispensing chum made from
an empty tin can and wooden handle.

As the chum slick develops and spreads, you'll see the oil form a wide band, which will extend for several hundred feet from the boat. The particles of bunker will sink to varying depths under the chum slick. Tuna and other fish will get the scent of the oil and blood and start feeding on the particles and follow them up to the boat.

Most tuna fishermen also get whole bunker and cut them up into chunks and toss these overboard into the chum slick as an added attraction. You can also cut up other fish such as butterfish, mackerel, herring, and whiting and throw these into the chum slick. This gives the tuna something bigger to swallow and holds their interest.

The next step, of course, is to bait up a big tuna hook with a whole bunker, herring, mackerel, butterfish, or whiting and let it drift out naturally in the chum line. Finally, you hope a big tuna will take it.

The same kind of chumming can be done for the smaller school tuna, only here you can use a small live mackerel on a tiny hook and let this out in the chum slick. Sometimes these school tuna will also take a small dead mackerel or a piece of fish bait, but live mackerel are usually better.

Off Bermuda anglers chum for Allison tuna using tiny hogmouth fry often mixed with some anchovies. This mixture is then crushed and scattered around the boat. Or you can mix the same tiny fish with wet sand, crush them together, and scatter handfuls of this chum in the water. Then hooks baited with either the fry or the anchovies are drifted out in the current in the chum slick.

The anglers who really go in for chumming in a big way are the bluefish fishermen. They also use ground bunker or menhaden and dump tons of the stuff into the Atlantic Ocean, mostly in southern New England, New York, and New Jersey waters. On weekends you will often see big fleets of several hundred boats all chumming for bluefish. And the fishing is done not only during the day but also continues into the night. This bluefish chumming can be done from an anchored or drifting boat.

When chumming for bluefish, you can bait your hook with a slice of butterfish and let this out in the chum slick. In the beginning you may have to let out 100 or even 150 feet of line to get a pickup from a bluefish. But as the fish work into the chum slick they come closer to the boat.

Usually you can let the bait out without any weight on the line. But if the tide is strong or if the wind is strong when drifting, you can add a clincher sinker on the leader to get the bait down deeper. Also, if you have to get the bait down deep, let out plenty of slack line fast from the reel spool. When a fish picks up the bait, let him run for a few seconds, then set the hook.

During the summer months along the Atlantic Coast when you are chumming for bluefish, you'll often notice false albacore and bonito feeding on the chum. They will often take a hook baited with a piece of butterfish or a small spearing or shiner. But they are more shy of hooks and leaders than even bluefish, and consequently they are harder to hook. Use the smallest hooks and thinnest leaders that are practical for them. At times the false albacore and bonito will also hit lures such as spoons, plugs, and jigs in the chum slick if these are jigged up and down where the fish are feeding and swimming.

Along the Pacific Coast chumming is also done from the "live bait" boats that leave from many ports in California. These boats are equipped with big bait tanks where sardines, herring, and anchovies can be kept alive. The live baitfish are thrown into the water a few at a time. The fish usually sought by these boats is the California yellowtail, a relative of the amberjack that puts up a tough, thrilling fight on light tackle.

Fishing for the yellowtail usually runs from April to October, and many of the live-bait boats leave from Southern California ports such as San Diego. You can use either spinning or conventional tackle for yellowtail, and lines testing from 15 to 30 pounds, depending on the flexibility of the rod. Usually the rods used from the live-bait boats are long—up to 9 or 10 feet—and limber in the tip section.

You'll hook more fish than with thinner lines and a small hook. Sizes No. 1 to No. 4 or No. 5 tuna hooks are used to hold the live anchovies. When you see yellowtail "boiling" near the boat attracted by the chum of live baitfish, hook one of the anchovies through the nose and cast it into the commotion. Let the anchovy swim around freely until a fish grabs it. Usually no weight is required when the yellowtail are near the surface, but if they are down deep, you may have to add a light clincher or clamp-on sinker to get the bait down. Yellowtail will also take live mackerel, squid, or other fish; or you can try casting out metal squids, spoons, or jigs and reel them back fast toward the boat.

The Pacific albacore are taken much the same way as the yellowtail. You can use the same rods and reels, hooks and live anchovies for these fish as for the yellowtail. First, the albacore are located by trolling with lures, and when some fish are hooked or a school is sighted, the chumming with live anchovies or sardines begins. When the albacore start boiling near the boat, you cast the live anchovy into them.

You can also catch Pacific tuna in the same way from the live-bait boats and on the same tackle and baits. White sea bass, barracuda, and bonito are also caught from these boats.

Another popular fish that is caught along the Atlantic Coast by chumming is the northern weakfish or squeteague. The chum usually used here is the small grass shrimp. These tiny, translucent shrimp can be bought by the quart from bait dealers and boat liveries in the popular weakfish areas in New Jersey, New York, and New England. But such grass shrimp are expensive and often hard to locate at tackle shops or bait dealers. You'll need anywhere from 4 to 8 quarts for a day's fishing. So many weakfishermen try to catch their own shrimp in tidal bays and creeks. A seine with a fine mesh can be used for this.

Once you get the grass shrimp, you keep them alive in a bait car or minnow bucket. The boat is usually anchored with two anchors, often crosswise to the current so that it stays put without wandering or swaying. Then you throw a few shrimp out at a time to start the chum slick going. It's a good idea to pinch the shrimp so that they aren't too active in the water.

Then, using a light spinning rod or bait-casting-type rod, you hook a sand worm or two or three of the small shrimp on a No. 1 or No. 2 hook, and let them out in the chum slick. After letting out about 150 feet of line, you can gradually reel in and let the line out again.

The same grass shrimp can be used for striped bass in inlets, bays, and creeks. It is especially popular in Chesapeake Bay, but here they often thread several of the small shrimp on the hook for bait. Chesapeake Bay anglers also like to use soft-shell clams as chum. The clams are mashed in a bucket or container, then scattered around the boat. Then a hook baited with two or three of the soft clams is drifted out in the chum slick.

Much the same thing is done for stripers in New Jersey and New York waters, only here they use the larger sea or surf clams called "skimmers." The big clams are shucked, and only the soft, meaty parts or bellies are used for chum and bait. The clams are also ground up like bunker chum before mixing with seawater and ladled overboard. Then a hook baited with a whole clam is drifted out in the chum slick.

Many years ago chumming from the shores of Rhode Island and Massachusetts was popular for big striped bass. Here ground-up bunker was used from specially built fishing stands or small piers or from the rocky points themselves. Usually they hired a "chummer" to chum all night, and then they arrived in the morning and cast hooks baited with pieces of bunker or lobster tail to entice the stripers. This is rarely done nowadays because of the expense and work involved.

Chumming is also highly effective when fishing for sharks. In fact, no serious shark fisherman would think of going out without bringing along cans of bunker chum to use to attract sharks up to the boat. You can also cut up some fish and throw these out from time to time. Other anglers bring along some buckets of beef blood to drop into the water. Almost any fish or animal can be cut up or allowed to bleed in the water. The bloodier kinds of fish such as tuna, mackerel, albacore, and bonito are best for this. You can use these same fish as bait either whole if small or cut up into chunks if big.

Mackerel of various kinds will also respond to chum and come to feed in the slick. Thus fleets of private boats and party boats head offshore in New York and New Jersey each spring and late fall to chum for the common Atlantic or Boston mackerel with ground bunker chum. Here you can use a shiny metal diamond jig or metal spoon or several tube lures on a hook to catch the mackerel in the slick.

You can do the same thing in southern waters for Spanish mackerel and king mackerel, using ground bunker or almost any other fish, crabs, or shrimp as chum. Then you can drift out a hook baited with a small fish or try casting lures such as jigs into the chum slick.

Anglers fishing for winter flounder have increased their catches by using chum. They often bring along a bushel of mussels, then crack the shells and scatter them around the anchored boat. Or you fill a mesh bag with the cracked mussels and lower it with a weight inside to the bottom on a line. Other anglers make or buy "chum pots," which are small wire cages filled with the cracked mussels. You can also use crushed or cracked clams, oysters, or other shellfish for chum. Every so often you can lift the chum pot or bag from the bottom and shake it to release some chum.

Flounder fishermen have also used such odd-ball chums as canned corn kernels, boiled rice mixed with sardines, and cat and dog food to bring flounders under a boat. As a matter of fact, cat and dog food makes an excellent chum for many salt-water species. They usually contain meat or fish of some kind, and these scatter and drift through the water and draw the fish. Punch some holes in the cans and let them sink to the bottom. Or you can open them up, mix the contents with some boiled rice or uncooked rolled oats and seawater, and ladle it overboard.

Mesh bag filled with chum and lowered to the bottom will attract many kinds of salt-water species.

Many other bottom fishes such as cod, porgies, sea bass, blackfish, or tautog can be chummed in northern waters. You can even "bait" the bottom for such fish a day or two in advance by scattering cracked clams, mussels, or crabs to bring the fish around.

In southern waters such as Florida, Bermuda, and the Bahamas, you can actually see the fish respond to your chum. Merely cut up some shrimp, needlefish, ballyhoo, mullet, or other fish and throw these overboard. In shallow water you'll soon see fish of all kinds rising from the coral reefs for the tidbits. Snappers, grunt, yellowtail, grouper, amberjack, and various reef fishes will all swarm around. Then you can bait a hook with a piece of the same fish used for chum or a live shrimp or a small whole fish and let it down around the waiting fish.

There are a few tips and tricks that help you to catch more fish when using chum. It is important not to chum too heavily or too lightly. The secret is to keep a steady stream of chum going at all times without any extended breaks. But don't dump the stuff over so lavishly that the fish get well fed and won't take your offering. The idea is not to satisfy their hunger but to give them just enough to tease them.

Chumming is most effective when there is some tide to keep the chum moving out some distance from the boat. But too fast a tide isn't very good because the chum will travel too high on the surface and go too far away from the boat to be effective. The same thing is true when the wind is too strong and the drifting boat moves too quickly away from the chum being thrown overboard. A slow, steady drift is best here.

And when letting your bait out in a chum slick, it is vital to have it drift out naturally. This means giving plenty of slack line so that the bait drifts without being hindered. Merely holding the bait on a tight line may get you a few fish, but not as many as a live baitfish swimming around naturally or a dead fish or bait moving out with the current or tide like a piece of chum.

Knowing just when to set the hook when chumming will come with experience and a sort of "feel" or "timing" when to come back with the rod. Usually it is best to let the line run off the reel spoon freely when a fish picks up the bait for at least a few seconds. With some fish you may have to give them up to a minute or more before setting the hook. The smaller the bait used the quicker you can set the hook, while larger baits take more time for the fish to swallow.

Chumming isn't a lazy man's game, and neither is it the

cheapest way to fish. It costs money to buy enough chum or you have to work hard to catch or obtain it. Then you have to keep it alive or fresh, grind or chop it up, and then ladle it overboard in a steady stream. This usually means two or three anglers taking turns or helping out with the chumming so that everyone gets a chance to fish. You often have a messy boat that must be scrubbed and cleaned after the fishing is done.

But as far as results are concerned, chumming is well worth the trouble. On many days it can mean the difference between catching fish or going home with no fish. So to be assured of sport and fun the next time you go fishing in salt water, bring plenty of chum and use it in your favorite spot.

16

Boat Casting

Surf anglers cast from beaches, rocky shores, or jetties and catch fish, but you'll catch a lot more fish by casting from a boat. You'll also catch a greater variety of fish both inshore and offshore casting from a boat. You'll also be able to cast and show your lure or bait to many more fish during a given fishing period or day than the surf or shore caster.

That's one of the great advantages a boat caster has over a surf or shore caster. He can try a spot for a few minutes or longer; then, if there is no action, he can scoot down to another spot in a short time and fish that area. By moving around and trying different spots, he increases his chances of running into fish. Of course, the surf angler or shore caster can also try different spots, but this takes more time and energy and often involves a lot of walking, so he is limited to two or three spots at the most.

The boat caster can also move out into deeper water quite a distance and search for fish or follow a feeding school of fish, but a surf caster or shore caster is limited to the distance he can reach with his longest cast.

Of course, boat casting can be more expensive than surf casting or shore casting. You either have to own a boat, charter one, or rent one. Even if you go out in a friend's boat, you usually have to share some of the expenses. And boat casting is usually more complicated and involved than shore casting. You not only have to cast from a rolling or pitching boat, but you also have to have someone who knows how to run and

handle the boat. This is especially true if you fish in dangerous or treacherous waters such as along beaches or rocky
shores with rough surf, in tidal rips and strong currents, or
among other boats.

But despite these few drawbacks, boat casting is a highly
successful way of catching more fish, and it can be even more
satisfying for the angler than other methods. Casting and working the lures is an art that must be mastered before you can
catch fish from a boat.

Anglers seeking striped bass do a lot of casting from boats,
and the so-called bass boats have been used for many years to
cast toward shore along beaches, rocky shores, and around
jetty ends, especially in such places as Martha's Vineyard,
Cuttyhunk, Cape Cod, along Rhode Island, at Montauk, and
at other Long Island spots.

This is often tricky business and involves going in close to
the beach or rocks or jetties so that anglers can reach the best
spots with their casts. These anglers prefer either spinning or
conventional-type surf rods, which may be a bit shorter in the
tip and butt sections than surf rods used from shore. They
cast such lures as surface plugs, underwater plugs, metal
squids, or heavy spoons, rigged eels, or plastic eels. For smaller
striper, they may use jigs.

Big swimming or popping plugs are especially effective for
this casting toward shore in the daytime. They should be cast
toward patches of white water, rocks, into swirling rips or currents, and along the edges of sandbars and reefs. You have to
work these plugs fairly fast so that they create a splash or
commotion on top of the water.

At night rigged eels or plastic eels or underwater plugs are
effective, especially for big stripers. Here, of course, you have
to know your waters and your best fishing spots. And the man
who runs the boat stays at the wheel at all times to be ready to
move the boat into the right position or out of danger.

Even small boats can be used to cast for striped bass near
shore, such as the 12- or 14-foot cartops used up in Cape Cod
and in other spots. They are launched from the beach and
head out to the offshore bars, rips, and holes where big strip-

ers lie. They even do this at night and cast the regular striper lures for hours, often coming back in the morning with a boat-ful of big bass.

During the fall months you can often catch the smaller school stripers by casting from a boat. Here you can use lighter one-handed spinning rods and cast the smaller poppers, underwater plugs, jigs, and spoons. The best fishing occurs when the fish are actually chasing baitfish on top and you can see them breaking. Then poppers are deadly. At other times, when they are deep, you can use jigs or spoons and let them sink before reeling them back up toward the surface.

Striped bass can also be caught in tidal rivers, bays, and sounds by casting from boats around likely spots such as rock or oyster bars, points of land, along marshbanks, around bridges, and at other striper hangouts. On some of the larger bays and sounds you can see birds working or fish breaking and cast to them.

Another great scrapper often caught by casting from a boat is the bluefish. They can be caught on the same tackle and lures used for striped bass. Here again, the best action will take place if you see the blues chasing baitfish and the birds diving. At such times lures such as surface plugs, underwater plugs, spoons, and metal squids will usually take them. If you don't see any blues feeding, you can still catch them by cast-ing into many spots alongshore at daybreak or toward dusk. They often feed in the surf or other spots where striped bass are also present. You can reel these lures somewhat faster than you do for striped bass, however.

One of the best ways to catch big channel bass is by cast-ing from a boat. This is done in Virginia and North Carolina waters, especially in the spring and fall when these fish move along the beaches or into bays in big schools. Here it doesn't pay to cast blindly, but instead you try to locate a school of channel bass. Once you see the fish, you can cast metal squids or Hopkins lures into them and reel these back toward the boat at a moderate speed but with occasional rod action. It is best not to approach the school too close to avoid spooking the fish.

Snook like to lurk under the roots and overhanging leaves of mangrove trees.

When fishing in southern waters you can cast from a boat to catch snook. For them a one-handed spinning rod or a bait-casting or "popping"-type rod can be used to flip a lure into tiny spots with accuracy. A 10-to-12-pound-test line is best with the spinning outfit, while a 20- or 25-pound-test line can be used with the bait-casting or popping outfit. Snook like to lurk around obstructions such as roots or piles, and you can't let them run too far in such places. You have to snub them and stop them and lead them out into more open water to fight and boat them without getting fouled or cut off.

Such boat casting is done in Florida in the Everglades and Ten Thousand Islands area. Here the snook like to lie in the shadows under the mangrove trees. You have to cast your lure right next to or even under the overhanging leaves to get a response from the snook. You can also cast in more open waters around shellfish, rock or sandbars, around the mouths of creeks, and where there are strong currents and rip tides. Snook also like to hang around bridges, and casting from a boat toward piles or shadows is often effective.

Snook will hit many types of plugs such as the poppers, swimmers, wounded minnows, darters, and underwater plugs.

They will also take spoons, plastic eels, and jigs. With jigs it's often a good idea to add half a shrimp to the hook.

The jig when cast becomes even more deadly if you add half a shrimp to the hook.

The best times to fish for snook is early in the morning, toward evening, and during the night. During the daytime they are more active on stormy, overcast days than on bright, sunny days.

Another southern fish that can often be caught while casting from a boat is the tarpon. They can be caught in many of the same waters and spots as the snook. And the smaller tarpon can be caught on the same fishing outfits. But if you are casting for the bigger tarpon in more open, deeper waters where they can run or sound, heavier fishing outfits are more practical.

And while snook often break water or splash on top, they don't come out as high in leaps as the tarpon. The tarpon almost always guarantees such a spectacular performance, especially when hooked in shallow and enclosed waters such as narrow rivers and tidal creeks.

Tarpon will hit top-water plugs such as swimmers, poppers, or torpedo types. If these don't produce, try shallow-running underwater plugs that wriggle, wobble, or dart. They also hit spoons, other metal lures, and various types of jigs. White, yellow, or red and white jigs are usually the best ones to use.

You can often see tarpon rolling on top of the water, and while they often won't be interested in taking lures cast from a boat, it's one of the best ways to locate a school of fish. And if you keep casting or try different schools, you're apt to hook some fish in the long run.

Tarpon also like to lurk in the shadows of mangrove trees,

piers, and bridges during the daytime and at night when they are waiting for the tide to bring shrimp, crabs, or a school of mullet or baitfish to them. But you'll also find schools of tarpon rolling or swimming in more open waters off the beaches, in inlets, rivers, and bays. They'll hit lures in the daytime but are more inclined to do so in the evening, early morning, and at night.

Also found in southern waters and a great fish to take on casting tackle is the barracuda. In shallow waters such as those found in the Florida Keys, the Bahamas, and other tropical spots, you can usually see the 'cuda lying motionless or swimming on the flats. They also hang around mangrove shores, over rock and coral reefs, and over offshore wrecks. In shallow waters the best fishing is usually around high tide.

An exciting way to take a barracuda is with a surface plug such as a popper or torpedo type. Sometimes you'll see several fish rush it at the same time, but most of the time the barracuda will be alone, especially the big ones. You can't reel a lure too fast for barracuda. If they want it they'll catch up with it and grab it. But they have a habit of following a lure but not hitting it. When this happens don't stop reeling or even slow down. Instead, speed up and activate the lure even more. This often excites them and results in a smashing strike.

In deeper waters you can use underwater plugs, spoons, various metal lures, and jigs, and let these sink before you start working them back to the boat.

On many of the same shallow flats where you find the smaller barracuda you'll also find bonefish. They come into even shallower water, often only inches deep. They provide top sport on a light spinning outfit and will often hit a light bucktail jig or a special bonefish jig. But they are pretty spooky, so you'll only get one chance to cast to single bonefish or a pair or a small school of them. Casting too close to a single fish or into the center of a school of bonefish will frighten them away. Instead, cast at least 10 or 15 feet ahead of them or beyond the fish, and reel the lure in so that it passes in front of the fish as they get there. With jigs it's often a good idea to let the jigs sink to the bottom and make them hop along so that they raise puffs of mud or sand.

Also in southern waters a boat caster can have a ball with southern weakfish or sea trout, often called "specks." They are found on many grassy flats, and by drifting slowly in a boat across these flats and casting various lures such as surface plugs, underwater plugs, jigs, and small spoons, you can often have a lot of fun and action. If the sea trout refuse to hit the lures, try using a "popping" cork or float about 2 feet ahead of a hook. Then bait this hook with a live shrimp and cast the whole rig out. Then slowly pop the float or cork so it makes a commotion. Sea trout will be attracted to the scene and will go for the live shrimp.

You can even catch many fish in the deeper offshore waters by casting from a boat. On days when school tuna can be seen in big schools near the surface but refuse to hit trolled lures, try casting a metal squid or heavy spoon into them with a surf fishing outfit. If they grab the lure, as they often do, you'll get a real workout from these speedsters.

Other tuna such as the blackfin tuna and their relatives such as the false albacore and bonito will also hit lures cast from a boat in offshore waters. They hit best if they are seen breaking on top or actually chasing baitfish. Then a plug, metal lure, or jig cast into them and reeled as fast as possible will often be taken.

If you run into a school of dolphin you can have some fast action by casting into them. Here it's a good idea to first hook a fish by trolling, then while one angler holds this first fish in the water with fairly heavy tackle, another angler can cast a lure near the hooked fish. Dolphin usually follow a hooked fish around and lurk near it. You can also try casting near floating logs, weeds, boxes, or even sea turtles for dolphin, which like to hang around such floating objects. They'll hit plugs, spoons, jigs, and other lures.

Some of the best offshore boat casting takes place in southern waters. Here you locate a coral reef, dropoff, sunken wreck, or offshore light tower and cast around these spots. You can try chumming with ground-up fish to attract king mackerel, amberjack, and cobia, and if you let your lure sink deep enough, you'll get grouper, snappers, and other so-called bottom fish.

In recent years casting from party boats such as the live-bait boats fishing Pacific waters has become popular. Using rods similar to surf tackle and fast-retrieve reels, they cast what they call "jigs" (usually metal squids, heavy spoons, or similar lures) into schools of albacore, yellowtail, barracuda, or bonito, and reel the "jigs" in at very fast speeds. The fish may be feeding on top or they may be well below the surface, so it pays to find out what level they are at and retrieve your lure there.

Even sailfish have been caught by casting from a boat. Here you have to wait until you see the fish or until you bring the fish up to the boat with fish strips trolled as teasers. Then you can try casting plugs near the teasers when you see sailfish following one. The best results are obtained if you wait until you see the sailfish slash at the teaser before you cast your plug near it.

Once you catch some fish while casting from a boat, you'll be less satisfied with such methods as trolling or bottom fishing. One of the great thrills in fishing is casting a surface plug, working it right, and having a big fish smash into it and get hooked.

17

Salt-water Fly Fishing

Many salt-water anglers looking for new thrills and challenges have taken up fly fishing in rivers, tidal creeks, canals, bays, and other inshore waters. They have even ventured offshore to tackle some of the smaller billfish and other deep-water fishes.

Fly fishing in fresh waters for trout, salmon, and bass is, of course, an old method. Some anglers also tried using the fly rod in salt water in England around the mid-1800s. In the United States a few anglers used the fly rod for tarpon, striped bass, shad, and other species in the late 1800s.

But the first real, serious attempts to catch fish on fly rods in salt water began in the 1920s when Tom Loving of Baltimore began catching striped bass up to 25 pounds on specially tied flies. Somewhat later, up in Rhode Island, Harold Gibbs was also catching striped bass on his well-known "Gibbs Striper" fly. Then just before World War II, a few men such as Red Greb, Homer Rhode, and Dick Splaine started using flies in the salt waters of Florida.

After World War II there was a revived interest in salt-water fly fishing, especially in southern waters. The man who did the most to spark and maintain this interest was the late Joe Brooks. He wrote a book and many magazine articles dealing with salt-water fly fishing. He traveled all over the world, and during his lifetime had caught over seventy-five different species of fish in salt water on a fly rod.

In recent years salt-water fly rodders have become more numerous than ever and can be seen fishing the waters of the Atlantic, Pacific, and Gulf of Mexico. Many salt-water fly fishing clubs have been established, and there's a national organization called the Salt Water Fly Rodders of America. Their address is Box 304, Old Court House, Cape May Court House, New Jersey 08210.

If you want to try salt-water fly fishing it is important to get the proper tackle, beginning with the fly rod. Although you can use some fresh-water fly rods such as Atlantic salmon, steelhead, and bass bugging fly rods for salt-water fishing, it is best to get a fly rod especially built for such fishing.

Nowadays most salt-water fly fishermen use sturdy glass fly rods with heavy walls and that have plenty of backbone in the butt section. They are made of noncorrosive metal parts and reel seats that hold the reel securely, and some of these salt-water fly rods can have an extension butt added to the lower end of the rod to help fight a big fish.

The length of the salt-water fly rod you get will vary according to the person who uses it and the kind of fishing you plan to do. For most salt-water species an 8½-foot fly rod is long enough if it has the right action and backbone. Many expert anglers prefer a 9- or 9½-foot salt-water fly rod. A long rod makes casting easier because you can get a high backcast. It is also easier to handle lures and fish that are hooked on a longer rod than a shorter rod, especially when wading in water up to your hips.

But no matter what length salt-water fly rod you get, make sure it has a slow action rather than a fast, stiff action. You'll make fewer false casts and even make longer casts with the soft-action rod.

Of course, shorter, stiffer rods with even more backbone may be used for bigger fish offshore such as small billfish, tuna, amberjack, and big tarpon. But for general "all around" salt-water fly-rod fishing, you'll find a lighter, softer rod about 8½ or 9 feet long most practical for most of the smaller species usually caught on a fly rod.

The fly line used with the salt-water rod is usually a forward-tapered line that floats. There are also weight-forward lines that sink for fishing flies in deeper water. And there are also "salt-water taper" lines that also float but that have a heavy belly section close to the end of the fly line. Choosing the correct weight fly line for your particular fly rod is very important if you want to cast efficiently. Fly lines are designated in numbers and letters, such as WF-9-F for a weight-forward No. 9 float-ing line or WF-9-S for a weight-forward sinking line. Usually most salt-water fly rods take a No. 9, No. 10, or No. 11 line.

The reel you choose for salt-water fly fishing is also very important and may make the difference between landing a big fish or losing it. There are many good Atlantic salmon reels made in this country and abroad that can be used for salt-water fly fishing. But in recent years many American tackle manufacturers have started making fly reels especially de-signed for salt-water fishing. These are built of strong non-corrosive materials and have smooth drags that stand up un-der the fast, long runs that many salt-water gamefish make.

Fly reels come in different sizes for salt-water fishing, with the smaller ones being used with the lighter salt-water fly rods for small or medium-sized fish, and the larger reels being used with the heavier rods for bigger fish. Every salt-water fly reel should have a big enough capacity to hold the fly line and also a backing line. For small fish that make short runs, 100 yards of nylon- or Dacron-backing line testing about 20 pounds are sufficient. But for bigger fish and when using the larger fly reels, you may need 200 to 250 yards of 25- or 30-pound-test line for backing.

Leaders used for salt-water fly fishing will vary from 6 to 14 feet in length with the 10-to-12-foot lengths used by most expert fly casters for the smaller fish or wary fish in clear, shallow water. The leaders should be tapered down from a 40- or 30-pound butt section to a tippet testing from 6 to 12 pounds. You'll get more strikes in clear, shallow water with the lighter leaders and tippets, but the heavier tippets are needed to hold the bigger fish. For big, heavy fish, salt-water fly rodders also use shock leaders about 1 foot in length testing 60, 80, or 100 pounds to take the wear and tear and chafing of the teeth, jaws, or lips of the large fish.

Most expert fly rodders prefer to tie their own leaders from nylon leader material to suit their tastes, preferences, and the fishing they plan to do. For this you'll need coils of nylon leader material in test from 40 pounds down to 8 or 6 pounds for the tippets. For some kinds of salt-water fly fishing you can use the ready-tied or knotless fly leaders sold in tackle shops.

Salt-water fly fishermen also need flies of various kinds to catch the different kinds of fish taken on the fly rod. While the bigger fresh-water streamers and bucktails and bass bugs will also catch salt-water fish, most salt-water flies are larger and are tied on stronger hooks. And instead of representing the different kinds of insects or fresh-water minnows, they are tied to imitate the different kinds of baitfish such as spearing, mullet, herring, shiners, anchovies, smelt, candlefish, small eels, and shrimp.

Some of the earliest flies tied especially for salt-water fishing such as the "Gibbs Striper" are still good and are being used by fly rodders. This fly had mostly a bucktail pattern, and since it was tied, many other types of bucktail flies have been created. The well-known "blond" patterns originated by Joe Brooks are tied with two bunches of bucktail: one at the head, the other at the tail of the fly, which results in a bulkier and longer fly. White, yellow, red and white, blue and white, and green and white bucktails are most effective in salt water.

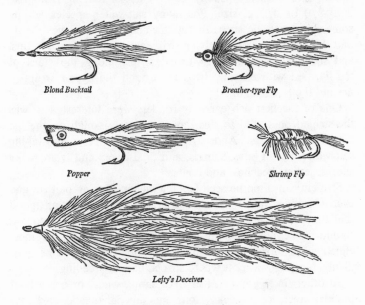

Blond Bucktail

Breather-type Fly

Popper

Shrimp Fly

Lefty's Deceiver

Salt-water flies.

The streamer type of flies tied with long feathers are also used by many salt-water fly fishermen. These flies come in different lengths and colors, and the "breather"-type flies have been used in the briny for many years. They are tied with anywhere from two to a dozen long feathers.

One of the deadliest lures you can use for many species with a salt-water fly rod is the "popper." These are similar to the fresh-water bass bugs and have cupped or slanted heads of cork, balsa wood, or plastics, and have hair or feather tails.

Other flies often used in salt water are the "shrimp" flies, which are tied to imitate tiny grass shrimp. These are usually tied in tan, pink, white, light brown, or yellow colors to imitate the small shrimp.

Then there are the larger patterns especially tied for offshore fishing for the smaller billfish and other fish, and they may run from a few inches to almost a foot in length. They are tied to imitate squid and the baitfish and small fish the gamefish feed on.

Salt-water flies are usually tied on hooks ranging from No. 2 to 3/0 or 4/0 in size. For many salt-water species adding some shiny metallic strips that glitter and flash improves the fly and draws more strikes. Mylar strips are usually used for this, and they can be added in broad strips, along the sides of the fly, tied with narrow strips all around the fly, or wrapped around the hook shank.

One of the first fish early fly rodders were interested in was the striped bass, and to this day the striper is high on the list with these anglers. And striped bass co-operate by taking salt-water flies in bays, sounds, and tidal rivers and from rocky shores, jetties, beaches, and boats.

Stripers can often be seen feeding on top-chasing baitfish and even breaking water. Then, of course, your chances are good that they'll take a fly-rod popper worked fairly fast on top. It should make a noise and throw a good splash to be most effective. In more open waters you'll often see birds or gulls diving, pinpointing spots where striped bass are feeding.

At other times you can fish from shore, wade, or use a boat in tidal rivers and creeks along marshy banks and cast into fast currents and rips, especially around bars and points. Here

A fly-rod popper is retrieved so it pops and makes a splash, which attracts fish.

you can also use fly-rod poppers, especially early in the morning and toward dusk or if you see surface action. But if the stripers are feeding below the surface, a streamer of bucktail fly worked below the surface at various depths is often better. Here a sinking fly line is more effective in getting your fly down than a floating one.

When stripers are feeding on grass shrimp, one of the small "shrimp" flies will take them when they won't look at the larger baitfish imitations. The "shrimp" flies work best when retrieved in short, slow, jerky movements, imitating the swimming of a natural shrimp.

There are many bays, sounds, tidal rivers, rocky shores, and beaches along the Atlantic Coast from Maine to the Carolinas where you can catch striped bass on a fly rod. The best fishing usually takes place in the spring, summer, and fall months.

Striped bass can also be caught on fly rods along the West Coast in Pacific waters. Here the best fishing is usually found in the bays, sloughs, rivers, and lagoons around San Francisco in California and Coos Bay, Oregon. Stripers here feed on anchovies, herring, smelt, small perch, and shrimp, so flies tied to imitate these foods are best. Although stripers can be caught almost the year 'round in many Pacific waters, the peak fishing usually occurs in the spring, early summer, and fall months.

Striped bass can be very finicky when it comes to the length of a fly. Sometimes they want a fly 2 or 3 inches long; at other times, a fly of 4 to 5 inches. So it pays to carry the different sizes with you at all times and try to find out which length the bass prefer on a given day in the spot you are fishing.

Another fish that provides top sport on a fly rod is the bluefish. Both the bigger jumbo blues and the smaller "snapper" blues can be caught on many of the same flies used for stripers. If you see blues breaking water or chasing baitfish, a popper is the one to use. When using sinking flies, use bucktails instead of streamers or those tied with feathers, since bluefish teeth will make quick work of the more delicate flies. Work your flies as fast as possible for blues.

In southern waters fly rodders find great sport with tarpon, from the small "baby" sizes weighing only a few pounds up to the giants going over 100 pounds. For the smaller tarpon, tiny flies and poppers are fished in canals, rivers, creeks, and shallow bays and coves. Here you'll often find the small tarpon back in the mangroves. Then you have to cast as close as possible to the mangroves and retrieve your fly in short jerks. At other times you can see the tarpon rolling and can cast to them. You can use your lightest salt-water fly rod for these small tarpon.

For the bigger tarpon, which lurk in deeper channels, under bridges, in wide rivers, along the beaches, and in the deeper holes on the flats, you need the heaviest fly rod, the strongest leaders, and the larger flies to succeed in catching them. These flies, usually bucktails, streamers, or poppers, are usually cast to fish that are seen cruising, lying below the surface or rolling on top. Bucktails and streamers should be retrieved in fairly slow strips of about a foot or so, then a pause to bring out the breathing motion of the flies. Poppers used for tarpon are also used slowly. They should be popped, then allowed to rest for a few seconds or even longer, then popped again, and this retrieve should be continued up to your feet or the boat. Tarpon will often follow such a popper all the way in and then decide to take it near the end of the retrieve.

Tarpon fishing can be good in the daytime, but they are most active early in the morning, in the evening, and during the night. They also feed more heavily during the new-moon and full-moon tides. In Florida the spring months and early summer months are best.

He's opening some clams to use for codfish bait. The empty shells with some meat attached can be thrown overboard as chum for cod, blackfish, sea bass, porgies, flounders, and other fish. (Photo by Vlad Evanoff)

Giant tuna are often attracted close to a boat with such chum as ground menhaden or bunker, herring, mackerel, or other fish. (Canadian Government Travel Bureau Photo)

Offshore anglers have taken a lot of big fish, such as this amberjack, on a fly rod. This one was taken off Hatteras, North Carolina. (Photo by Joel Arrington)

You can even catch small sharks by wading and casting lures or baits in the Florida Keys or other tropical waters. (Florida News Bureau Photo)

Salt-water anglers from Canada to the Carolinas often wade in the water to catch small striped bass on the flats in bays, tidal rivers, and beaches. This angler is walking the waters of East Lake near Manns Harbor, North Carolina. (Photo by Joel Arrington)

Many salt-water fish are caught around lighthouses and light towers, both inshore and offshore. This is Diamond Shoals off North Carolina. (Photo by Joel Arrington)

Gamefish are always easier to spot from a great height, such as these giant tuna swimming in a school off Cat Cay in the Bahamas. (Bahamas News Bureau Photo)

Even a smaller boat such as this Aquasport can be equipped with a flying bridge or tower as an aid in spotting fish. (Aquasport, Inc., Photo)

Channel bass can be taken by casting from a boat, especially in Virginia and North Carolina waters. These fishermen are in North Carolina's Pamlico Sound. (Photo by Joel Arrington)

This is a white marlin caught off Fort Lauderdale, Florida. It is smaller than the other kinds of marlin but is one of the gamest of billfish. (Photo by Vlad Evanoff)

Big snook like this one are a prize trophy, since they are hard to fool and difficult to land or boat. This one was caught in the St. Lucie River in Florida. (Florida News Bureau Photo)

In many of the same waters where you find the tarpon you'll also find the snook, and he'll take many of the same flies and provide top sport on a fly rod. The only trouble with them is that instead of fighting fair like a tarpon and leaping high in the air in more open water, snook will try to run your line around the nearest mangrove root, stump, rock, pile, bridge support, or other obstruction. And they often succeed in doing so. Or they'll cut your leader with one of their sharp gill covers.

When fly fishing for snook, work the shorelines along the mangroves, around islands, oyster bars, sandbars, inlets, and the mouths of creeks early in the morning, in the evening, or at night. Snook hit the breather-type flies best, but will also take poppers. These should be retrieved slowly but with plenty of action.

At times you can also see big snook cruising on top in canals or chasing a school of tiny minnows. Then you have to use a smaller fly to match the size of the minnows the fish are feeding on.

Another southern favorite of the fly-fishing clan is the bone-fish. They are caught either from a shallow-draft boat poled along the flats or by wading in the shallow water. Fly fishing is the hard way to take bonefish, since they spook easily, and on most occasions you can't approach too closely. So long casts are usually required. And there is usually a fairly stiff wind blowing across the flats, and you often have to cast into it. It is easier to catch a bonefish on a spinning rod or fishing with bait such as live shrimp.

But the salt-water fly angler has one big advantage over the lure caster: His flies do not sink as fast as most lures, so he can work it in very shallow water without hanging up on the bottom as often. So most bonefish flies are small and tied on small hooks so that they don't sink too fast. Small bucktails, combination streamer bucktails, and shrimp flies are favored for this fishing.

Bonefishing with a fly rod—or any tackle, for that matter—also means hunting. You have to first locate the fish, then cast to them. Usually they move up on the flats with incoming water singly, in pairs, or in small schools. And you usually have only one cast at them and must make that one count. The best procedure is to cast well ahead of the fish and beyond them so that you can retrieve your fly to pass in front of the fish where they can see it.

Also found on the flats in many of the same waters as the bonefish are the channel bass (or redfish, as it is called down in Florida) and barracuda. Channel bass will take a streamer or popper if you cast it close enough and hard enough so that it catches their attention. And you have to retrieve your lures slowly for the redfish. But for barracuda you can't retrieve fast enough. They like a fast-moving fly or popper and a noisy one, so you should pop the lure hard, making it throw a big splash. If you see a barracuda and he's interested, keep casting to make the fish excited or mad enough to hit.

The spotted weakfish or sea trout is often caught on a fly rod in southern waters from boats or by wading. They like grassy flats of bays and sounds, but are also found in channels, tidal rivers, and inlets. Multiwing streamers or poppers retrieved slowly are the tickets for them.

You can also have a lot of fun catching the smaller sharks on the flats in such places as the Florida Keys and the Bahamas on a fly rod. Several species of the small sharks venture on the flats into shallow water to feed, and they can be seen cruising around. Some of them will hit the bigger streamer flies if the flies are retrieved very close in front of the sharks where they can see them. It may take several casts before they notice the fly. To land a shark you'll need a short wire leader next to the fly.

In recent years many salt-water fly fishermen have ventured offshore to do battle with many species. One of these fish, the dolphin, is made to order for fly fishing. It doesn't run too big, but any size you hook will give you a great fight. They'll hit bucktails, streamers, or poppers. The smaller tuna of various species and the bonitos and albacores will also take a fly readily if you can locate a school of them feeding on top. Or you chum for these fish with live bait or ground fish and hold them close to the boat, where you cast a fly to them.

And the more expert fly rodders have even taken on the smaller billfish such as sailfish, white marlin, and striped marlin and have succeeded in boating these fish in weights up to 150 pounds or so. To get them you usually have to attract them close to the stern of the boat by trolling teasers, and then when the billfish come up to grab the teaser baits and are teased repeatedly to make them excited and angry, the fly caster places his fly close to the fish where it can see it and take it. This requires teamwork among the pilot of the boat, the man working the teaser, and the fly caster.

Even so-called bottom fish can be caught on a salt-water fly rod if you use a sinking line and let it down deep where such fish as croakers, halibut, cabezon, lingcod, rockfishes, snappers, and pompano can see it. To get down deep enough you usually have to use a section of lead-core line in front for casting weight and to sink to the right depths. About a 30-foot length of 18-to-20-pound-test of lead-core trolling line can be used. This is tied to a 20- or 30-pound-test monofilament backing line.

Salt-water fly fishing is still in its development, and experimental stages and new tips, kinks, and tricks are always being developed or discovered to improve the sport. One of the best books I can recommend for anyone who is serious about salt-water fly fishing or wants to know more about it is *Salt Water Fly Fishing* by George X. Sand, published by Alfred A. Knopf, New York. It is the most complete book ever published on salt-water fly fishing.

18

Wade Fishing, Jigging, and Night Fishing

When you think of wade fishing you usually picture an angler silently wading in a stream or river and casting a fly rod for trout or Atlantic salmon. In salt water the typical wade fisherman is a surf angler who wades out into the tumbling surf to cast a lure or bait. But the wade fisherman we will be writing about here is the guy who wades the bays, sounds, rivers, flats, and tidal creeks. The wade fisherman doesn't stand out like the trout fisherman or surf caster, but there are hundreds of thousands of wade fishermen in the protected shallow inshore waters, and they catch a lot of fish.

Wade fishermen use all kinds of salt-water tackle such as light surf rods, spinning and spin-casting rods, bait-casting rods, and fly rods, depending on where they fish and what they are trying to catch.

The clothing and other gear you wear will also vary with the area being fished and the climate and the season. In northern waters where the water is cold or the weather is bad or in the spring and fall, you'll do best with a pair of chest-high waders. Even during the summer months, if you fish the salt waters of New England, especially Maine, or in Canada, you'll find waders best for comfort. Even farther south, if you fish a lot at night, waders will keep you dry and warm.

Where there are a lot of rocks and where the water is very cold, you should use a pair of heavy, all-rubber waders. But in warmer water and along sandy or muddy bottoms, a light, plastic pair of waders will usually do the job.

Hip boots can also be used if you are wading in shallow water and do not have to go out deeper than up to your knees. But even then you have to watch out for waves created by passing boats. And around inlets and close to the beaches you may have some surf to watch out for in order to prevent water from getting into your boots.

During the hot summer months you can often wade in bathing trunks or a pair of old pants and tennis shoes or sneakers. This is the way they fish in Florida and tropical waters. I wouldn't recommend going around barefooted because you might step on glass, coral, broken shells, or a stingray. Long pants also prevent sunburn, as does a peaked hat.

The wade fisherman can't tote around a tackle box with him, so he needs some kind of shoulder bag or pouches to hold his lures and other tackle. Fly fishermen and spinning anglers can make use of the special vests made for this purpose. You can also get a web belt or other wide belt and attach a couple of pouches to it to hold the lures.

The same belt can also hold a fish stringer about 8 or 10 feet in length, a small hand gaff, and a fishing knife. If you plan to use live baits such as shrimp you'll need a small floating bait box, which you can pull along with a string as you wade along.

Wade fishermen seek all kinds of fish, and anglers have been wading for many years seeking striped bass, not only in the surf, but also in the bays, sounds, inlets, and tidal rivers. The big advantage the wade fisherman has over the boat angler is silence. A boat usually frightens or alerts striped bass in shallow water, but the wade fisherman can move very slowly and quietly and have fish feeding and breaking almost at his feet.

Then, of course, you can use a spinning or fly rod and cast a small popping plug or bug and often hook stripers with short casts.

At other times you'll find a bucktail jig or fly worked deep more effective. In fact, when fishing blind, an underwater lure is usually best, but since you will be fishing mostly in shallow water, you can often raise stripers with surface lures. These work best early in the morning, toward dusk, and at night.

These are the times when striped bass come into shallow water near shore to feed. They also come in more often on overcast, cloudy days than on bright, sunny ones.

It is in southern waters that the wade fisherman is in his glory and can fish for many different kinds of fish. In the Florida Keys and the Bahamas he can wade and cast for bonefish, permit, barracuda, and small sharks. Here a pair of Polaroid sunglasses are a must, not only to protect your eyes, but also to make it easier for you to spot the fish.

Bonefish are ghostly, pale, camouflaged phantoms on the flats, and they are not easy to see when you first try fishing for them. After a while you begin to see them better. Often you look for the shadow they cast on the bottom rather than for the fish itself. They are also very spooky, and if you approach too close or splash a lure too close, they'll take off at top speed. But even here the wade fisherman can usually approach these fish closer than the boat angler.

Permit are even more difficult to locate since they are not as numerous and do not come in to feed on the flats everywhere. They also require deeper water than bonefish and are more inclined to feed along dropoffs and edges of channels. Both the bonefish and permit are easier to catch if you cast natural baits such as live shrimp, crabs, and pieces of spiny lobster tail rather than lures.

Barracuda on the tropical flats can be caught with surface plugs, underwater plugs, spoons, and jigs, but don't approach them too closely. You'll do better if you make long casts. They are curious fish and will often follow you around on a flat but are no threat to the wading angler. They always keep their distance, but if too close are not inclined to take a lure as readily.

One fish often caught by wading anglers in southern waters is channel bass or redfish. This type of fishing is popular in the Gulf of Mexico, especially in the shallow bays in Texas. Redfish will come into water only a few inches deep to feed, and then a gold or silver spoon cast to them will draw a strike. Redfish will also hit surface plugs, shallow-running underwater plugs, and jigs, but cast them beyond the fish and reel them about 2 or 3 feet in front of the fish so that they see them. Instead of lures, you can also cast a live shrimp. These fish can usually be

A popping float and live shrimp is a good way to catch sea trout when wade fishing.

seen on the flats or by the wake they create as they swim along.

In many of the same waters as the channel bass or redfish you also find the sea trout or spotted weakfish. Fishing for them is good all year 'round, but the spring, fall, and winter months are usually best. They like the grassy flats of most bays and will come into water from 1 foot to 2 or 3 feet in depth. Wading anglers take many big sea trout up to 8 or 10 pounds on surface plugs, underwater plugs, plastic worm jigs, bucktail or nylon jigs, and spoons. For big sea trout fish early in the morning, in the evening, and during the night. You'll also find good wade fishing for sea trout in inlets that empty into the ocean. Here you usually can't wade as far as on the flats, but go out mostly on sand- or rock bars or oyster bars or underwater reefs.

The wading anglers will also run into bluefish, tarpon, Spanish mackerel, pompano, jacks, and other species in southern waters.

If there is any "ace in the hole" in salt-water fishing it is probably the method of angling called "jigging." Here you lower a lure down to the depths, usually just above the bottom, and then "jig" or work the lure up and down so that it rises and sinks in an erratic, enticing manner; at least the fish think so, and they go for the crazy-acting lure and get hooked not only in the mouth, but also often in the head, back, belly, or some other part of the body.

In fact, any angler who fishes from a boat should carry some jigs in different weights and use them when other methods of fishing fail to produce. You'll not only save the day and have some fun and sport but also will be able to take home some fine-eatin' fish.

The tackle you need for jigging is much the same as you use for regular casting and bottom fishing. Thus in shallow water you can use a one-handed spinning rod, small reel, and 8-pound-test line. In deeper water you can use bait-casting or "popping"-type rods, and in still deeper water you can use heavy spinning rods with 15-to-20-pound-test lines or conventional-type boat rods with revolving-spool reels and lines testing 30 to 50 pounds. Jigging works best, however, with light lines, so spinning tackle is usually favored.

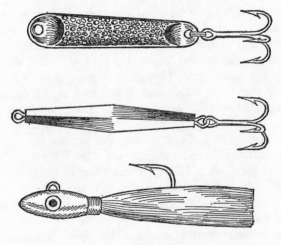

Lures used in jigging.

There are various types of lures that can be used in jigging. The most popular up in northern waters are the metal lures such as heavy spoons, metal squids, Hopkins lures, and diamond jigs. These will range from 1 or 2 ounces in very shallow water for small fish up to 14 or 16 ounces or even more in very deep water. The slim Norwegian-type jigs are very good in these heavy weights.

The other lure that is often used in jigging in both northern and southern waters is the regular lead-head bucktail, feather, or nylon jig. These range in size from 1 or 2 ounces for shallow-water jigging for small fish up to 3 or 4 ounces for deep-water jigging for bigger fish. Usually white and yellow or orange are the best colors, but a few darker red, brown, or blue jigs can be tried also. Adding bright, metallic Mylar strips around the jig also helps in obtaining more strikes.

Where you do your jigging is, of course, very important. Usually the best fishing is over wrecks, rocky bottoms, coral reefs, mussel, clam, and oyster beds, and similar bottoms that attract fish. In deeper water the so-called offshore banks, plateaus, mountains, and other higher elevations than surrounding waters are fish hangouts where jigging is effective.

In North Atlantic waters when jigging in shallow waters you'll catch mackerel, bluefish, striped bass, bonito, and false albacore by simply casting out or letting your jig sink to the bottom, then reeling it back toward the surface with up-and-down rod action. These fish may hit at almost any level but usually higher off the bottom than the bottom species.

Such bottom species as porgies, sea bass, whiting, and even fluke will take a small jig if it is lowered to the bottom, then worked up and down in an attractive manner. This can be done from a drifting or anchored boat. If the current is strong, you may cast or flip the jig away from the boat uptide so that the jig will sink to the bottom, or change to a heavier jig and let it down straight. It won't go down exactly straight, since in the running tide the line will belly out, but at least it will reach bottom. You may have to let out some line, feel it hit bottom, jig a few times, then let out more line so it hits bottom again. You keep doing this until too much line is out, then reel in and repeat the same technique.

Another fish that is taken on heavy metal jigs such as the diamond jigs from 3 to 16 ounces in weight is the cod. They will often be caught on such jigs in fairly shallow water in the spring and fall months near shore in New England waters. In

Maine and Canada you can catch them on jigs even in the summer months. Here you let the jig down to the bottom, then reel in a couple of feet or so and start working the jig with sharp upward lifts of the rod, then lower the tip so that the jig flutters back toward the bottom.

While jigging for cod you'll often hook pollock on the same jigs—in fact, these fish are more active than cod and more inclined to hit the shiny metal. But pollock also rise higher above the bottom than cod, and when seeking pollock it's a good idea to let your jig down to the bottom, then jig it a few times there, reel in a few feet, jig it again, and keep doing this until the jig is all the way up. Then lower it to the bottom and repeat the process. Pollock, bluefish, striped bass, and mackerel will hit jigs worked this way. Of course, once you find out what level the fish are at, you can mark your line with plastic tape and lower it straight to the correct level and do your jigging there.

Because there's a greater variety of fish in southern waters you'll catch even more species when jigging in these tropical fishing spots. In shallow water you can jig for grunt, snappers, pompano, yellowtail, small grouper, bluefish, Spanish mackerel, sheepshead, channel bass or redfish, black drum, and many other species. Here you can let your jig down to the bottom and work it up and down in the regular manner. Or you can cast some distance away from the boat and bounce your jig along the bottom.

In deeper waters in the South while jigging over reefs, wrecks, rocky bottoms, or coral, you're apt to hook almost anything. On the bottom, jigging will get you the larger snappers such as red snappers and larger groupers. On the way up closer to the surface you're apt to hook king mackerel, amberjack, barracuda, blackfin tuna, false albacore, dolphin, cobia, and various jacks and mackerels.

Along the Pacific Coast anglers also jig for various bottom and top species. When jigging just off the bottom over rocks or kelp, the fishermen catch white sea bass, black sea bass, rockfish, lingcod, and even halibut. If the jig is worked at intermediate depths or closer to the surface, you can hook barracuda, yellowtail, albacore, bonito, and other species. For the latter species it is often better to cast a good distance, let the jig sink, then work it back fast toward the boat.

The effectiveness of jigs is often improved by adding a strip of pork rind, strip of fish, or a small whole fish to the hook or hooks. When using such a combination it is often a good idea to add an extra hook or two to the jig so that the bait is held more securely and hooks more fish, which grab the tail of a bait.

No matter what type of fishing you do in salt water, you'll often improve your score and catch more fish if you fish at night. There are many species that come close to shore to feed at night, and even in deeper water they continue feeding after the sun has gone down. It is also easier to fool fish at night, especially the more cagey, wary big fish, which are hard to fool during the daytime.

This is well known by many surf anglers who seek big striped bass. Stripers tend to stay in deeper water during the daytime and are hard to reach with a cast from the beach or shore. But as it gets dark, many baitfish such as mullet, spearing, herring, and other small fish move in closer to the beaches, rocky shores, coves, inlets, and rivermouths for protection in this shallow water. They are usually safe from many of the larger gamefish that stay in deep water. But striped bass, and even channel bass, weakfish, and snook, often follow the baitfish right into the surf or shallow water.

Surf anglers can catch striped bass and other fish at night on lures, such as surface and underwater plugs, jigs, and plastic eels, or you can use natural baits such as seaworms, clams, squid, shedder crabs, mullet, and other baitfish.

Boat anglers fishing for striped bass also find they often catch more big fish at night trolling or casting big plugs, rigged eels, plastic eels, or jigs, or drifting with live eels or other live fish. This can be done along beaches, rocky shores, around inlets and rivermouths, or in bays.

Big channel bass feed at night along the beaches of Virginia, North Carolina, and farther south in Florida and the Gulf of Mexico. Even the smaller channel bass called "reds" will feed at night. The three days before and three days after a full moon are especially good for these fish.

Another southern fish that is noted for its night feeding habits is the tarpon, especially the big ones that come in close to shore or under bridges. They'll hit many lures such as surface and underwater plugs, jigs, plastic baits, and live mullet. You can troll or cast these lures in the same spots where you see tarpon rolling during the daytime. You can sometimes hear them at night as they chase or feed on baitfish or shrimp.

In the same spots that you catch tarpon you'll often find snook—another notorious night feeder. They also hit many of the same lures as tarpon, only in smaller sizes. Live shrimp also make a good bait for them, especially when fished from piers, bridges, or docks. Snook often feed on the stormiest nights, and they like the strong rips and currents that trap baitfish, shrimp, and other marine life.

Also in many of the same spots you'll see big sea trout or spotted weakfish looking for food, and here a live shrimp will make the best bait. Many sea trout fishermen suspend lights from a bridge, pier, or dock and fish late into the night for these fish.

Bluefish are also noted for feeding at night in northern or southern waters. Off New York and New Jersey, fishermen chum for the bluefish at night from party boats and private boats and catch more fish and bigger fish than in the daytime. They do the same thing in the Gulf of Mexico off Louisiana, but instead of chumming, they cast spoons and other lures around the gas and oil rigs offshore.

King mackerel can also be caught at night by drifting with a whole balao or other fish bait rigged on two hooks. Many drift boats in Florida leave about 7 P.M. to fish for the kings at night and come back around midnight. Here again, you'll usually catch bigger king mackerel than if you troll or drift the same waters in the daytime.

Off California other anglers fish for the big white sea bass at night using squid for bait. Here too, many party boats make special night trips for these fish around Catalina Island and other spots.

Even bottom species such as whiting or silver hake, cod, croakers, snappers, and other species will feed at night. It is often easier to fool and hook the cagey mangrove snapper, for example, at night than during the daytime.

Of course, as any shark fisherman knows, these fish are nocturnal and do a lot of feeding at night, as do a lot of billfish such as swordfish and marlin. But this fishing does have its dangers and discomforts. Many anglers prefer to catch billfish on top and see them leap. This is one of the big thrills in fishing, of course, but night fishing has thrills of its own. Many anglers find that there is a great deal of mystery and suspense in hooking something big on a black night and wondering what it is.

Finally, in these days of crowded beaches, shores, piers, bridges, and waterways, night fishing is almost a must in the more popular resort areas or fishing areas. There is just too much boat traffic, swimming or bathing, and other fishermen around to relax and enjoy yourself or fish the way you want to. But such congestion and crowding disappears after dark in most places and you can have the place to yourself or share it with only a few other night owls. But the biggest advantage is that most gamefish and bottom fish return to normal feeding habits or start feeding at night, and you will catch more and bigger fish.

19

Locating
Salt-water Fish

Like the fresh-water angler, the salt-water angler also must first find the fish before he can catch them. If anything, locating fish in salt water is usually more difficult than in fresh water simply because the ocean is big and you have more water to fish. Even many bays or sounds are bigger than most fresh-water lakes. To add to the problem, salt-water fish move around more with the tides and also make seasonal migrations. So you have your work cut out for you when you try to locate salt-water fish.

Locating fish is, of course, much easier for the veteran or regular angler who has fished a certain area for many years. He knows when fish will appear in a certain area because he has fished that spot for so many years that he can figure out when certain species will show up there. He also knows which tides and wind and weather conditions produce best in different spots. And because he usually knows several hot spots in an area, he can try a few of them until he finds fish that are feeding or taking baits or lures.

The average salt-water angler who doesn't fish often or goes to a strange spot is handicapped and cannot locate fish as readily because he has little information to go by. Of course, there are obvious ways of finding fish, such as asking local fishermen, tackle dealers, boat liveries, marinas, or watching where other anglers are fishing. Nowadays with so many anglers fishing the more popular spots, you'll often see them lined up or boats congregated at a hot spot, and you can join them if they are catching fish.

Of course, if you hire a guide or charter a boat or go out on a party boat, you don't have to worry about locating the fish. The men on these boats will take you to the best fishing spots and even tell you how to fish. The same thing is true if you are lucky enough to know a skilled fisherman who knows the area and where to fish. If he takes you along on fishing trips or tells you where to go, you have it made.

Gulls or terns wheeling and diving often indicate that gamefish are feeding on baitfish.

But most salt-water anglers are usually on their own and have to find fish themselves with little outside help, such as gulls, terns, or other birds wheeling, diving, or hovering over the water. This often indicates that a school of big fish is driving smaller fish or baitfish to the surface. It always pays to investigate such bird activity, even though it sometimes may turn out to be a false alarm. Even one or two birds hovering over a spot or sitting on the water can mean fish under them.

At other times there may not be any gulls or birds, but you'll see the fish breaking water or the baitfish skittering or leaping out of the water. Here again, it's always a good idea to run over to the spot and start casting or trolling.

Even the presence of schools of baitfish or small fish can

lead to good fishing. In fact, the best advice you can give is "find the baitfish" and you'll often locate the bigger fish. Thus if you see big schools of mullet, spearing, sand eels, bunker, shiners, herring, ballyhoo, anchovies, sardines, or other fish, hang around that spot and try fishing it. Sooner or later the larger gamefish will also find the baitfish and start feeding on them.

Baitfish will usually ripple or ruffle the water or show up as dark patches and can be seen from a good distance. It pays to investigate any variations of the norm, such as changes in color, dark spots, ruffled or rippled surface, oil slicks, splashes, and other disturbances.

When it comes to locating a certain species, it pays to know something about its habits, food preferences, type of bottom or water conditions it prefers, and where it is most prevalent. Thus when seeking big stripers in the ocean you look for them in the strongest rips and tides, around rocks, reefs, bars, dropoffs, and holes. Offshore boulders or rocks where the waves break or even submerged rocks will attract them. Rocky points, jetty ends, and mouths of inlets and rivers are all good spots to try.

Big stripers do not feed as often as the smaller ones, so it is mostly a waiting game. Your best bet is to fish at daybreak or just before, at dusk, and during the night. Trolling deep near the bottom will also take them at various hours, especially if the day is cloudy or stormy with plenty of surf or chop.

You can sometimes see stripers underwater if the water is fairly calm and clear, especially if you run a boat fairly fast and watch for fish scooting away from the approaching boat. At night stripers will do the same thing, only here you will see the trails of phosphorescence they leave as they dart away from the boat.

The smaller stripers found in bays, sounds, and rivers hang around sandbars, rock bars, oyster and clam bars, banks of marshes, islands, flats, the edges of channels, and along dropoffs. Look for spots where tides and rips create swirls, usually around rocky points and other obstructions. Bridges spanning rivers attract stripers, and the stripers gather below high dams or falls that block their migrations upstream.

Anglers fishing for channel bass in bays and sounds from boats cruise around looking for these fish near the surface.

Polaroid sunglasses are a big help here, as in any fish spotting. This fishing is done mostly in Virginia and North Carolina in the spring and fall. Here you look for changes in the color of the water, since channel bass may show up as gold, copper, brown, bronze, or even tan or purple. If the water is not too rough and the day is not overcast, you can often see the school of fish clearly or even see individual fish.

Compared to other fish, tarpon are usually easy to spot, since they have the habit of rolling and revealing their presence in this manner. Even if they aren't showing, you can look for telltale trails of bubbles or foam on the surface of the water. In clear water such as the Florida Keys you can see schools of tarpon or single fish swimming along in the deeper spots. Tarpon tend to feed in brackish rivers, bays, creeks, and along mangrove shores.

Snook can also be seen cruising along the beaches or in canals, but most of the time they remain well hidden in the depths or lie along the piles and supports of piers and bridges or under mangroves. They particularly like to lie in the shadows during the day or on moonlit nights waiting for baitfish or shrimp to drift by. You can also see them chasing mullet in the morning, evening, and during the night.

Bonefish are ghostly and difficult to see, even in shallow water on the flats, unless they break the surface with their tails when trying to swim in very shallow water or when feeding and grubbing in such water by lowering their head and bringing their tail out of the water. They also muddy the water when feeding, and then you look for such muddy spots. It is easier to spot bonefish when standing on a casting platform of a boat than when wading. So some wading anglers bring along stepladders and climb up on top for a better look over a wider area. They even cast and hook the fish from this elevation.

Another fish of the flats that will break the surface of the water with its tail and dorsal fin is the permit. Being a deep-bodied fish, it can't help but expose itself when feeding in shallow water.

Pompano can sometimes be seen cruising along the beaches in the surf if the water is fairly calm and clear. Or you can fish for them in inlets and rivers emptying into the ocean, especially where the waves break over sandbars. They feed on sand fleas or bugs and small crabs and shrimp washed out or tossed around by such wave action.

Another fish in southern waters that often comes in close to the beaches and piers is the cobia. Anglers fishing for them from the surf ride around in beach buggies rigged with towers to help them see the fish. They also rig such towers on small boats when looking for cobia in deeper water. Cobia are dark and easy to see if the water isn't too rough. Cobia also hang around light towers, oil rigs, and buoys, and even keep company with big rays and turtles.

Anglers fishing the Gulf of Mexico look for commercial shrimp boats emptying their nets in the morning throwing away trash fish, crabs, and tiny shellfish, and this sort of chumming attracts many fish such as king mackerel, amberjack, false albacore, cobia, jack, crevalle, and other species.

Many southern fish also hang out around the offshore light towers and oil rigs and natural-gas structures found off Florida and in the Gulf of Mexico. Some of these are lit up at night and attract baitfish, which in turn attract such larger fish as bluefish, king mackerel, amberjack, barracuda, grouper, and snappers.

When it comes to locating fish in offshore waters, a boat equipped with a flying bridge or tuna tower is a big help in spotting fish at a distance or below the surface. A good pair of binoculars aboard can also aid in locating buoys, landmarks, other boats, birds, bait, and the fish themselves. When searching for fish in the ocean, good vision, especially at a distance, is a big help. Scanning the horizon and the waters in front of it in all directions is a good way to start.

If you are looking for swordfish or marlin, you can often see them lying or cruising on top, with their dorsal and tail fins protruding above the water. Sharks also swim on top and reveal their fins above the surface, but these are wider and not as rigid as those on billfish. At other times you can see schools or individual fish swimming just below the surface, especially when the water is calm and clear. In fact, such surface or near-surface sighting is best done on days when the water isn't too rough.

Schools of fish and individual fish are more readily spotted from a height, and in recent years light planes have been used to locate swordfish, marlin, tuna, channel bass, striped bass, and other fish.

Members of the tuna family often reveal themselves by leaping out of the water. School tuna and the smaller tuna of various species will often do this. The albacores and bonitos will also leap, and when feeding will turn the water to a white froth as they chase baitfish.

The larger giant tuna can often be seen "pushing" the water as they swim along on top, or they can be spotted breaking and feeding on squid, herring, mackerel, capelin, and other fish. Giant tuna will also gather around commercial draggers, trawlers, and herring seiners to feed on the trash fish thrown overboard or on herring or other fish that are lost from the nets. Fishing near these spots with dead or live baits is, of course, a good way to hook these big fish.

When fishing for sailfish, look for these fish "balling" baitfish such as pilchards. Several sailfish will surround a school of these small fish so that they form into a tight ball. Then trolling baits or drifting with live baits near the scene of such activity is a sure way of hooking these billfish.

Also offshore in southern waters near the Gulf Stream, look for "weedlines" or patches of sargassum weed because dolphin, tuna, jacks, and other fish hang out near such weedlines. Big marlin often lurk in weedy areas to feed on these smaller species. So it pays to troll along such weedlines and near the patches of weed. The same is true for floating objects or debris such as trees, logs, boxes, dead fish, whales, and turtles. These are favorite hangouts of the dolphin.

Offshore anglers also study the currents and color of the water as guides to finding fish. Oil slicks often reveal bigger fish feeding below the surface, because when they chop up the smaller fish, the oil released from these fish floats to the surface.

While running offshore, the anglers watch the color of the water, which is usually greener and dirtier-looking than the deeper water farther offshore. They usually look for an "edge" where this green water meets and merges with the blue ocean water or the Gulf Stream. This is a good spot to troll for billfish and other fish.

Anglers fishing along the West Coast usually chum with live

baitfish such as anchovies, sardines, or herring to locate such fish as tuna, yellowtail, albacore, and other fish. Then when they see the fish "boil" behind the boat, they troll or cast for them. Yellowtail usually hang around the offshore islands and kelp beds. Albacore prefer the warmer "blue water" about 25 to 35 miles offshore during the summer fishing season.

Anglers seeking Pacific salmon look for birds working or baitfish such as herring, anchovies, or candlefish, which the salmon feed on. Here too, salmon will ball up or herd such baitfish into tight schools. Coho or silver salmon can often be seen chasing schools of pilchards, forcing them to the surface.

At other times you can locate the salmon in water from about 30 to 150 feet deep. The coho salmon will be closer to the surface, while the king or Chinook salmon will be down deeper. Salmon like to hang out over ledges and holes and channels close to shore or around points or along kelp beds and tidal rips. The mouths of rivers and the rivers themselves are very good spots because salmon gather there prior to their upstream spawning runs.

If you know your bottom, you'll have a better idea of the kinds of fish that live there. Thus a rocky or broken bottom will attract cod, pollock, sea bass, porgies, and blackfish in North Atlantic waters. In the South such bottoms will draw grouper, snappers, grunt, yellowtail, and many other species. Often you don't need a large rocky area to hold fish. A small patch of rocks in a largely sandy bottom will attract a few fish.

Coral reefs in tropical waters also attract many bottom species such as grouper, snapper, grunt, barracuda, amberjack, and the various smaller reef fishes. Shellfish bottoms and mussel, clam, oyster, and scallop beds also attract many fish. So do seaweeds such as eelgrass, which in bays is the favorite hangout of striped bass, weakfish, fluke, flounder, and croakers. Rockweed found growing on rocky bottoms, jetties, and breakwaters harbors worms, shrimp, crabs, and smaller fish, which in turn attract larger fish. Kelp beds in the Atlantic and Pacific also harbor numerous species.

As mentioned earlier in this book, sunken wrecks are prime bottom-fishing locations. They attact many species, depending on where they are located. The trouble with sunken wrecks is that they are not always in convenient spots or easy to reach

Salt-water fish of many kinds will congregate around a submerged wreck.

or locate. So in recent years many artificial reefs have been created by sinking old cars, boats, tires, concrete blocks, rocks, and other material. These soon become covered with moss, barnacles, and mussels, which in turn bring crabs, worms, and smaller fish. These then attract the larger fish. Some of these reefs are clearly marked by floating buoys.

One of the quickest ways to learn the type of bottom in your area is to study a chart published by the U. S. Coast and Geodetic Survey. These are the same charts boatmen use for navigation and indicate the type of bottom and depth of the water and the location of buoys and channels that can be used to pinpoint the best fishing spots. Also, in some areas, the Coast and Geodetic Survey publishes special "fishing charts" or maps showing favored fishing spots for certain species. These can usually be bought at local fishing tackle stores or marinas.

Finally, the modern angler fishing in salt water depends on electronic depth sounders and fish finders as aids in locating baitfish and gamefish and learning the depth of the water and type of bottom in his fishing area. There are now many types of such electronic equipment on the market, from small portables for small boats to larger, permanent models for bigger boats.

Popular Salt-water Fishes

WHERE, WHEN, AND
HOW TO CATCH THEM

Striped Bass

NAMES AND SPECIES: The striped bass (*Roccus saxatilis*) is also called the striper, linesides, rock, rockfish, greenhead, and squidhound.

RANGE: The striped bass is found along the Atlantic Coast from the Gulf of St. Lawrence to Florida and in the Gulf of Mexico. In the Pacific, striped bass are found from the Columbia River to San Diego Bay. They are most plentiful around San Francisco and Coos Bay, Oregon.

FISHING METHODS: Surf fishing, spinning, fly fishing, trolling, boat casting, and still fishing.

LURES: Surface and underwater plugs, metal squids, spoons, spinners, jigs, eelskin lures, rigged eels, tube lures, plastic eels, bucktail, streamers, and poppers.

NATURAL BAITS: Blood worms, sand worms, crabs, shrimp, squid, mullet, spearing, sand eels, herring, mackerel, menhaden, and sardines.

WHERE TO CATCH THEM: In the surf, look for them around rock and wood jetties, breakwaters, rocky shores, in coves, off points and reefs, sandy beaches, in sloughs and holes, and on sandbars. Any of the surf spots are best if there's a good surf or strong current, rip, and tide. In rivers and inlets look for stripers around piers, bridges, trestles, and in the stronger currents and channels. In bays and sounds they will be on the flats, along marshy banks, edges of channels, and in tidal creeks.

WHEN TO CATCH THEM: Early in the morning, at dusk, and during the night are the best hours, and before, during, and after a storm; also when the surf is rough and during the tide changes. Cloudy, overcast days are better than bright, sunny ones. Spring and fall months are best along the Atlantic Coast. From March to November along the Pacific Coast.

HOW TO CATCH THEM: Use surface plugs when stripers are chasing mullet or other baitfish. Underwater plugs and spoons, tube lures, and jigs for trolling. Metal squids and other heavy metal lures are good for surf and boat casting when the water is rough. Jigs are good for trolling and casting for small and medium-sized bass.

Channel Bass

NAMES AND SPECIES: The channel bass (*Sciaenops ocellatus*) is also called the red drum, drum, red bass, and redfish.

RANGE: The channel bass is found from Virginia to Florida and in the Gulf of Mexico.

FISHING METHODS: Surf casting, bait casting, spinning, spin casting, fly fishing, trolling, boat casting, and still fishing.

LURES: Metal squids, spoons, underwater plugs, surface plugs, and jigs.

NATURAL BAITS: Cut mullet, menhaden, herring, squid, shrimp, clams, crabs, spot, whiting, and other fish.

WHERE TO CATCH THEM: The biggest channel bass are caught in the surf and bays of Virginia and North Carolina. Smaller fish range along the Atlantic Coast to Florida and in the Gulf of Mexico. They like inlets and rivermouths entering into the ocean.

WHEN TO CATCH THEM: The best fishing in Virginia and North Carolina is in the spring and fall. They can be caught in Florida and parts of the Gulf of Mexico all year 'round. Morning, evenings, and night are best, especially during an incoming tide.

HOW TO CATCH THEM: Bait fishing in the surf, using cut mullet or other fish for bait. Casting from a boat with metal lures when schools are sighted. Trolling with spoons for big channel bass in the North and the smaller ones in the South. Casting while wading or from a boat on the flats in bays, rivers, and inlets. Jigs are good lures and so are plugs at times. Fishing on the bottom with live shrimp is good in these inshore waters.

Bluefish

NAMES AND SPECIES: The bluefish (*Pomatomus saltatrix*) is also called the skipjack, fat back, snapping mackerel, snapper blue, and greenfish.

RANGE: Bluefish are found in many parts of the world. Along the Atlantic Coast they range from Maine to Brazil. They are also found in the Gulf of Mexico.

FISHING METHODS: Surf casting, bait casting, spinning, fly fishing, trolling, chumming, and still fishing.

LURES: Surface and underwater plugs, metal squids, spoons, jigs, eelskin lures, salt-water flies, and tube lures.

NATURAL BAITS: Whole or cut menhaden, mullet, butterfish, mackerel, herring, or other fish. Squid and shedder crab can also be used. Chumming with ground bunker will bring them up to the boat.

WHERE TO CATCH THEM: Bluefish are found in schools well offshore, along the surf, in inlets, bays, and tidal rivers. They prefer to feed in strong currents and rips.

WHEN TO CATCH THEM: Bluefish feed day and night. Offshore chumming and trolling are productive. Surf anglers catch most of the bluefish early in the morning and evening. Summer months are best in northern waters, and the winter months are good in Florida.

HOW TO CATCH THEM: Trolling with spoons, plugs, jigs, or tube lures at various depths. Wire lines are used when they are deep. When they are seen breaking or chasing baitfish, use surface plugs and metal squids. They like fast-moving lures better than slow ones. Chumming with ground bunker will bring them close to a boat, and then a chunk of butterfish or other fish can be drifted out with the tide. Bluefish will also take baits on the bottom in the surf, inlets, or deeper water. Jigging with shiny metal lures is also a good way to catch them.

Common Weakfish

NAMES AND SPECIES: The common weakfish (*Cynoscion regalis*) is also known as the northern weakfish, gray weakfish, gray trout, squeteague, and salt-water trout.

RANGE: The common weakfish is found from Cape Cod to Florida but is most plentiful north of the Carolinas.

FISHING METHODS: Surf casting, bait casting, spinning, fly fishing, trolling, still fishing, and also chumming.

LURES: Underwater plugs, metal squids, spoons, jigs, streamer and bucktail flies.

NATURAL BAITS: Seaworms, squid, shrimp, shedder crabs, cut mullet, and other fish.

WHERE TO CATCH THEM: Weakfish run in the surf, bays, channels, inlets, and tidal rivers and creeks. They prefer the deeper spots in such places, but will venture into the surf to feed at times.

WHEN TO CATCH THEM: In the surf the spring, summer, and early fall months are best. The spring and early summer months are best in bays and sounds. They bite during the day, but the big ones are more active early in the morning, toward evening, and during the night.

HOW TO CATCH THEM: Casting in the surf with metal squids, plugs, jigs, and bait fishing with cut baits and squid or shrimp. Chumming with grass shrimp in the bays and using a sand worm for bait. Casting in the evening with a spinning rod or fly rod in tidal rivers and inlets.

Spotted Weakfish

NAMES AND SPECIES: The spotted weakfish (*Cynoscion nebulosus*) is best known as the sea trout or speckled trout.

RANGE: The spotted weakfish is found from Virginia to Florida and in the Gulf of Mexico.

FISHING METHODS: Surf casting, spinning, bait casting, fly casting, trolling, and still fishing.

LURES: Surface plugs, underwater plugs, spoons, metal squids, jigs, plastic worms, and fly-rod lures.

NATURAL BAITS: The best bait for sea trout is a live shrimp, but they will also take cut fish and shedder crabs.

WHERE TO CATCH THEM: In the surf from beaches and piers. In inlets, tidal rivers, and bays the year 'round in many places. They are often caught from bridges and small boats.

WHEN TO CATCH THEM: They run best during the spring, fall, and winter months in many areas. Early-morning, evening, and night tides are very good.

HOW TO CATCH THEM: Casting from a small boat over tidal flats with surface plugs, underwater plugs, or jigs. A popping float with a live shrimp can also be used in this shallow water. Along the beaches cast with lures or shrimp bait. From piers or bridges you can cast jigs or fish with live shrimp. Hang a light from the pier or bridge close to the water to attract shrimp, baitfish, and later the weakfish.

Atlantic Mackerel

NAMES AND SPECIES: The Atlantic mackerel (*Scomber scombus*) is also called the Boston mackerel and the common mackerel; small ones are called spikes and tinkers.

RANGE: The Atlantic mackerel is found from Canada south to the Carolinas. It is very plentiful in Maine and the rest of New England.

FISHING METHODS: Shore casting, spinning, chumming, trolling, and still fishing.

LURES: Tiny spoons, diamond jigs, other metal lures, tube lures, and flies.

NATURAL BAITS: Pieces of fish, squid, shrimp, and seaworms.

WHERE TO CATCH THEM: Mackerel come close to shore in many spots, especially in the colder, northern waters of New England, Maine, and Canada. Offshore schools in deeper water are caught while chumming off the coasts of New York and New Jersey. When close to shore they can be caught from rocks, jetties, piers, and bridges.

WHEN TO CATCH THEM: Mackerel bite best during the daytime, with high tides best in shallow-water areas. Evening tides are good for shore casting or bridge or pier fishing. Summer and early fall months are best for shore fishing, while spring and late fall are best for offshore fishing.

HOW TO CATCH THEM: Offshore mackerel can be caught by chumming with ground bunker, and then tiny metal lures, jigs, and tube lures can be used to catch them. Casting from a boat or shore with small spoons, metal squids, or spinners is effective. Trolling with such lures can also be done.

Codfish

NAMES AND SPECIES: The codfish (*Gadus morhua*) is also called the rock cod, and young ones are often called "scrod" by commercial fishermen.

RANGE: Cod are found in many parts of the world in cold waters. Along the Atlantic Coast they range from Canada to North Carolina. Best fishing is from New England to New Jersey.

FISHING METHODS: Bottom fishing with bait, jigging, and occasionally taken while trolling.

LURES: Diamond jigs, Norwegian jigs, other metal lures, and tube lures jigged or trolled very slowly.

NATURAL BAITS: Clams, squid, whelk, sea snails, herring, and other small fish or pieces of fish.

WHERE TO CATCH THEM: Caught close to shore in northern waters that are cold, but farther south they stay in deeper water, especially during the warm months. Cod are most numerous on so-called banks or underwater mountains and reefs, which are shallower than surrounding areas. Also around sunken wrecks and rocky, mussel, and shellfish bottoms.

WHEN TO CATCH THEM: The best fishing takes place along their southern range during the winter months, but they can be caught all year 'round in deeper water and colder northern waters.

HOW TO CATCH THEM: Most cod are caught bottom fishing with a sinker and bait such as clams. But they will also go for a diamond jig or other shiny metal lure worked up and down near the bottom. Occasionally they will hit a slowly trolled lure near the bottom.

Summer Flounder

NAMES AND SPECIES: The summer flounder (*Paralichthys dentatus*) is also called the fluke and northern flounder.

RANGE: The summer flounder ranges from Cape Cod to Florida. It is most common from Rhode Island to the Carolinas.

FISHING METHODS: Drifting or still fishing with baits. Occasionally by slow trolling along the bottom and by jigging.

LURES: Will sometimes hit spinners, underwater plugs, spoons, metal squids, and jigs.

NATURAL BAITS: Small fish such as spearing, sand eels, shiners, killies, strips of fish, or squid.

WHERE TO CATCH THEM: Fluke are found in the ocean close inshore from the beaches and rocky shores up to a mile or two offshore. They also come into bays, sounds, inlets, tidal rivers, and creeks, and other inshore waters. Look for them on the flats and along dropoffs and edges of channels.

WHEN TO CATCH THEM: The summer and early fall months are best. While some fluke are caught at night, most fishing takes place during the daytime.

HOW TO CATCH THEM: The most popular method is to drift in a boat and drag a rig with a live killie or dead spearing or strip of squid. When you catch the first small fluke you can cut it up for bait and use the strips on a hook. They can also be caught slow trolling along the bottom when there is no wind or tide for drifting.

Porgies

NAMES AND SPECIES: The northern porgy (*Stenotomus chrysops*) is also called the fair maid, ironsides, and scuppaug. There are other species such as the southern porgy, jolthead porgy, and saucer-eye porgy found in southern waters.

RANGE: The northern porgy is found from Massachusetts

south to the Carolinas. The other species replace it in southern waters.

FISHING METHODS: Mostly caught on the bottom with baits, but can also be taken by jigging.

LURES: Diamond jigs and bucktail and nylon jigs.

NATURAL BAITS: Clams, seaworms, mussels, shrimp, and squid.

WHERE TO CATCH THEM: Porgies like rocky bottoms or those covered with seaweed, mussels, oysters, clams, or other shellfish. But smaller porgies will also be found over sandy bottoms. Porgies can also be found around sunken wrecks close to shore, around jetties and breakwaters, and in inlets and bays.

WHEN TO CATCH THEM: The best fishing for northern porgies is in the summer and early fall months. Farther south the species found in those waters can be caught the year 'round.

HOW TO CATCH THEM: Bottom fishing with sinkers and hooks baited with clams, seaworms, or shrimp. They are attracted by a moving bait, so lift and lower your rig every so often or let it move out with the tide. Porgies can also be caught by jigging a lure such as a diamond jig up and down near the bottom.

Atlantic Sailfish

NAMES AND SPECIES: The Atlantic sailfish (*Istiophorus americanus*) is also called the spearfish, spindlebeak, and sail.

RANGE: The Atlantic sailfish is found from the Carolinas to Florida in the Gulf of Mexico, and in the Caribbean.

FISHING METHODS: Trolling and drifting with live baits. Occasionally by casting lures such as plugs.

LURES: Will sometimes hit feather, nylon, and plastic lures and plugs.

NATURAL BAITS: Ballyhoo, mullet, and strip baits cut from the sides or bellies of dolphin, bonito, mackerel, or other fish.

WHERE TO CATCH THEM: Sailfish will sometimes come close to shore if there is deep water around islands or sharp drop-offs from beaches. They are even caught from some Florida piers at times. But usually they hang around along the edges of the Gulf Stream or in the Stream itself. In Florida the East Coast from Fort Pierce to the Keys is best. They are also plentiful in the Gulf of Mexico.

WHEN TO CATCH THEM: In northern waters the summer months are best. In Florida they are caught the year 'round, with the winter months the best. In the Gulf of Mexico they can be caught from May to October.

HOW TO CATCH THEM: Trolling whole small fish or strip baits from outriggers. Drifting with whole live fish such as blue runners. Cast lures when you see them "balling" or herding baitfish.

Pacific Sailfish

NAMES AND SPECIES: The Pacific sailfish (*Istiphorus greyi*) is also called the spearfish and pez-vela.

RANGE: They range from Monterey, California, to Mexico and the Gulf of California.

FISHING METHODS: Trolling is the most popular method.

LURES: Will occasionally hit artificial lures.

NATURAL BAITS: Whole mullet, sardines, mackerel, flying fish, and small bonitos, as well as strips cut from various fish.

WHERE TO CATCH THEM: Sailfish appear off the southern part of California for only a short period in the late summer. Most of the time you have to go to Mexico, the Gulf of California, or Panama to get them. In many of these places they are found fairly close to shore and around islands if the water nearby is deep.

WHEN TO CATCH THEM: As mentioned earlier, late summer is best off California. They are caught the year 'round off Mexico, with the Pacific side best during the winter months and the Gulf of California best during the spring and summer months.

HOW TO CATCH THEM: Trolling the whole fish or strip baits from outriggers is the most effective method. The same "drop-back" method is used for Pacific sails as for the Atlantic variety and other billfish. This gives them slack line from the outrigger to mouth the bait so that the hook can be set.

White Marlin

NAMES AND SPECIES: The white marlin (*Makaira albida*) is also called the small marlin and billfish.

RANGE: Along the Atlantic Coast white marlin are found from Massachusetts to Brazil, with the greatest numbers from Maryland to Florida and in the Gulf of Mexico. They are also common around the Bahamas and in the Caribbean.

FISHING METHODS: Trolling and drifting with whole dead baits or live baits.

LURES: Marlin will occasionally hit feather and nylon lures or plastic fish or squid and other artificials.

NATURAL BAITS: Squid, ballyhoo, mullet, eels, and other fish. Also strips of fish.

WHERE TO CATCH THEM: White marlin are found in and along the Gulf Stream and over offshore reefs or banks. Look for the "edge" where the clean, blue offshore water meets and merges with the greener, dirtier inshore water.

WHEN TO CATCH THEM: They are most plentiful in North Atlantic waters during the summer and early fall months. They can be caught during the winter months in tropical waters. Marlin will hit throughout the day, but the early-morning and late-afternoon hours are better. And choppy or rough waters are better than glassy, smooth water.

HOW TO CATCH THEM: Trolling baits from outriggers on top. Such baits as squid, ballyhoo, and rigged eels or fish strips should skip on the surface for best results. Drifting live fish down deep can also be tried.

Striped Marlin

NAMES AND SPECIES: The striped marlin (*Makaira mitsukurii*) is also called the spikefish and billfish.

RANGE: Striped marlin are found in many parts of the world and particularly in the Pacific Ocean. In California they are found from Santa Catalina Island south to the Los Coronados Islands. They are very plentiful off Mexico and around the Hawaiian Islands.

FISHING METHODS: Trolling with whole fish.

LURES: Striped marlin will hit artificial lures such as the Knuckleheads and plastic imitations of fish and squid.

NATURAL BAITS: Flying fish, sardines, mackerel, squid, and other small fish.

WHERE TO CATCH THEM: Around Santa Catalina and San Clemente islands off California. Off Mexico from boats sailing from Acapulco, Mansanillo, Mazatlan, Guaymas, and La Paz. Around the Hawaiian Islands.

WHEN TO CATCH THEM: Off California fish for striped marlin from July to October. During the spring, summer, and winter months in Mexican waters. During the fall months around Hawaii.

HOW TO CATCH THEM: Trolling such natural whole baits as squid, flying fish, sardines, and mackerel from outriggers. Trolling such lures as Knuckleheads, plastic fish, and squid at fast speeds. At times they will also take a whole live fish drifted below the surface.

Bluefin Tuna

NAMES AND SPECIES: The bluefin tuna (*Thunnus thynnus*) is also known as the horse mackerel, great albacore, and tunney. Small ones are called "school tuna," while the bigger ones are called "giant tuna."

RANGE: They are found in many parts of the world in the Atlantic and Pacific. In the Atlantic the best fishing is from Canada to the Bahamas, with New England, New York, and New Jersey offshore waters the most productive. In the Pacific they range from Oregon to Baja California.

METHODS OF FISHING: Trolling, chumming, and drifting with live baits.

LURES: The smaller tuna will hit metal squids, spoons, cedar jigs, nylon and feather jigs, plastic baits, and plugs.

NATURAL BAITS: Dead and live menhaden, herring, mackerel, butterfish, whiting, ling, flying fish, sardines, anchovies, and squid.

WHERE TO CATCH THEM: Tuna may roam vast sections of the ocean and appear almost anywhere. But certain spots such as the Bahamas, offshore New Jersey and New York, Rhode Island and Massachusetts, Bailey Island, Maine, and the coasts of Nova Scotia, Prince Edward Island, and Conception Bay, Newfoundland, are noted for tuna fishing.

WHEN TO CATCH THEM: Tuna fishing is best off the Bahamas in May and early June and from July to October along most of the Atlantic Coast. In the Pacific, tuna run from May to October. Tuna fishing is mostly daytime fishing.

HOW TO CATCH THEM: Trolling fast with lures will catch the school tuna. Chumming with ground bunker will attract both the smaller and the bigger tuna, and then a live or dead bait can be drifted out in the chum slick. Trolling with whole fish baits or "daisy chains" of several baits can be done for the giant tuna.

Mako Shark

NAMES AND SPECIES: The mako shark (*Isurus oxyrhynchus rafinesque*) is the one found in the Atlantic. The one in the Pacific (*Isurus glaucus*) is similar in appearance and habits. They are also called mackerel sharks, sharp-nosed sharks, leaping mako, and bonito sharks.

RANGE: The Atlantic mako is found from Cape Cod to the tropics. They are fairly common off Florida. In the Pacific, makos may appear off the southern part of California but are more common throughout the South Seas, and especially around New Zealand.

FISHING METHODS: Although makos have been known to hit artificial lures and trolled fish baits, chumming is best for them.

LURES: Will occasionally hit feathers, plastic baits, and jigs.

NATURAL BAITS: Almost any small whole fish or piece of fish.

WHERE TO CATCH THEM: Mako sharks hang out in offshore waters and will often be found in the company of schools of mackerel, tuna, or where swordfish and marlin are found.

WHEN TO CATCH THEM: Mako will hit day or night, but most anglers prefer to fish during the daytime because these sharks are noted for their high leaps. They are found in northern wa-

ters during the summer and early fall and in southern waters
the year 'round.

HOW TO CATCH THEM: Chumming with ground bunker is best
to attract them up to the boat. Then drift a dead or live small
fish such as a mackerel, herring, bunker, butterfish, or bonito
out in the chum slick. They'll also hit a trolled whole fish
bait or lure at times.

Dolphin

NAMES AND SPECIES: The dolphin (*Coryphaena hippurus*) is
also called the dorado and mahimahi.

RANGE: Dolphin are found in most of the warmer waters of
the world. Along the Atlantic Coast they range as far north
as Massachusetts but are more plentiful from North Carolina to Florida and the Gulf of Mexico. In the Pacific they
are found from Oregon to Mexico, but are common from the
southern part of California to tropical waters.

FISHING METHODS: Trolling, casting, and drifting.

LURES: Dolphin will hit plugs, feather lures, jigs, spoons, and
plastic baits.

NATURAL BAITS: Dolphin will hit whole fish baits and strip
baits.

WHERE TO CATCH THEM: Dolphin are mostly fish of the
warmer waters and will stay close to the Gulf Stream along
the Atlantic Coast. They are especially attracted to floating
weedlines, weed patches, boxes, crates, and logs, and this is
where most trolling is done. But you can start trolling for
them once you are a few miles from shore and can look for
flying fish, on which they often feed.

WHEN TO CATCH THEM: In northern waters the late summer
and early fall months are tops. In tropical or southern waters
they can be caught the year 'round.

HOW TO CATCH THEM: Trolling is the best method. But once
you hook a dolphin, keep it near the boat and then cast
lures next to the hooked fish to catch others attracted by
the first fish. You can also try chumming with small whole
fish or cut fish to keep them near the boat. Casting near floating objects or weed patches can also be done.

Amberjack

NAMES AND SPECIES: The amberjack (*Seriola dumerili*) is also called the great amberjack, amberfish, coronado, and great jack.

RANGE: They range as far north as New York or New Jersey, but are more plentiful from the Carolinas south to Florida and the Gulf of Mexico.

FISHING METHODS: Trolling, casting, drifting with live fish, or chumming with cut fish.

LURES: Amberjack will hit plugs, spoons, jigs, plastic fish, and other artificials.

NATURAL BAITS: They will take many small fish such as pinfish, yellowtail, mullet, grunt, snappers, or strips or chunks of these fish.

WHERE TO CATCH THEM: Although a few amberjack may venture close to shore, they are mainly fish of the outer reefs, rocky bottoms, and around light towers and sunken wrecks. The Florida Keys are especially noted for the amberjack prevalent in those waters.

WHEN TO CATCH THEM: They may be taken in northern waters off North Carolina in the summer and early fall months, but the winter months are best off Florida and other tropical waters—here they are found the year 'round.

HOW TO CATCH THEM: Trolling with whole fish, strip baits, or lures is good. So is drifting with a live bait. You can also try casting plugs or other lures around likely spots.

Great Barracuda

NAMES AND SPECIES: The great barracuda (*Sphyraena barracuda*) is also called the common barracuda, sea tiger, tiger-of-the-sea, salt-water pike, and cuda.

RANGE: Although some barracuda may range as far north as the Carolinas, they are most common around Florida, the Bahamas, the Gulf of Mexico, and in the Caribbean.

FISHING METHODS: Spinning, bait casting, fly casting, trolling, and still fishing.

LURES: Surface and underwater plugs, spoons, jigs, and feathers.

NATURAL BAITS: Barracuda will take almost any small fish, especially if it's alive. They also hit trolled dead fish and strip baits.

WHERE TO CATCH THEM: The great barracuda are most plentiful over offshore reefs and wrecks, but they will come in close to shore around piers, off beaches, in inlets, and into bays. They can usually be seen cruising or lying still in shallow, clear water.

WHEN TO CATCH THEM: Barracuda are most plentiful during the summer months, especially close to shore in shallow water. In deeper water they are present during the winter months and most of the year. They are mostly caught in the daytime and may hit a lure or bait at any time.

HOW TO CATCH THEM: One of the best ways to catch a barracuda is by drifting with a live fish or presenting a live bait when you see the barracuda. Trolling is also a good way to catch them along mangrove banks and offshore over reefs or wrecks. Casting can also be done when you see the fish.

Bonefish

NAMES AND SPECIES: The bonefish (*Albula vulpes*) is also known as the white ghost, gray ghost, white fox, banana fish, big-eye herring, and bone.

RANGE: Occasionally range as far north as the Carolinas, but are most plentiful in southern Florida, especially the Florida Keys. They are also plentiful in the Bahamas.

FISHING METHODS: Casting with spinning rod, by bait casting, or with fly rod. Still fishing with bait.

LURES: Bonefish will hit tiny plugs, pork chunk, spoons, jigs, and flies.

NATURAL BAITS: Conch meat, hermit crabs, sand bugs, and shrimp.

WHERE TO CATCH THEM: In this country the best grounds are the flats in the Florida Keys, or in the Bahamas. You pole or wade the flats looking for the fish "tailing"—showing their tails above the surface or "mudding," creating puffs of mud on the flats. At other times they can be seen cruising around alone, in pairs, or in small schools.

WHEN TO CATCH THEM: Bonefish move up on the flats to feed on an incoming tide. The water should be fairly clear and calm to see them. On windy, rough days or when the water is muddy, it is difficult to spot them. Warm weather is also better than cold snaps, which may send them into deeper water.

HOW TO CATCH THEM: Casting lures toward single fish or a small school of fish not too close to frighten them, but working the lure in front of them so that they see it. Casting a live shrimp also in the path of the fish so that it can see it. Chumming with ground conch meat and drifting a bait out in the tide toward approaching bones.

Tarpon

NAMES AND SPECIES: The tarpon (*Tarpon atlanticus*) is also called the tarpum, silver fish, grande ecaille, sabalo, and silver king.

RANGE: The tarpon is found in the South Atlantic, the Gulf of Mexico, and the Caribbean. They go as far north as Virginia but are not too plentiful in those waters.

FISHING METHODS: Spinning, bait casting, fly casting, trolling, drifting live baits, and still fishing.

LURES: Surface and underwater plugs, spoons, jigs, plastic baits, and salt-water flies.

NATURAL BAITS: Crabs, shrimp, and small fish, dead or alive, such as mullet, pinfish, squirrel fish, catfish, and others.

WHERE TO CATCH THEM: The best fishing in the United States is along both coasts of Florida and along the Gulf of Mexico. They are found in the passes, inlets, rivers, and canals. They also swim far up into brackish water in fresh-water rivers.

WHEN TO CATCH THEM: Anything, day or night, but best results are usually obtained early in the morning, in the evening, and during the night. Full-moon and new-moon tides are most productive. Fishing is best from March to November, with May, June, and July the top months.

HOW TO CATCH THEM: Cast surface and underwater plugs and jigs when you see the tarpon rolling on top. Or cast along mangrove shores or when you see tarpon cruising along the beaches or over flats. Trolling with spoons and plugs can also be done in tarpon waters. Fishing with small live fish or crabs and drifting these under a float in shallow water and down deep near the bottom in deeper water.

Snook

NAMES AND SPECIES: The snook (*Centropomus undecimalis*) is also called the sergeant fish, salt-water pike, and robalo.

RANGE: The snook is found in Florida, the Gulf of Mexico, and in other tropical waters.

FISHING METHODS: Spinning, bait casting, fly casting, trolling, and still fishing.

LURES: Surface and underwater plugs, spoons, jigs, plastic lures, eelskins, and salt-water flies.

NATURAL BAITS: Live shrimp, mullet, pinfish, and other small baitfish.

WHERE TO CATCH THEM: Snook are most plentiful in Florida, especially in the southern part of the state around the Everglades, Ten Thousand Islands, and in the Florida Keys. Snook like the inlets, beaches, shore flats, and bars. They also like to hang around under piers and bridges and around jetties and mangrove-lined shores.

WHEN TO CATCH THEM: Early in the morning, in the evening, and during the night. The last of the outgoing tide in inlets and rivermouths. The best fishing in Florida is during the spring and summer months. Stormy weather and rough water often produce better fishing than clear, calm water.

HOW TO CATCH THEM: Cast surface plugs into likely spots and work them back fairly slowly but with plenty of action. In canals and rivers and along mangrove shores and over deep holes, trolling is often productive. When the surf is rough, they come in close to shore to feed on mullet and other baitfish. A live shrimp or mullet or other small fish can be lowered from a pier or bridge at night to take them.

Chinook Salmon

NAMES AND SPECIES: The Chinook salmon (*Oncorhynchus tschawytscha*) is also called the king salmon, spring salmon, quinnat salmon, tyee, and king.

RANGE: The Chinook salmon is found from California to Alaska, with the best fishing in Oregon, Washington, British Columbia, and Alaska.

FISHING METHODS: Spinning, bait casting, trolling, and mooching or drifting.

LURES: Plugs, spoons, spinners, and jigs.

NATURAL BAITS: Herring, anchovies, sardines, or fillets cut from these fish.

WHERE TO CATCH THEM: Most of the larger rivers entering into the Pacific have runs of Chinook salmon. They are caught out in the ocean up to several miles offshore, but the best fishing is in the inlets, bays, and mouths of rivers. They are found close to the bottom in strong currents, rips, and along sharp dropoffs.

WHEN TO CATCH THEM: The best runs take place when the salmon enter the bays, sounds, and rivermouths prior to their upstream spawning migration. This could happen anytime from March to November, depending on the location of the river.

HOW TO CATCH THEM: Although some Chinook salmon are caught by casting from boats or shore in bays or rivers, the majority are taken by trolling lures or herring baits. They are also caught from drifting boats trailing lures or herring baits.

Pacific Yellowtail

NAMES AND SPECIES: The Pacific yellowtail (*Seriola dorsalis*) is also called the amberfish, Pacific amberjack, California yellowtail, yellowtail, and white salmon.

RANGE: It is found in the Pacific from Monterey, California, south to Mexico, Baja California, the Gulf of California, and South America.

FISHING METHODS: Casting, trolling, and chumming with live baitfish.

LURES: Plugs, metal squids, spoons, jigs, and plastic baits.

NATURAL BAITS: Anchovies, sardines, herring, smelt, mackerel, and strip baits.

WHERE TO CATCH THEM: Yellowtail are found around rocks, kelp beds, reefs, islands, bays, and coves. In the southern part of California many live-bait or party boats leave San Diego, Long Beach, and Newport-Balboa to fish for these fish. Farther south in Mexican waters they are even more plentiful.

WHEN TO CATCH THEM: In California they appear around April, and the fishing continues until September. In Baja California and other Mexican waters they are taken the year 'round.

HOW TO CATCH THEM: Some yellowtail can be caught by trolling lures, but the most dependable method is to chum with live anchovies or sardines and bring them up to the boat. Then a live anchovy is hooked and cast into the feeding yellowtail. They'll also hit lures such as metal squids, heavy spoons, and jigs cast into them or allowed to sink toward the bottom, then reeled in fast.

Pacific Albacore

NAMES AND SPECIES: The Pacific albacore (*Thunnus germo*) is also called the long-finned albacore, long-finned tuna, chicken-of-the-sea, and white-meat tuna.

RANGE: They may run as far north as Alaska, but are usually found off California, Oregon, Washington, and other temperate waters of the Pacific.

FISHING METHODS: Trolling, casting, and chumming with live baitfish.

LURES: Spoons, metal squids, bone lures, and jigs.

NATURAL BAITS: Anchovies, sardines, herring, and smelt. At times will also feed on or take squid, shrimp, and strip baits.

WHERE TO CATCH THEM: Pacific albacore are usually found well offshore in water that is between 60 and 70 degrees F.

They are fast swimmers, and schools will roam over vast areas and are very difficult to locate.

WHEN TO CATCH THEM: Off California the months from May to September are best, with August and September usually the top months. The live-bait boats leaving from California ports will go out for Pacific albacore if they are running.

HOW TO CATCH THEM: Trolling with spoons, metal lures, or feathers is done fast to catch them and also to locate a school. Then chumming with live anchovies, herring, or sardines is done to hold them near the boat, after which you can cast a live anchovy to the fish or even try casting metal lures. The latter must be reeled in very fast to bring strikes.

California Halibut

NAMES AND SPECIES: The California halibut (*Paralichthys californicus*) is also called the southern halibut, chicken halibut, halibut, and alabato.

RANGE: California halibut are found from Monterey Bay, California, to Baja California.

FISHING METHODS: Drifting and still fishing.

LURES: Halibut will occasionally hit flies or other lures worked slowly.

NATURAL BAITS: Squid, anchovies, herring, queenfish, and other small fish.

WHERE TO CATCH THEM: They can be caught from party boats or small boats drifting off the beaches or inshore in bays and sounds. Pier fishermen catch them at times, and occasionally shore or surf fishermen get them. They are most abundant over sandy bottoms in water from a few feet deep to about 60 or 70 feet deep.

WHEN TO CATCH THEM: Halibut can be caught the year 'round off California, but the best months are usually from February to May.

HOW TO CATCH THEM: The best procedure is to drift with the sinker holding a live anchovy or queenfish down near the bottom. You can also still fish from a boat, pier, or shore.

Slow trolling will sometimes take them on lures worked close to the bottom. You can also try jigging for them with lures.

Rockfish

NAMES AND SPECIES: There are so many different kinds of rockfishes that we can group most of them together here. There are about sixty species of these fish found along the Pacific Coast.

RANGE: Rockfishes are found from California to Alaska, depending on the species.

FISHING METHODS: Casting, still fishing, and drifting.

LURES: Rockfish will take small lures such as spinners, jigs, spoons, and flies at times.

NATURAL BAITS: Seaworms, clams, mussels, sand crabs, shrimp, herring, anchovies, and other fish or cut bait.

WHERE TO CATCH THEM: Rockfish of various species may be found from close to shore along the beaches out to depths of several hundred feet. They usually prefer rocky shorelines or bottoms and the deeper holes and pockets close to shore. They are also found around jetties and breakwaters, docks, and piers. Other species prefer kelp beds.

WHEN TO CATCH THEM: Many species of rockfish can be caught the year 'round in Pacific waters, while others run best in the summer and fall.

HOW TO CATCH THEM: Although some kinds of rockfish can be caught by slow-trolling lures or casting from shore or boats, most of them are caught on one of the natural baits listed above. Drifting with such baits is a good idea, so that they drag along the bottom. Since these fish are found over rocky bottoms or kelp beds, it's a good idea to use small bags of sand or pebbles for sinkers rather than more expensive lead ones, which are lost too readily.

Salt-water Perch

NAMES AND SPECIES: This is a fairly large family of small fish numbering about eighteen species, so we'll group them together here rather than choose just one or two kinds.

RANGE: They are found from California to Alaska and are common along the California, Oregon, and Washington coasts.

FISHING METHODS: They will occasionally hit trolled or cast lures, but most of them are caught by still fishing. A few kinds are taken by surf fishing.

LURES: Spinners, tiny spoons, jigs, and flies at times.

NATURAL BAITS: Pileworms, mussels, sand crabs, shrimp, clams, and cut fish.

WHERE TO CATCH THEM: Some species such as the barred perch come close to the beach and can be caught by surf casting. Others are caught from rocky shores or piers. Some can also be caught from boats in bays and tidal rivers.

WHEN TO CATCH THEM: They can be caught the year 'round in many spots along the California coast. Usually the summer and fall months are best.

HOW TO CATCH THEM: Surf fishing with worms, mussels, sand crabs, or shrimp for bait. Fishing from boats or rocky shores or jetties and piers on the bottom with a sinker using similar baits.

Index